Frontispiece. John Cotton Dana. New Jersey's foremost library pioneer.

A History of
New Jersey Libraries
1750–1996

Edited by
Edwin Beckerman

The Scarecrow Press, Inc.
Lanham, Md., & London
1997

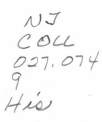

SCARECROW PRESS, INC.

Published in the United States of America
by Scarecrow Press, Inc.
4720 Boston Way
Lanham, Maryland 20706

4 Pleydell Gardens, Folkestone
Kent CT20 2DN, England

British Cataloguing-in-Publication Information Available

B&T   58.00   6/97

Library of Congress Cataloging-in-Publication Data

A history of New Jersey libraries, 1750–1996 / edited by Edwin
    Beckerman.
    p. cm.
    Includes bibliographical references and index.
    ISBN 0-8108-3272-0 (cloth : alk. paper)
    1. Libraries—New Jersey—History. I. Beckerman, Edwin, 1927— .
    Z732.N6H57 1997
    027.0749—dc21   96-45323
                                                  CIP

ISBN 0-8108-3272-0 (cloth : alk. paper)

To Roger McDonough,
who has inspired and guided New Jersey librarians
for over a half-century,
this book is fondly dedicated.

Contents

Appendixes:

Preface

New Jersey is a particularly rich subject for study, since its history parallels the development of the nation as a whole, as one of the original thirteen states of the union. The development of New Jersey libraries also reflects a pattern of growth typical of the Northeast, the cradle of library development in the nation. What happened in New Jersey library development is not isolated and peculiar to the state, but rather a reflection of broad regional patterns of growth. Even where the parallels are less direct, the patterns of library growth as it relates to societal influences make a review of library growth within one state a useful exercise.

Public and school libraries in America tend to follow a pattern of development consistent with the nature of local and school governance, of which these institutions are a part. Thus, in such states as Maryland with large library districts, public libraries are few in number and tend to serve large numbers of people. Similarly where school districts are consolidated, fewer independent school media centers exist. In "home rule" states, typical of New England and the Middle Atlantic states, many small public and school library districts exist, reflecting the fact that the local community is the prime unit of government.

When one looks at New Jersey, a strong "home rule" state, it is hardly surprising therefore to see an abundance of local libraries serving municipalities and school districts. In recent years, New Jersey has also experienced the development of regions, networks and other cooperative library ventures, as the modern world grows in complexity; these cooperative arrangements are increasingly visible in the New Jersey.

A careful examination of the past can aid us in discerning trends for the future. And, surely as important, it can help us to examine our values, as we explore how we have grown into what we are, with the values we hold. This is particularly important for those libraries which are public institutions, driven both by the values of the society as a whole and by the canons of their unique calling.

This history brings together a series of chapters dealing with broad elements of library development in New Jersey. The idea for such a book originated with Roger McDonough, retired director of the New Jersey State Library. While some chapters of the history were completed as early as 1984, for a variety of reasons the project languished, with a few unsuccessful attempts in the interim to proceed with new editors. Finally, in 1995 Roger asked me as an author of one of the original chapters, if I would be willing to take on the role of editor and complete the history. This was agreed and this volume is the result. It will be noted that some of the chapters have multiple authors: much of this occurred because some chapters were written more than a decade ago and needed to be revised and updated.

Chapter 1 charts the development of the public library from 1750 to the present.

Chapter 2 looks at the history of the State Library, certainly one of the prime agents for change on the New Jersey library scene, as well as the library regulatory agency for the state. The influence of the State Library on statewide library development is typical of the influence that state libraries have had on library development in many other states in the nation.

Chapter 3 follows the development of county libraries from their beginnings in 1920 to the present time. While county libraries are of course public libraries, their history is unique among public libraries in the state, as are the statutes which authorize them and provide the framework for their operation. Their status differs so much from that of municipal libraries in the state that we must look separately at their history.

Chapter 4 reviews the history of New Jersey's premier public library, the Newark Public Library. Over the years this library provided leadership not only in New Jersey, but in the nation as well.

Chapter 5 looks at the state library system and state aid over the past fifty years, and how they helped to shape the current scene.

Chapter 6 reviews the impact of federal library aid on service to the people of New Jersey.

Chapter 7 looks at professional development for librarians through certification and education, from the earliest days of State Library-sponsored summer training classes, to the development of the Rutgers University School of Communication, Information, and Library Studies.

Chapter 8 follows the development of school media centers from their earliest days to the present.

Chapter 9 looks at the development of academic libraries from the colonial period to the present. Chapter 10 covers the development of special libraries, including libraries serving business and industry, government, trade associations, non-profit agencies, etc.

Chapter 11 looks at the history of the New Jersey Library Association and its impact on libraries.

Chapter 12 sums up the general position of libraries in New Jersey today, how it compares with the general status of libraries in the United States, and its prospects for the future.

In addition to the contributions of many individual authors, this work also results from the interest of the many people who have taken the time to talk about their views and their experiences, and to provide material invaluable to the completion of this history. Note should be taken as well of the influence of Scarecrow Press on the professional life of librarians in New Jersey, during the many years its headquarters was located in Metuchen. The presence over the years of such figures as Ralph Shaw, the Daubs (father and son), Eric Moon, Bill Eshelman and Norman Horrocks has enriched the library dialogue in New Jersey and done much to advance the cause of librarianship. Along the way the manuscript benefited from many helpful suggestions made by Bernard Bush, former Executive Director of the New Jersey Historical Commission. This book owes much to his insights. Most of all, a huge debt is owed to Roger McDonough, the man most responsible not only for this history, but for much of library development in New Jersey over the past half-century.

Foreword
The New Jersey Scene

Roger McDonough

To understand the framework in which libraries operate in New Jersey, it is essential to have at least a fundamental understanding of the state's history, geography, population characteristics, traditions, and not least of all, its interesting albeit complicated legal and political structure.

History

New Jersey is one of the thirteen original states of the union and was the scene of many important battles during the Revolutionary War. Washington spent much more time in New Jersey than he did at Valley Forge, and his victories at Trenton and Princeton were critical in keeping alive the colonies' hopes for victory. As the new nation began to organize following the end of the war, New Jersey became the third state to ratify the new Constitution in 1787, and the first state to ratify the Bill of Rights in 1791.

The Civil War found New Jersey deeply divided. While it provided its quota of men for the Union, it twice voted against the election of Abraham Lincoln, in both 1860 and 1864. General George B. McClellan, the losing candidate in 1864, later became Governor of New Jersey, and served from 1878 to 1881.

The early 20th century was notable for the election of Woodrow Wilson, New Jersey's second U.S. President (1912–1920), who had been President of Princeton University and then Governor of New Jersey (1910–1912) until he moved on to the White House. Since then New Jersey has been a swing state, dividing control of the Governor's office and the legislature almost equally between the Democratic and Republican parties. In 1992 the state followed the national trend and the Republicans took firm control of the Governor's office and both houses of the legislature control which they have since maintained. Governor Christine (Christy) Todd Whitman, the state's first woman governor, proved to be not only an able and vigorous politician/campaigner, but one of the most powerful and dominant governors in the state's history.

Geography and Population

New Jersey is one of the smallest states in the union ranking 46th among the states in size. It is located in the Middle Atlantic region of the country, bordered on the north by New York, on the east by the Atlantic Ocean, on the south by the Atlantic Ocean and Delaware Bay, and on the west by Pennsylvania and Delaware. A long, narrow state, it is only 168 miles long and approximately fifty miles wide. The geography is varied, however, ranging from gentle hills in the north to the land below Trenton, known as the Coastal Plain, a region noted for its flatness and sandy soil, home of the picturesque Pine Barrens. The state is flanked by two major rivers: the Delaware, which forms the western border, and the Hudson, which forms part of its northern boundary.

From the earliest days of European settlement, perhaps because of its strategic location, New Jersey has had a remarkably heterogeneous population. The Dutch arrived first, settling in the northern and central portions of the colony, followed by the Swedes who settled along the Delaware River and Delaware Bay. In time English and Scottish settlers began to outnumber the Dutch and Swedes, and New Jersey became an English colony. In the process the peaceful native Lenape (or Delaware) Indians were "encouraged" to move West, the majority settling eventually in Oklahoma. The population swelled dramatically during the 19th century as mass migrations of Irish, Italians, Germans, Hungarians, Poles and others came to the state to work on the railroads and canals and in the burgeoning industrial centers: Newark, Paterson, Jersey City and Trenton.

Although it is a little known fact, New Jersey was one of the strongest slave colonies north of the Mason-Dixon line, and many of the descendants of these slaves still live here. The African-American population of New Jersey swelled after World War I and World War II, and major cities like Newark and Trenton now have black mayors and governing bodies. More recently an influx of people of Hispanic origin have come into New Jersey from Puerto Rico, Cuba, Guatemala and other Latin American countries, a large number of them settling in Hudson County. In addition, immigrants from Asia arrived in increasing numbers, many settling in central New Jersey. The total population of New Jersey today numbers almost eight million—and is growing.

Agriculture

New Jersey's nickname, "The Garden State," may seem an anomaly in a state where open space is being gobbled up at an alarming rate, but the appellation was accurate in the 19th century when farming was the major occupation. A growing population and urban sprawl have made farming unprofitable in most areas, and the acreage lost to agriculture has been replaced by businesses, homes and the omnipresent shopping centers. Surprisingly, although largely confined to the southern part of the state, agriculture is still an important occupation. New Jersey farmers produce great quantities of garden vegetables, fruit, berries, poultry and dairy products, a substantial portion of which goes to such giant concerns as the Campbell Soup Company for canning.

Business and Industry

Now a heavily industrialized state, New Jersey in the 19th century experienced a transition from an agricultural to an industrial economy, a trend that was spurred by the rapid development of railroads and canals such as the Delaware and Raritan Canal, which for many years played an important role in transporting coal and raw materials for manufacturing. Among the industries they served were those producing steel and iron. The steel wire produced by the Roebling plant in Trenton, for example, was used in the construction of the Brooklyn Bridge. Other important new industries included the Paterson silk mills, rubber and paper mills, pharmaceutical industries such as Johnson and Johnson in New Brunswick, and the leather and brewing industries in Newark. Many of these heavy industries have moved to other states or other countries by now and have been replaced in part by oil refining, electric goods and chemical manufacturing. Increasingly the state has become more dependent on service occupations and retail trade, but manufacturing still provides a substantial portion of wage and salary income to state residents. The continuing importance of business and industry to the state's economy is illustrated by the fact that a large number of the Fortune 500 companies are headquartered here or have ongoing operations within the state. In addition, hundreds of concerns, including the famous Bell Laboratories, are engaged in industrial research and development, and their expenditures amount to about ten percent of all the money spent for this purpose in the United States.

Environmental Protection

In recent years public opinion has put increasing pressure on those industries known as heavy polluters, and the New Jersey Department of Environmental Protection, created in 1970, has established a stricter code for emission standards. Similar restrictions are now in effect for private and commercial automobiles and trucks. In addition, the DEP is engaged in a continuing battle with developers seeking to exploit vanishing wetlands for private gain. One successful defense against further encroachment has been the highly successful "Green Acres" program under which the state acquires open space and converts it into parkland and other similar uses.

Transportation

Rail and Highway. New Jersey's location at the epicenter of the Washington, D.C.-to-Boston corridor requires that the state have a well developed transportation system, and New Jersey has an excellent one. While the railroads have lost ground to the highways, they still carry thousands of commuters to New York City and other destinations, and excellent bus lines serve those who cannot use the railroads. The state's major highway, the New Jersey Turnpike, is familiar to millions of motorists who never see any other portion of the state and leave with the impression that New Jersey is nothing but an industrial wasteland. The Turnpike is a vital artery, however, transporting enormous quantities of freight on a daily basis to and from all parts of the United States. Traffic flows more smoothly on the Garden State Parkway, which follows a curving route from southern Cape May to the New York State Thruway, and except for a few urbanized portions, passes through pleasant, quiet countryside for its entire length; and it is closed to truck traffic.

Air Transportation. The state has only one major airport, The Newark International Airport, but this is growing rapidly and now rivals Kennedy Airport as the major center for air traffic for northern New Jersey and the New York metropolitan area.

Education

Primary and Secondary. A long-standing requirement of New Jersey's constitution is that the state provide free public education for all children between the ages of five and eighteen. A further refinement specified that the education provided was to be "thorough and efficient," a vague phrase whose exact meaning has eluded generations of Jerseyans. Nevertheless, it has helped provide the climate for ever-increasing levels of funding for education at state, county, and local levels to support the state's well-articulated system of education from kindergarten through graduate school. The state has 594 local school districts, 29 regional school districts, and 49 regional high school districts. In 1993 these districts enrolled 1,126,420 pupils. In addition, parochial schools enrolled 287,194 school children in the same year. The public elementary and secondary schools are supported locally but receive substantial amounts of state aid. The courts have made clear that state government has a financial responsibility under the state constitution to equalize educational opportunity to all New Jersey children, however poor the local school district in which they may attend school.

Higher Education. New Jersey has many institutions of higher education, the most prominent and prestigious being Princeton and Rutgers, both colonial colleges dating respectively from 1746 and 1766. As the State University, Rutgers is the principal unit in a system embracing more than a dozen state colleges and universities. The main Rutgers campus is in New Brunswick, and other large campuses are located in Camden and Newark. There are, in addition, seven state colleges located in Montclair (now Montclair University), Wayne, Union, Jersey City, Trenton and Ewing, Glassboro, and Stockton. Undergirding the four-year institutions and graduate schools are the two-year community colleges located throughout the state. In addition, there are more than thirty private colleges and universities. The state is also home to such well-known institutions as the Institute for Advanced Study, the Princeton Theological Seminary, and the University of Medicine and Dentistry, New Jersey (UMDNJ), a network of facilities located throughout the state.

Recreation and Cultural Activities

Recreation. New Jersey's dependence on New York City and Philadelphia for its cultural and recreational activities has lessened considerably in recent decades as the state has moved to provide its own facilities. The Meadowlands Sports Complex, for example, is now home to the New York Giants and New York Jets, which have retained their New York identities but play all of their home games in New Jersey, as does the New Jersey Devils hockey team.

New Jersey's major recreational asset is the New Jersey Shore, a string of beaches running from the southern tip of Cape May to Sandy Hook in the north, which forms part of the National Gateway Recreational Area and is within view of New York City. In addition, a wealth of state and county parks offer endless opportunities for wholesome, inexpensive recreation.

Music and Theater. Opportunities to hear professional concerts of popular and classical music and to see good theater are growing, and theaters such as the McCarter Theater in Princeton, the New Jersey Arts Center in Newark, and the State Theater in New Brunswick offer a wide variety of artistic offerings including both classical and modern ballet. The New Jersey State Opera summer series at the Lawrenceville School and other concert series at Waterloo Village and the Garden State Arts Center in Holmdel draw increasingly larger audiences.

Museums. The state is also blessed with several excellent museums, of which the Newark Museum and the State Museum are the largest and most varied, with holdings ranging from local artifacts to first-rate collections of modern art. Both museums also have state of the art planetariums. In addition, smaller museums with excellent collections, such as the Montclair Art Museum, the Morris Museum, the Paterson Museum and the university museums of Princeton and Rutgers, are all open to the general public. The Liberty Museum of Science in Liberty State Park and the New Jersey State Aquarium in Camden have also proved to be popular attractions.

Historic Sites. There are a number of places of historic interest in various parts of the state. Two of the most important and attractive are the Morristown National Historical Park, where Washington spent the bitter winter of 1779–80, and the Washington Crossing State Park near Trenton, which celebrates Washington's famous crossing of the Delaware on Christmas night, 1776.

Politics and Government

Considering its size, New Jersey has an extraordinarily complex political structure. Only slightly larger than one of California's largest counties, New Jersey has 21 counties of its own, 567 municipalities, and 623 school districts, only 20 of which serve more than one municipality. Although many voters and legislators and almost all political scientists agree that the existing structure of municipal government is wasteful and inefficient and should be replaced by some more logical pattern, all efforts to accomplish this have failed. The tradition of "home rule" is so deeply ingrained that few politicians are willing to alienate their constituents by advocating consolidation of municipalities. Only a major financial crisis, it would appear, could bring about such consolidation, but with major cutbacks looming in state and federal aid, change may be in the making. Some progress toward consolidation seems to be occurring in the area of school organization, where, despite the public's dedication to the principle of "home rule," 40 percent of school districts now serve the children of two or more municipalities. This principle of "home rule" is of more than passing interest to libraries. Just as a multiplicity of local government jurisdictions can lead to inefficient government, so this same pattern of government leads to problems in library organization. Indeed, much of recent public library history can be seen as an attempt to cope with the multiplicity of local library districts by creating larger units of service in the form of area and regional cooperatives.

New Jersey is now governed under its third constitution, which was approved by the voters in 1947, following a Constitutional Convention. The Constitution makes the governor one of the most powerful in the nation by providing him or her with a line-item veto over the state's budget, a power that American presidents covet. In addition, the governor exerts great power through the appointment process. The governor is the only statewide official elected by popular vote. All other such officers (for example, the attorney-general, cabinet heads, justices and judges) owe their appointments to the governor.

The Legislature. The Constitution also provided for a bicameral legislature—the Senate and the General Assembly. The upper house consists of 40 members, elected for four-year terms that run concurrently. The General Assembly has 80 members who are elected for two-year terms.

The Judiciary. New Jersey has one of the best court systems in the United States, because the entire system of courts is directly responsible to the New Jersey Supreme Court, which relies on an administrator of the courts to carry out its rules and regulations. The Superior Court, the workhorse of the system, consists of appellate, law and chancery divisions. At the next level are the county courts, each with one or more judges according to the need.

County Government. The twenty-one counties are governed by boards of chosen freeholders, each elected for three-year terms. Their chief functions are to maintain the roads and to operate county institutions of various kinds. The freeholders are not limited to these functions, however, and only recently one county, Mercer, has built a baseball stadium in order to attract a minor-league team. Five of the twenty-one counties are administered by elected county executives who serve for four-year terms. The remaining counties appoint administrators who serve at the pleasure of their respective boards of freeholders.

State Taxation and Finance. Although New Jersey is one of the wealthiest states, historically its citizens have been distinctly averse to spending money, or, more properly, to paying taxes for the government to spend money on their behalf. This fact of life was demonstrated by Governor Whitman's proposed 30 percent reduction in income taxes in the years 1993–95. This sharp reduction was assailed by critics who claimed it would raise local property taxes because the social programs eliminated or reduced by the cuts would inevitably have to be provided by county and municipal governments. The irony of this debate is that it had taken almost a generation to persuade the public and the legislature to accept an income tax, and it was only when Governor Brendan T. Byrne had pushed for the tax that it was finally enacted in 1976. Despite the passage of this tax, New Jersey still relies heavily on regressive measures such as property taxes and sales taxes of various kinds for a large portion of its revenue. These taxes were augmented in 1976 by a tax on Atlantic City casino gambling, which was approved by the voters with the understanding that part of the state's revenue from gambling would be used to assist senior citizens and the disabled.

So there we have it: New Jersey, a state once so dominated by New York and Philadelphia that it seemed to lack any clear identity of its own, but is now a vibrant force, both economically and politically, in the affairs of the nation. Admittedly crowded in its narrow geographical confines, it is still, as a recent public opinion poll demonstrated, a residence of choice for the majority of its eight million inhabitants.

New Jersey has been a library leader for most of the twentieth century. With the emphasis now shifting to the shape of things to come in the next century, the library community faces the future with confidence in the leadership demonstrated by the New Jersey Library Association and its close allies, the trustees and the myriad "friends of libraries." New Jersey librarians also have in Rutgers, The State University, one of the largest and strongest library schools in the country. Now, with the hope of new, dynamic leadership at the State Library, New Jersey appears ready to participate fully in the Internet and all the other challenges and opportunities that loom ahead in the 21st century. New Jersey, in short, is a good "library state" and intends to remain so.

1

Public Libraries

Roger McDonough

The public library movement in New Jersey began in the mid-18th century, when the first "library companies" were formed in Trenton (1750), Elizabeth (1755), and Burlington (1758). The creation of similar institutions followed quickly in many other New Jersey communities, and by 1800 twenty-one municipalities had one or more such libraries in operation.

Company Libraries

These "company" or "society" libraries were private in the sense that they were supported entirely by membership dues or the purchase of shares. They were public because membership was open to any person who could afford to join or become a shareholder. The majority of the members came from the educated portion of the community—the clergy, school men, and men of property who could afford to buy books. They were the progenitors of the more than three hundred public libraries that are now part of New Jersey's educational and cultural life.

The colonial beginnings of these libraries were linked to developments elsewhere. In Trenton, for example, the founding of the company library was associated with Benjamin Franklin and his pioneer efforts in starting the Library Company of Philadelphia in 1731. Dr. Thomas Cadwalader, a Philadelphia surgeon who was a collaborator of Franklin's in starting the Philadelphia library, resided in Trenton from 1743 to 1750. Before returning to Philadelphia, Cadwalader gave a substantial sum of money to Trenton for the establishment of a library.[1] This handsome gesture produced quick results. Only two years later Benjamin Franklin, who had been engaged to procure books for the new library, wrote to the London bookseller William Strolman: "The books for the Trenton Library arrived safe and I believe gave satisfaction."[2] Records for the period are scanty, but from advertisements in Philadelphia newspapers, usually notices of meetings, it appears that the library progressed satisfactorily for a quarter century until 1776, when enemy troops, presumably Hessian, "wantonly" destroyed "an elegant public library in Trenton."[3]

We may assume that "elegant" refers to the books and not to the building, because it is likely that the modest collection was housed in a small rented room. Nevertheless, the book-burning represented a setback, and it took many years for the library to recover. By 1798, however, the company had been reorganized and had printed a pamphlet entitled *Laws and Regulations of the Trenton Library Company Agreed to . . . May 1797*. In 1804 a *Catalogue of Books*, classified by subject, was published and provided a useful guide to the more than seven hundred books in the library. A similar catalogue was printed in 1819.[4]

A period of decline then set in, and by the 1830s library use dwindled rapidly: 833 books circulated in 1832, but by 1847 only 32 books were borrowed, and by 1850, its 100th birthday, the library was almost a dead institution. This decline and fall after a century of service is understandable when one recalls that the original founders had all died and competition in the form of an "Apprentices Library Company," founded in 1822, and the Trenton Library Association, begun in 1852, further undermined the Library Company's stability. In 1855 the company went out of existence and transferred its holdings to the Trenton Library Association.[5]

The Burlington Library Company was founded in 1758 under a charter granted by King George II. The Company could properly lay claim to a number of firsts. It still operates today under the same royal charter, and most of its early records are extant. In 1789 it became the first New Jersey library to erect a library building. Also in the year of its founding it became the first New Jersey library to print a catalog of its holdings, then the most extensive collection in the colony.[6] The progressive spirit manifested in the library's founding was a reflection of the town's early history. Founded by English Quakers in 1677, the settlement soon became a thriving port, and William Penn thought enough of its favorable location on the Delaware River to consider it as a site for the capital of his projected colony. Philadelphia was selected instead, but Burlington reaped its own share of honor later in 1681 when it became the capital of the Province of West Jersey, and still later, when it alternated with Perth Amboy as the capital of New Jersey, following the union of East Jersey and West Jersey in 1702. In 1776 the little city of 1,000 people served as the meeting place of the Provincial Congress which adopted the first constitution for the new state.[7]

The library history of Burlington is a success story of a private library begun over 200 years ago by the leading gentlemen and clergy of the bustling 18th-century community and continuing with uninterrupted service to the public (even through the Revolutionary War years) to the present day. There were many changes over the years, the most important being the acceptance by the city, beginning in 1898, of fiscal responsibility for the library's operations. The current situation thus represents a unique admixture of old and new, with the library still functioning in what is only its second library building, erected in 1864, but providing modern, efficient library service to the citizenry.

Since the colonial libraries were begun by the leading citizens of the community—the clergy, schoolmasters, and men of property—their book collections reflected the interests of these relatively few educated citizens. Plutarch's *Lives*, the *Odes* of Horace, Swift's works and Robertson's *History of Scotland* were among the books purchased by the Burlington Library Company. However, these works were leavened by the inclusion of such works as Fielding's *Life and Works*, which probably included the racy novel, *Tom Jones*.

The works of Voltaire and other "free-thinkers" presented a more serious problem in some communities, as evidenced in the history of the Shrewsbury Library Company in Monmouth County. Voltaire's works in thirty-five volumes were purchased in 1766, but there were numerous objections to having them in the library. In 1770 it was "ordered that Voltaire's work be sold or exchanged. . . ." No action was taken, however, until 1773, when (according to the Company minutes of February 22) it was "ordered that the members may have the reading of Voltaire's book until the meeting of the next board. . . ."[8] Such threats to the established order continued to be of concern. In 1778 Josiah Holmes, one of the library's leading spirits, assured prospective subscribers that the books purchased would promote virtue and true religion "and that works of a contrary nature had already been ordered out."[9]

While the censorship problem was resolved over a period of time, the fortunes of the Shrewsbury Library Company waned. Several times the Company voted to dissolve itself and sell its books, only to have such action forestalled. The Revolution seems to have brought the library almost to a complete halt, although records continue to show some activity until 1790, about the time of the death of its founder, Josiah Holmes. In 1862 a new company was formed, the Shrewsbury Library Association, which was incorporated in 1872 and continued in existence until 1918.

The Trenton, Burlington and Shrewsbury libraries were not the only ones incorporated before 1800. Eighteen other communities are on record—scanty though those records may be—as having libraries. They include Haddonfield, Mount Holly, New Brunswick and Newark, according to Samuel Smith's 1768 *History of New Jersey*. Swedesboro began a library in 1783, Arneytown in 1789, Morristown in 1792, Orange in 1793, Woodbury in 1794, Bloomfield in 1795 and Rahway in 1797. Most of these municipalities have libraries today; several, like the New Brunswick Public Library, still possess many of the books from the original collections.

The local library movement received encouragement from the state by the passage in 1794 of an "Act to incorporate societies for the promotion of learning." This law was amended in 1799 to "include all library companies that now are, or shall hereafter be formed in any of the counties of this state, which have not been, by letters patent or act of assembly, already incorporated." This statute was to serve as the basic legal authority for the organization of local libraries until 1879, when the Municipal Library Act was passed. This act, as amended in 1884, and at various times over the years, still provides the basic framework covering municipal library organization, governance and administration.

Apprentices' Libraries

New Jersey's early library experience was similar to that of Massachusetts and other New England states. In all of these the majority of the elite library companies gradually declined and gave way in the early part of the 19th century to what were to become known as "apprentice libraries," a development reflecting the change from an agricultural to an industrial economy. Business and community leaders became increasingly concerned about the welfare of men in their teens and early twenties who had left the family farms to seek work in the factories and were now exposed to vices and temptations in their new, and frequently sordid, surroundings. The creation of some apprentices' libraries appears to have been due to a combination of forces: young men banding together and desirous of education to improve their position in society, and the "do-good spirit" which was prevalent in all the industrial states of the North and which led citizens in many communities to work for the benefit of the young apprentices.

The apprentices' libraries were a part of the broad humanitarian movement which accompanied expansion of industry and emergence of a 'working class.' Every plea made for their support shows how fully class distinctions had become recognized. Apprentices were 'a most interesting part of our community,' a 'numerous and important class,' an 'interesting portion of our society.' Moreover, they were a class perilously exposed to temptation. To rescue them from this, and to form them into useful citizens was the primary purpose of those who founded libraries for them. 'In this country,' the apprentice was told, 'the industrious mechanic is as honored and as worthy of honor as the professional man.' There was 'no barrier to his access to the highest stations.' The example of Franklin and of other boys who had risen from apprenticeship to fame was constantly held before him. He was exhorted to accept the opportunity which the library offered; to strive for that equality which, though it seemingly had been withheld, was rightfully his.[10]

The first apprentices' libraries opened in Newark and Trenton in 1821. Burlington followed in 1822 and Elizabeth in 1825. A bookplate of the New Brunswick Mechanics Association is in the Rutgers University Libraries, but nothing more is known about this organization. It is likely that other towns initiated apprentices' libraries, but no records exist concerning them. Newark seems to have been the most successful, perhaps because the library was established as part of the existing Newark Library Society. At one time after its founding in 1821, it had 500 members, but interest dwindled and the library appears to have disbanded about 1830. We know little about the operation of the library in Elizabeth, but it operated from 1825 to the 1850s in a room in the county courthouse. Moral earnestness marked the beginnings of the Apprentices' Library Company of Trenton as this statement by the first Board of Managers (1825) illustrates:

> These facts are highly honorable to our youth, and encouraging to this society. They prove that *they* properly estimate our motives, and set a just value on this institution, while they are *a pledge to us* that our continued and increased exertions to place useful knowledge within their reach will not be in vain.
> Let it be further observed, to their credit, that the library . . . contains no novels, romances, or plays, which are so apt to captivate juvenile imaginations, but is composed of works of more sterling value and lasting usefulness . . . on religion, morality, and science, history, biography, travels, voyages, etc. . . . The collection . . . now contains two hundred and sixty-seven [volumes].[11]

Small wonder that uneducated youths looking for diversion in the evenings after a twelve-hour day of work in shop or factory would find little in the book collection to keep them interested.

There are no further records of the Apprentices' Library Company of Trenton until 1828, when, according to the *Trenton Federalist*, the library's books were turned over to the Trenton Literary Society, which offered to lend books "under the like guarantees as formerly."[12] In 1845 a notice in the *State Gazette* asked for the return of all books belonging to the Apprentices' Library, for it was "proposed to place the Library in charge of a Society recently organized, under whose direction the books may be made useful to a large portion of our citizens."[13]

This new organization, the Trenton Library Association, was active until the late 1860s, when the Young Men's Christian Association opened a library which ran for about ten years. Its collection included books from the Library Association together with many volumes that had originally belonged to the Apprentices' Library. In 1879 the YMCA Library was transferred to the Women's Christian Temperance Union, which in 1883 erected a headquarters building. The WCTU provided space to another library organization, the Union Library Company, which continued as Trenton's principal community library until the present municipal Free Public Library of Trenton was incorporated in 1900.[14]

The history of the libraries of Trenton has been given in some detail because it mirrors the library history of the other major industrial and business communities of the state: Camden, Elizabeth, Newark, New Brunswick, Jersey City and Paterson. In each of these cities, which now have substantial municipally supported free public libraries, the institution started as a small private library, which suffered many vicissitudes and changes of name before emerging as a modern public library. The idea and ideal of free public library service persisted. Much is owed to the thousands of individuals who carried on the work of the hundreds of small independent libraries that were established in every part of the state from pre-Revolutionary times onwards.

Municipal Free Public Libraries

The persistent growth of libraries in the state throughout the 19th century is all the more remarkable because New Jersey had no outstanding library leaders to inspire and guide public opinion about the value of libraries as social institutions. Public library leaders of national reputation emerged in New Jersey only in the early years of the 20th century, when John Cotton Dana came to the Newark Public Library and Sarah Byrd Askew became head librarian of the New Jersey Public Library Commission.

By contrast, the agitation for a public library in Boston in the mid-19th century by such public figures as Edward Everett, noted orator and statesman, and George Ticknor, distinguished Professor at Harvard, had brought the idea of tax-supported libraries to an ever-widening audience throughout New England. The differing views of Everett and Ticknor as to the nature of the projected library—Everett envisioned a scholarly reference facility while Ticknor favored a more democratic general circulation library—further served to heighten public interest and support for the project. Ticknor won the friendly debate with Everett, and the philosophy he espoused became widely accepted. Essentially it differs little from the philosophy and practice of today.

Ticknor hoped to "begin by making it a really useful library; by awakening a general interest in it as a City institution, important to the whole people, a part of their education, and an element of their happiness and prosperity."[15] He was eloquent in his advocacy of the then radical notion of buying multiple copies of popular works. "Books that will be asked for . . . should be provided in such numbers that *many* persons . . . can be reading the same work at the same moment, and so render the . . . literature of the day accessible to the whole people at the only time they care for it . . . that is, when it is living, fresh and new. Additional copies, therefore, should be bought as long as they are urgently demanded, and thus, by following the popular taste . . . we may hope to create a real desire for general reading; and by permitting the fresh circulation of the books that is consistent with their safety, cultivate this desire among . . . the greatest number of people in the city."[16] As Ticknor the evangelist saw it, "A free public library, if adopted to the wants of our people, would be the crowning glory of our public schools."[17]

Moved by Ticknor's eloquence and with the ground having been already carefully prepared, the City Council quickly passed the enabling ordinance, and in 1852 the Boston Public Library became a reality. There is no mention of money in Ticknor's appeal, but the distinguishing feature of the new library was the fact that for the first time a major city in the United States had a tax-supported library institution. The city had petitioned the state for permission to levy a tax on real estate in support of a library, and the enabling legislation was passed in 1848.

In Boston, as in New Jersey and other states, the growing trend toward a more democratic, classless society, coupled with a belief in public education as a foundation of a free society, provided the open atmosphere in which public libraries began to develop in the 19th century. The company libraries, the mercantile libraries, the libraries established by YMCAs, the temperance societies and other similar groups, had all performed useful if limited service. But they were gradually giving way under the influence of a growing public consensus that, in a democracy, only libraries founded, operated and maintained by the people themselves could meet the needs of modern society.

The change in New Jersey was slow in coming. It was only in 1884 that the legislation was passed to make public support of municipal libraries possible. Before that occurred, however, a substantial number of libraries had already been created. By the mid-19th century 57 libraries had been operating in New Jersey, with numerous other efforts having been dissolved earlier.[18] Curtis notes that between 1850 and 1883, before the passage of the 1884 public library legislation, 81 new libraries had been established in New Jersey. From 1884 through the end of the century, an additional 57 libraries were established, 22 of these under the provisions of the new statute.[19]

By modern standards, most of these libraries were a poor lot (particularly those not established under the 1884 statute, and having no assured means of support). They had nondescript collections of gift books, often out-of-date, a volunteer in charge, and a building (more often a small room) that was open to the public for only a few hours each week. Such libraries could provide an illusion of library service without the substance to realize its full potential. Unfortunately, the public image of library service was molded by several generations of New Jersey residents who had grown up in communities with just such libraries and had no conception of what a good, well-supported, professionally-managed public library could offer. In effect, the majority of the New Jersey libraries of this period were on a par with the typical one-room school, affectionately looked back upon by thousands who had graduated from them but who now wanted something better for their children and grandchildren. They were typical also of the first primitive libraries established in schools, colleges, corporations, and institutions.

Not all of these early libraries deserve such harsh judgment. Many, particularly in the larger communities, were struggling to provide good service and needed only a solid basis of financial support to bring them onto higher ground. Paterson, a prosperous manufacturing community, was to provide the individual who would push through the landmark legislation authorizing municipalities to support libraries using public funds.

Paterson, like other large manufacturing centers in the state, had experimented with the creation of a half-dozen or more libraries of various kinds over the years. But as "these efforts were based upon voluntary subscriptions and donations, and as they acquired no permanent endowment, they flourished for a while, then gradually died away, as do so many projects which have to depend for support on private contributions."[20] It was against this background that the Reverend William Prall proposed a legislative solution. Influenced by the success of Boston and other New England communities, Prall worked with other leading citizens, and with the backing of the *Paterson Daily Press*, to get a public library established under a law enacted in 1879, sponsored by Senator George Ludlow of Middlesex County, authorizing municipal governments to establish and maintain public libraries. The effort failed. In 1883, Assemblyman Patrick Shields of Passaic County introduced a bill which would permit the establishment of a public library supported by municipal funds but placing it under the jurisdiction of the local board of education. The bill never became law.

In 1884 Prall, then a member of the General Assembly, introduced a bill which subsequently became law under the title, "An act to authorize the establishment of free public libraries in the cities of this State." Prall had definite ideas about how libraries were to fit into the general municipal scheme of things, and the legislation clearly reflected his philosophy. The library was to be established as a separate entity: it was to be tied to the governing body of the municipality and the public school system but was to be kept out of politics. The legislation, signed into law on April 1, 1884, incorporated these basic objectives by authorizing, following a successful referendum, the creation of a seven-member public library board of trustees, five to be appointed by the Mayor, with the remaining two, the Mayor and the Superintendent of Schools, to serve ex-officio. The key provision of the new law was fiscal: libraries were to be supported from municipal funds by a minimum one-third of a mill property tax on every dollar of assessed valuation. The importance of this landmark legislation can scarcely be overestimated. It gave libraries organized under its provisions a sound structure of governance and an assured minimum base of tax support.

The City of Paterson rose to the challenge. Following a vigorous public campaign in 1885, the creation of a free public library was approved by an overwhelming majority of the voters. The city became the first municipality to incorporate its library under the new law. William Prall was elected president of its first board of trustees.[21] In 1890, when the New Jersey Library Association was organized in Trenton, Prall was elected its first president. His bill, which became the basic law governing public libraries, remains, after numerous amendments, the fundamental law under which public libraries organize and operate.

Libraries continued to proliferate. By 1901, 102 libraries were reporting to the newly established Public Library Commission, 52 of these being free and 38 being subscription libraries.[22] However, the real progress in the creation of new public libraries took place after the turn of the century. The Public Library Commission noted in 1911 that 214 libraries were currently reporting to it.[23]

During this period at the turn of the century direct state assistance to public and school libraries began in the form of traveling libraries, collections of books distributed by the State Library to communities lacking adequate library facilities. The traveling libraries created a considerable stir in this agricultural state, and the State Grange, the State Federation of Women's Clubs and other organizations began to agitate for a permanent state library extension agency to promote the establishment and efficiency of free public libraries. The State Library, which had previously confined itself to its traditional law library and general reference functions, supported the move. On March 20, 1900, the act creating the new Public Library Commission was signed into law. The act authorized the Commission to donate up to one hundred dollars, for the purchase of books on a matching basis, to public libraries having less than five thousand books. One thousand dollars was made available for this purpose during the Commission's first year, but this modest state aid program provided the first tangible evidence of the State's willingness to contribute a share of the cost of local library service.

The Askew Era

The Public Library Commission limped along until 1905, when it appointed its first head librarian, Miss Sarah Byrd Askew of Alabama, who was to dominate the New Jersey library scene until her death in 1942. Miss Askew's original title was Secretary and Organizer (the title was changed to Secretary and Librarian in 1913), but I knew her well and recall hearing her refer to her position as librarian and "missionary." And missionary indeed she was, for under her leadership the number of libraries increased to 316 and the county library law, enacted in 1920 largely through her efforts, resulted in the creation of county libraries to serve the then predominantly rural counties. A woman of great personal charm and intelligence, she was also a gifted public speaker, whose skill in persuading public bodies to establish and support libraries was unrivaled. If Miss Askew's record was flawed, it was perhaps because she succeeded too well, for many of the libraries she started were established on too flimsy a fiscal and population base and never became really successful institutions.

One of Miss Askew's major contributions was the summer school for librarians established in 1906 and conducted at various times in such locations as Asbury Park and Ocean City, and during the winter months at the Newark Public Library. The training school, which issued certificates to its graduates, was eventually taken over by Trenton State College and operated as an extension program leading to a Bachelor of Science degree in library science. During its existence the summer training school exerted a profound influence on the hundreds of individuals who attended its sessions. Beatrice James, for example, retired director of the Bergenfield Public Library, recalls her training period there with respect and affection. "The courses were taught by excellent instructors," she states, "and they were difficult but practical and down-to-earth, and we learned a great deal. And, of course, Miss Askew was always on hand to inspire us to love libraries and to serve the public well as 'trained librarians'."[24]

The Carnegie Buildings

By a fortunate coincidence the emergence of the Public Library Commission in 1900 was paralleled by the beginning of grants of Carnegie Library buildings to New Jersey communities. Through Andrew Carnegie's well-known benefactions, twenty-nine communities in New Jersey received grants for the construction of thirty-four library buildings—twenty-eight main buildings and six branch libraries.[25]

Twenty-nine of the thirty-four buildings are still standing, and only five have been demolished. Of the twenty-nine extant, twenty are still in active service as libraries, while the remaining nine continue useful lives as city offices, senior citizen centers or commercial centers. Librarians, like me, who have had to administer one of these frequently inefficient buildings could wish that Carnegie had not built quite so well, but no one can doubt that he got his money's worth on his New Jersey philanthropies. His concern that the buildings be practical and not overly monumental was evidenced in his reply to a letter from the Secretary of the Belleville Public Library. "The architect states that your building is of monumental design with a large amount of granite steps. It is in fact a monument and not a Library Building at all."[26]

The Carnegie buildings were not outright gifts but required a commitment by the community to support the library by budgeting annually at least ten percent of the building's cost for its maintenance. The problem with this arrangement was that in too many

Carnegie Library Buildings in New Jersey

Active Main Libraries	*Used for Other Purposes*

Active Main Libraries

Avon-by-the-sea
Bayonne
Belleville
Belmar
Caldwell
Camden
Edgewater
Elizabeth
Freehold
Kearny
Long Branch
New Brunswick
Nutley
Perth Amboy
Union City
Verona

Branch Libraries

East Orange—Elmwood
East Orange—Franklin
Montclair—Upper Montclair
Union City—West Hoboken

Used for Other Purposes

Main Libraries

Atlantic City—City Offices
East Orange—Municipal Court
Englewood—Bank Offices
Lakewood—Storage (Prospective
   Local History Museum)
Montclair—Church Offices
Vineland—Senior Citizen Center
Westfield—Ladies Shop

Branch Libraries

Camden—East Camden—Regional
   Health Center
Elizabeth—Liberty Square—City
   Offices

Demolished Main Libraries

Collingswood
Cranford
Little Falls
Plainfield
Summit

instances local officials thought that a "building" was a library and failed to appropriate sufficient funds for the other two important elements that make libraries work: books and trained staff.

It is difficult, three-quarters of a century later, to assess accurately the full impact of the Carnegie grants on New Jersey libraries. Coming as they did at a time when Sarah Byrd Askew was persuading local communities to start new libraries and improve existing services, the challenge grants for library buildings added an important dimension to library development in the first years of this century.

1920–1945, The Years Between

With the exception of the County Library Law of 1920, library development from 1920 through 1945 appears to have been driven more by external events to the library world than by initiatives from the library world itself. These events included both the Great Depression and World War II.

The "Roaring Twenties"

The 1920s largely witnessed the completion of the feverish cycle of the creation of new local libraries triggered by the passage of the forward-looking public library legislation of 1884 and the zealous promotion of library service by the Public Library Commission beginning in 1900. By the end of the decade the number of public libraries reporting to the Commission had grown to 325.[27] Succeeding decades would reduce rather than increase the number of public libraries in New Jersey.

The 1920s also saw the continuation of the trend to provide more ample funding for the many public libraries now in existence.

> In spite of the cry of high taxes more New Jersey municipalities last year voted to give tax support to libraries than have ever voted in one year, and this was in addition to the county and township libraries established by popular vote.
>
> Local library appropriations have more than doubled in the past three years, and during the period covered by this report more library buildings have been constructed in this state than ever before in one year, although the Carnegie Foundation has discontinued giving money for this purpose.[28]

Perhaps the most significant development of the 1920s was the creation of larger units of service to meet the needs of New Jersey residents. This largely took the form of county libraries, forestalling the creation of small new independent community libraries, and even reducing the number of such libraries as many became branches of county libraries. In a parallel development in counties not served by county libraries, between the years 1922 and 1934, twenty-seven small community libraries were united into three township libraries, with the old libraries serving as branches of the new enlarged system. As late as the 1960s this continued to occur, for example with the eight libraries serving Woodbridge Township merging into one municipal system.

The Depression Years

The decade of the 1930s marked a sharp departure from the seemingly unending progress which marked the earlier decades of the century. The period from 1900 to 1929 had generally witnessed constantly improving support for the rapidly growing number of public libraries. The 1929 stock market crash brought all of this to a screeching halt. At first it was primarily "association" libraries (referred to by law as "private reading rooms") which suffered, many losing from five to sixty percent of their funding. This was undoubtedly true because municipalities were not required by law to provide any support to these libraries, underscoring the wisdom of those who pressed for the mandated level of support of "free public libraries" enacted in the 1884 library law.

With the deepening of the depression even free public libraries began to feel the pinch, particularly as a declining economy was accompanied by increased use of public libraries. "Demands have increased in all lines of service rendered by the Public Library Commission. During this crisis people are turning to libraries in ever increasing numbers. The number of card holders in libraries from reports received show an increase of as high as 40 percent. The number of books borrowed has increased in many instances more than 50 percent and most of this increase has been in the use of nonfiction."[29]

One of the major casualties of the crisis was library book budgets: ". . . all libraries have had their book appropriations reduced. Therefore, their book stocks are also being depleted with few or no additions to take the place of the discarded books."[30] Still later the Commission reported: "The greatest cuts have had to be in the book funds so that the entire book stock in New Jersey libraries is at present in bad condition—from their lack of money to add new titles and to replace old ones when worn out. With reports showing more than six hundred thousand borrowers this condition is much aggravated. . . ."[31]

One of the ways that libraries were able to cope during this crisis of diminishing resources and expanding use was through the assistance of workers supplied with federal assistance. "It would have been impossible for the libraries of the State to render efficient service this past year if it had not been for the workers supplied by the Emergency Relief Administration."[32]

As the decade wore on libraries began to recover. "As a whole there has been a gain in library appropriations. . . . In some libraries salary cuts are still in force but not in many."[33] Putting library difficulties in perspective, noted the Commission deep in the depression, ". . . New Jersey libraries as a whole have been fortunate as compared with libraries in other states. More were closed during the past year although as said before it was through the help of the E.R.A. [Emergency Relief Administration] that a number of the association and endowed libraries were kept open. Many have had their appropriations badly cut because of the inability of the town to continue appropriations which had been given in the past but on an average libraries have been cut less than a number of other departments."[34] This suggestion, that public libraries may have suffered less than other institutions or libraries in other states, may once again be related to the mandatory level of support required for those organized as "free public" libraries.

Libraries Go to War

Just at the point when libraries were beginning to emerge from the difficulties of the depression into a more normal world, the country found itself in a major world conflict. Once again the energy of libraries began to focus on the most pressing job at hand. "Of course by far the greater part of the energy of the Library Commission staff, as well as of all libraries in the State, has gone into the service of our defense forces. During the earlier part of the year these energies were concentrated on supplying books and valuable material to the workers in defense areas in order to aid them in speeding up our wartime production. It also has been the task of the libraries to supply the families of these men with recreational reading."[35]

One of the difficulties to be overcome related to library book collections. "The war has, of course, brought a demand for an entirely different type of book and all libraries are exploring every possible avenue in their attempt to meet the new demand."[36] It can be surmised that the difficulty lay in supplying a more varied diet of non-fiction books to readers.

In the midst of the war period Sarah B. Askew died, and the Commission replaced her in 1943 with a new Secretary and Librarian, Raymond C. Lindquist. His proved to be a short tenure when the Commission was merged with the State Library in 1945. In his last report of the Public Library Commission before the merger, Lindquist assessed the public library world he found:

> . . . though most people in New Jersey have access to some public library service, most of the libraries are so starved financially that both the quality and quantity of the service they can give is decidedly limited. The American Library Association's 'Post-War standards for Public Libraries' has recommended that $25,000 annually for library purposes is the desirable minimum. However, 80% of New Jersey's libraries have less than that amount for annual support. The American Library Association's standards state further that until such time as the $25,000 minimum annual support . . . can be achieved, the very minimum on which any public library should undertake to operate is

$6,000 per year . . . 54% of New Jersey libraries have . . . less than $6,000 per year.[37]

The solution he suggested reflected a growing professional perception. "The solution may lie in consolidation of library areas into units that can pay at least $6,000 per year for a public library, and, preferably, a very much higher figure."[38]

The Post-War World

The end of World War II found the public library world in the United States in a ferment of self-examination regarding the future of national public library policy. One of the most influential of such efforts was the publication of the *Public Library Inquiry*, a series of studies undertaken by the Social Science Research Council at the behest of the American Library Association, and published by Columbia University in 1948–1950. These and other publications began to focus the attention of the public library community on key post-war issues, and the consensus that developed began to be worked into federal and state legislation. These national and state efforts have done much to shape the library world in which we function today.

Post-War public library development in New Jersey owes much to federal and state initiatives which began to be enacted from the 1950s onward, in response to the questions being raised within the library community. These initiatives began to look at some of the kinds of questions raised by Lindquist in his 1944 report: the lack of financial resources of many public libraries, and the question of whether some libraries were too small to provide an adequate basis for service. Also, even with the development of numerous county libraries in New Jersey, some rural counties remained largely unserved (Gloucester and Salem counties, for example) and many counties still had communities with no planned access to public library service.

Many of these concerns were addressed by the federal Library Services Act of 1956. In the state, they were addressed by the New Jersey Library Association's Library Development Committee in its 1954 publication, *Books for the People of New Jersey*. That was followed by a legislative commission to study library issues whose recommendations were published in its 1956 report, *Better Libraries for New Jersey*. The concepts contained in these federal and state actions, the legislation which emerged from these and later actions, and the later legislative initiatives of government to influence library developments have been varied and profound in their effects, and because of this they are considered fully under separate chapters in this history.

We will consider, as well, in a separate chapter, one of the more significant events to occur in the early 1950s, from the perspective of public libraries: the creation of a Graduate Library School at Rutgers University.

Public Library Trends in the 1950s and 1960s

1. The period following the Second World War witnessed the growing involvement of federal and state government in the affairs of public libraries. This has taken the form, on occasion, of the development of standards and/or operational criteria. It has been reflected in the promotion of library research, and in the collection and dissemination of information about public libraries. Perhaps most importantly, it has involved making funds available from other than local sources to support the operations of public libraries. In New Jersey both federal and state funds have provided important support for public library programs. Particularly with the creation of the "Area Library Program" as a result of state legislation in 1967, library development came to be increasingly dominated by state legislation.

2. One of the more important by-products of federal and state programs nationally has been the encouragement of cooperative action among libraries. Even when such cooperation has not been mandated by statute, public libraries, having been encouraged to look at things cooperatively, tend to seek out cooperative means of achieving their objectives. This has been evident in New Jersey, for example, in the development of such local cooperatives as the Bergen County Library Cooperative (BCCLS) and the Middlesex County Cooperative (LMX). What has taken place, in fact, has been a cultural shift in the way local public librarians view their world.

3. The world we inhabit in New Jersey today is a more prosperous one than the post-war world we entered in 1945. New Jersey public libraries have shared in this prosperity generally, not only through state and federal action but also through increased appropriations at the local level. However, this experience has been mixed. New Jersey's development in the past half-century is characterized by the development of suburban communities, to the point today that many traditionally rural counties like Sussex, Warren and Hunterdon are experiencing substantial growth. In developing suburban and exurban com-

munities, libraries have fared well, with expanding budgets and new buildings. However, for older urban communities, both large and small, communities like Newark and Paterson, the loss of taxable property has led to a serious strains on library financing at the very time they are needed most to serve populations requiring enhanced services.

4. Given the fragmentation of opinion on many critical issues in our national life, highlighted by the Vietnam war, it was perhaps inevitable that this would spill over into our statewide professional dialogue, much as it did nationally within the American Library Association. Particularly during the early 1970s rhetoric within the New Jersey Library Association began to reflect the national dialogue. Sharp divisions arose between those who wanted the Association to take stands on social issues and others who felt the Association should concentrate only on issues of immediate interest to libraries. It is perhaps a reflection of the genuine goodwill that normally flows between members of the New Jersey library community that however sharp the divisions may have grown, they never quite succeeded in fracturing the civility that characterizes relations among professional colleagues within the state.

The 1970s and Beyond

While a period as long as a quarter century has obviously witnessed many trends and cross-currents in library development, a number stand out above the rest.

The Development of Technology

The growth of new technology is certainly not peculiar to New Jersey, but it is proving central to library development in the state. Events may have begun as a small stream, but by the mid-1990s they have grown into a torrent. From such modest beginnings as microfilm catalogs of the Newark Public Library and State Library holdings, we now find many New Jersey libraries with access to huge databases and online services. Most larger libraries in the state and many smaller ones have developed electronic databases of their own holdings, and many public libraries have made provisions for dial-up access. Some cooperatives such as BCCLS in Bergen County have developed area-wide databases of their holdings. Automated charging systems are now commonplace.

Almost all public libraries in the state now have regular access to remote databases to enhance reference and information service, either through their own resources or through utilization of the services of regional cooperatives as part of the New Jersey Network. Access to the Internet is becoming more common, with an increasing number of libraries making provision for direct patron access to Internet searching. The effect of many of these technical innovations is to expand the horizons of small libraries in the state, making them increasingly more viable as service institutions. At the same time, these technical innovations stretch the professional capacities of even larger libraries, as they struggle to create training opportunities for their staffs.

Increasing Emphasis on Cooperative Effort

Increasingly, the attention of public libraries has gravitated toward cooperative effort. In the mid–1970s the New Jersey Library Association, acting primarily through the work of its Library Development Committee, began to look at the statewide cooperative "area center" library effort, eventually suggesting the creation of even larger regional units of service. In the late 1970s and the 1980s the Association supported efforts to develop a new system of multitype cooperative library regions. Much of this effort has focused on harnessing technology through coordinated action of local independent libraries of all kinds. Beginning in the mid-1970s, library professionals increasingly began to see themselves as members of a unified profession rather than as hyphenated fragments of a scattered profession, such as public-librarians, school-librarians, special-librarians, etc. This is not to suggest that such designations have become meaningless, but rather, that they appear to be declining in New Jersey.

Uncertainties in Public Funding

Funding trends for public libraries in New Jersey have been inconsistent since 1970, with peaks and valleys dotting the landscape as public attitudes toward public funding have ebbed and flowed. However, it is fair to say that the trends have been primarily downward. In other parts of the country, such as California and Massachusetts, strong public pressure forced state government to limit expenditures for public purposes by either state or local government. The federal government has also been under increasing pressure to balance its budget by strictly limiting the amount it expends for public purposes. In New Jersey in 1976 this kind of sentiment took the form of legislation which placed a "cap," or limit, of five percent on the amount of an increase local government could promulgate from one budget year to the next.[39] When first implemented this legislation had a severe impact on library budgets and programs, particularly since in many of these years the level of inflation often exceeded the level of the increase permitted.

This condition persisted until 1985, when a bill under the sponsorship of Assemblyman Joseph Palaia of Monmouth County was passed eliminating the "cap" as a factor in the funding of municipal libraries. In 1988 this law's application was extended to "association" libraries, not organized under the municipal library statute,[40] and to Joint Libraries, under a separate statute which brought these institutions, which served two municipalities jointly, under the same provisions of the law generally affecting municipal libraries.[41] Despite this, the "cap" continued to be a factor in library funding, with many local officials refusing to treat the library as a special case, even though they were no longer required to limit library budgets by the "cap" law.

In the mid-1970s and the early 1990s as well, severe cuts in state aid were suffered by New Jersey libraries, adding to their general discomfort. In 1993 public sentiment against increases in public financing crystallized when the public turned against Governor Jim Florio, mainly due to his having raised taxes at the beginning of his term, and to the promise of his opponent, Christine Todd Whitman, to cut taxes if she were elected.

Despite the long-term negative trend noted above, public library progress has continued in New Jersey since 1970. Over the years, automation, expensive as it has been, has proceeded. Also, even with the serious reduction that has occurred in some libraries in the state, on the whole most libraries have at least managed to hold their own. For librarians, the negative effects of recent economic events on general library employment prospects appear to have caused the greatest difficulty, with prospects for advancement within one's own library and in the profession generally somewhat diminished.

If funding pressures have ushered in difficult times for New Jersey public libraries, another event has helped to balance this picture. As noted earlier, communities which organized public libraries under the public library statute of 1884 were mandated to provide a level of support at least equal to one-third of a mill, calculated on the *assessable* value of the property in the community. However, while in theory each community is supposed to assess property for tax purposes at its true value, in practice different communities assess at different levels. One community may decide that it will set its rate of assessed valuation at 49 percent of true value, while another may decide to assess at 75 percent of true value. Also the ratio of assessed to true value is apt to change from year to year. In effect, therefore, the 1884 law permitted different levels of support for different communities.

In fact, based on the ratio of assessed to true valuation, some communities in the state were mandated to receive support equal to double the amount of other communities. The mandated support for other community libraries was negligible. One of the proposals suggested to eliminate this difficulty, as well as to set a meaningful mandatory minimum figure for library support, was to no longer base the one-third of a mill minimum on an assessed valuation figure, which fluctuated from community to community. Instead it would be based on the true taxable value of a community, by utilizing an "equalized valuation" figure generated annually by the state, for the purpose of equitably setting state tax rates from community to community. Efforts were made in 1981 and 1982 to mandate library support at the level of one-third of a mill on equalized valuation, but the efforts failed. In 1985, under the sponsorship of Senator Matthew Feldman, of Bergen County, a law was passed embodying this concept. It was estimated that in the year following the passage of this law, an additional $3 million dollars was raised for library support from local sources.

Intellectual Freedom

One of the constant sources of concern for librarians has been the periodic attempts by some members of the legislature to pass legislation to restrict public access to material deemed "obscene and pornographic." Some of these efforts have specifically mentioned libraries among their provisions. By and large, the legislature has recognized the constitutional "free speech" issues involved in much of this legislation, and it has declined to pass measures which clearly could not withstand legal constitutional tests. From time to time, however, public pressure mounts for the legislature to take action as authors and publishers press ever onward in extending the boundaries of free expression, and periodically censorship bills of various kinds are introduced and considered by the legislature. In most cases proposed legislation never makes it out of committee, as committee members question the legality of the proposals or wish to avoid a bruising fight on the floor of the legislature, or often, a little bit of both. Occasionally, a bill does reach the floor of one or more of the legislative houses. This can be serious for those concerned with intellectual freedom, for legislators often do not want to be seen opposing such legislation and will vote in the affirmative to avoid being targeted by the bill's supporters in the next election.

On one occasion, in 1965, one such bill, attempting to define obscenity and banning it in libraries among other places, was introduced during the last days of a legislative session, when legislators are usually so pressed by pending measures that they are hardly aware of the provisions of many of the bills on which they vote. The bill quickly passed both houses with barely a comment from legislators. Jarred into a state of alarm by the sudden action of the legislature, members of the library profession mounted a massive campaign urging then Governor Richard Hughes to veto the bill, and, after a short period of anxiety and apprehension, Governor Hughes responded with a veto. "I have received an unusually large number of letters and telegrams from persons, especially those involved in the teaching of our youth, who have questioned seriously this bill's provisions. The New Jersey School Library Association, the New Jersey Library Association, the New Jersey Education Association and many other groups and individuals whose concern for our children is beyond reproach . . ."[42] This sent a powerful message to members of the profession: always be particularly alert at the end of a legislative session, when the logistics of legislative management make possible effective action by small groups to pass legislation that would ordinarily die a lingering death.

On another occasion, another kind of intellectual freedom issue was raised in the legislature. Early in the 1980s, reports from various states indicated that law enforcement authorities were increasingly trying to gain access to library records in order to determine "who was reading what." NJLA decided to take preventive measures by seeking to have legislation introduced that would protect the confidentiality of library records. Senator Matthew Feldman introduced a bill accomplishing this, and it was passed by the legislature and signed into law in 1985 by Governor Thomas Kean. As it turned out, New Jersey was fortunate in having such a law. In 1987 and 1988 the FBI conducted a series of investigations involving library circulation records in many parts of the country, but because of New Jersey's protective law the state was not affected.

Some Other Concerns

A number of other actions of the state assisted public libraries in meeting a variety of potential problems. Librarians, in New Jersey and elsewhere, have been continually concerned by problems of maintaining their collections against the danger of theft. Given the litigious nature of our society, there was particular concern that staff and the library might be liable for legal action if they acted in good faith to prevent theft. The concern existed, as well, that the laws against theft of library material should be strengthened. In 1985 a bill was passed exempting staff from criminal or civil penalties in any action causing the arrest of anyone believed to have stolen library material.[43] Action was taken later to protect library trustees, granting them exemption from liability for damages for exercise of their duties as trustees unless their "actions evidence a reckless disregard of the duties imposed by the position."[44]

The hazards of operating a public library in the present climate are illustrated by a case which attracted national public attention. In 1991 the Morristown Public Library barred a man from the library alleging his behavior in the library and his lack of hygiene made patrons uncomfortable. Initially, a federal district court supported the patron, ruling that the library had erred in adopting its regulations governing conduct in the library and in its application of several of these to the patron. Later, a superior court reversed the initial decision, noting that the library's policy was within "well established constitutional privilege." The case pitted the New Jersey library community (who were generally supportive of the library's position) against the community of librarians represented by the American Library Association, some of whom appeared to show more concern for the rights of the patron in question than they did for the concerns of the library and its service to the public.[45]

Conclusion

As the end of the century approaches, public librarians view the future with a mixture of anticipation and anxiety. They sense that libraries will be altered dramatically as public needs change and as technology alters the way we meet those needs. Yet one also senses a feeling of confidence born of the success that public libraries in New Jersey have experienced in the past. While librarians are always conscious of their shortcomings and the goals they have yet to reach, they have also gained a firm sense of their abilities, and this is likely to serve them well in the years to come. In terms of training, ability and self-knowledge, no generation of librarians has been better prepared to wrestle with the future.

Notes

1. Howard L. Hughes, *Public Libraries in New Jersey, 1750–1850* (Trenton, N.J.: New Jersey Library Association, 1965).
2. *Ibid*: 8.

3. *Ibid*: 10.

4. *Ibid*: 11.

5. *Ibid*: 11.

6. *Ibid*: 17.

7. *New Jersey . . . Guide . . . Federal Writers Project (WPA)* (New York: Hastings House, 1956), 218.

8. Hughes: 22.

9. *Ibid:* 22.

10. C. S. Thompson, *Evolution of the American Public Library, 1653–1876* (Washington, D.C.: Scarecrow Press, 1952), 94, 95.

11. Hughes: 12, 13.

12. Hughes: 13.

13. Hughes: 13.

14. Conversation with Veronica Cary, Director of the Trenton Free Public Library, retired.

15. Thompson: 184.

16. Thompson: 184, 185.

17. Thompson: 180.

18. Hughes. Hughes records the history of libraries in 57 New Jersey communities, most of which were still operating, in some form, by the mid–19th century.

19. Cordelia Curtis, "Chronological List of Public Libraries Before 1900 in New Jersey." Taken from thesis, *"Development of the Public Library in New Jersey*, submitted to the Faculty of Political Science, Columbia University, 1935.

20. *Fiftieth Annual Report of the Free Public Library, 1935* (Paterson, N.J.: Paterson Free Public Library, 1936).

21. Irene James, *Early History of Libraries in Paterson* (Paterson, N.J.: 1949).

22. *Second Report of the Public Library Commission of the State of New Jersey* (Trenton, N.J.: John J. Murphy Pub. Co., 1901), 6.

23. *Twelfth Annual Report of the Public Library Commission of the State of New Jersey* (Trenton, N.J.: State Gazette Pub. Co., 1912), 13.

24. Interview with Mrs. James, October 14, 1985.

25. Richard A.Hazen, *Carnegie Libraries in New Jersey; A Summary.* Unpublished manuscript, September, 1985.

26. Timothy Rub, "The Day of Big Operations: Andrew Carnegie and His Libraries." *Architectural Record*, July, 1985, 81–85.

27. *Thirtieth Annual Report of the Public Library Commission of the State of New Jersey, 1929–1930*, 1.

28. *Twenty-third Annual Report of the Public Library Commission of the State of New Jersey, 1922–1923*, 1.

29. *Thirty-second Annual Report of the Public Library Commission of the State of New Jersey, 1931–1932*, 1.

30. *Thirty-third Annual Report of the Public Library Commission of the State of New Jersey, 1932–1933*, 2.

31. *Thirty-fifth Annual Report of the Public Library Commission of the State of New Jersey, 1934–1935*, 7.

32. *Ibid*: 6.

33. *Thirty-eighth Annual Report of the Public Library Commission of the State of New Jersey, 1937–1938*, 10.

34. *Thirty-fourth Annual Report of the Public Library Commission of the State of New Jersey, 1933–1934*, 8.

35. *Forty-second Annual Report of the Public Library Commission of the State of New Jersey, 1941–1942*, 2.

36. *Ibid*: 12.

37. *Forty-fourth Annual Report of the Public Library Commission of the State of New Jersey, 1943–1944*, 2.

38. *Ibid*: 2.

39. Chapter 68, Laws of 1976. State of New Jersey.

40. Chapter 66, Laws of 1988. State of New Jersey.

41. Chapter 38, Laws of 1988. State of New Jersey.

42. *Veto Messages of Hon Richard J. Hughes Governor of New Jersey* (Trenton, N.J.: State of New Jersey, 1965–1969), 74.

43. Chapter 373, Laws of 1985. State of New Jersey.

44. Chapter 171, Laws of 1989. State of New Jersey.

45. For a discussion of the Morristown case see Alice Gertzog and Edwin Beckerman, *Administration of the Public Library* (Metuchen, N.J.: Scarecrow Press, 1994), 324–326.

2

The New Jersey State Library

Edwin Beckerman

The generally accepted date for the beginning of the New Jersey State Library is March 18, 1796, when the General Assembly resolved that its Clerk, Maskell Ewing, "be directed to enter on the Minutes of the House of this Day, the Titles and Names of the several Books now belonging to the Legislature, and that he be further directed to procure at the expense of the Legislature a suitable Case for the keeping and Preservation of such Books; and further also, that he be responsible to the Legislature for the safe keeping and Preservation of the same."[1] Some clues to the kind of collection being developed was indicated by the Assembly a week earlier, when it authorized the Clerk "to purchase during the recess of the Legislature, the following books for the use of the Legislature, viz.

Two sets of Cunningham's Law Dictionary
Two sets of Sheridan's Dictionary
Two sets of Blackstone's Commentaries
Two sets of Montesquieu's Spirit of Laws
Two sets of Paley's Moral Philosophy
Two sets of Vattel on Law of Nations
Two sets of Ferguson's Political and Moral Science
Two sets of the constitutions of each state in the union"[2]

Collection building during this early period clearly focused on a combination of intensely practical tools for the edification of the legislature and works on the general moral and ethical basis of law and government, for their further guidance.

Although, in a formal sense, we can date the beginning of the State Library to this action of the legislature in 1796, the origin of the library collection actually predates this event by some 58 years.

In 1738 a gift of D'Ewes' "Journal of Parliament" was recorded by the Royal Governor, Lewis Morris, in a note to the colonial legislature, and subsequently additional volumes were gradually added to the collection.[3] The early use of this collection may have been cumbersome, owing to the peculiar development of the colony. In fact, it may have spawned the nation's oldest "traveling library." New Jersey was originally composed of two colonies, East Jersey and West Jersey, reflecting the separate interests of the two proprietors, Lord Berkeley and Sir George Carteret. While the two colonies were united under a royal charter in 1702, until after the Revolution meetings of the legislature continued to alternate between Perth Amboy in East Jersey and Burlington in West Jersey, and did so until a state capital was finally chosen in Trenton. For almost a century all of the trappings of government, including records and books, had to be transported between these (then) distant points, or duplicated for use in the two capitals.

The State Library in the 1800s

The fledgling State Library continued to grow after the turn of the century and by 1804 included some 195 volumes, as well as a large number of pamphlets and journals issued by the United States House of Representatives and Senate. In that year it was reported that at least eight volumes were missing and that it was suspected that this was true of other volumes as well, which "they have no means of discovering,"[4] a circumstance that has troubled many librarians of a later age. Accordingly, an Assembly committee proposed that all books be put under the care of the Clerk of the Assembly, even though Maskell Ewing, as Clerk of the Assembly had *already* been given custody of the collection eight years earlier. The committee also proposed that each member of the Assembly, when borrowing an item, record it properly in a book to be provided by the Clerk, that all books be stamped with the words "New Jersey Legislature," and that only members of the Assembly be entitled to borrow from the library. Finally, it enjoined that all "bindings be of leather, strong and neat."[5]

Custody of the State Library was vested in the Clerk of the Assembly until 1822, when the legislature determined that "a suitable person shall be annually appointed, by the council, and general assembly of this state, in joint meeting, as librarian of the two houses of the legislature, to serve for one year, and until another shall be chosen in his stead."[6] The act further provided that the librarian should have custody of the books and papers of the two houses, that books and papers be organized and a catalog prepared, and that the compensation for the librarian be set at $2 per day when employed on state business. The act also appropriated $200 for the library. Accordingly, William L. Prall was appointed the first State Librarian of New Jersey in 1822. He served only one year and was replaced by Charles Parker, who served the first extended term as appointed State Librarian from 1823 to 1828.

In 1824, the legislature began to appropriate funds on a regular basis for the support of the State Library. It provided for the "gradual increase of the State Library" through an annual appropriation of $200 for the improvement of the collection, a sum it authorized for the succeeding ten years, to be disbursed by the State Librarian.[7] Perhaps the "gradual increase" of the State Library was not as gradual as anticipated, for by 1828 a committee of the Assembly recommended the erection of additional shelving for the library, and in a sybaritic burst of self-indulgence recommended that a cloth be put on the table and a carpet on the floor. During these early years the library was first housed on shelves placed adjacent to the legislative chambers. Later, as the collection grew, it was transferred to a room nearby. Evidence of continuing interest in the library was also provided by the Assembly's action in 1835, when it extended the annual $200 grant to the library for another ten years.[8]

Until 1837, the State Supreme Court maintained a separate law library, but in that year the legislature authorized the State Librarian to prepare a room adjoining the State Library to house the law collection. Consolidation of the two collections laid the groundwork for the development of one of the pillars of the present State Library, the Law Collection. This action was supplemented in 1855 when the legislature directed the State Librarian to add to its law collection the library belonging to the Law Society of New Jersey, for the use of the legislature, the courts and the bar of New Jersey.[9]

State Library Act of 1845

While rules for the operation of the State Library were adopted in 1804, it was not until 1845 that any comprehensive statement regarding the State Library was made by the legislature. The "Act to Regulate the State Library," enacted in 1845 and amended in 1846, provided the following:

1. The State Librarian was to be elected on a triennial basis by a joint meeting of the Assembly and Senate.

2. The Library was to be kept open from 9 a.m. until 6 p.m. during the sessions of the legislature and courts.
3. The Library was open to use, among others, by members of the legislature, judges and other officers involved in the legal system, members of the executive departments of state government, and "all others who have been or may be at any time entitled by law, when at the seat of government."
4. The Librarian, with the consent of the Governor, Treasurer, and Secretary of State (or any two of these), was directed to prescribe rules and regulations for the operation of the Library, posting such rules in a conspicuous place in the Library. The Librarian was authorized to resort to court action, if necessary, to recover fines or any other debt owed.
5. The Librarian was directed to arrange and preserve books, maintain records of books borrowed, maintain a catalog of holdings and keep account of expenditures for the Library.
6. Two hundred and fifty dollars was provided annually for book acquisition and maintenance.
7. The Librarian would receive and preserve all bills and joint resolutions of the legislature.
8. A sum of $2 a day was voted for the services of the Librarian while the legislature and courts were in session, and $1 a day for all other duties.
9. A joint committee of the legislature was created to examine the condition of the Library, order necessary repairs and recommend improvements.[10]

While the 1845 Act increased the acquisition budget of the Library only slightly, from $200 to $250 annually, the funds were not always fully used. In 1848 the legislature was forced to direct the State Librarian to expend the entire budget of the State Library and to secure the complete Statutes of New Jersey and have 500 copies printed. It also authorized the Governor, the Secretary of State and the Assembly Education Committee to publish any material in the State Library worthy of reproducing.[11] Clearly, the State Library operation was growing in scope and was increasingly regarded as a statewide resource, a judgment confirmed by the legislature again in 1853 when it authorized publication of 500 copies of the State Library catalog of holdings.[12]

The improvement in the prospects of the State Library also extended to its physical facilities. In 1845 space was created for an expanded library on the third floor of a new addition to the State House, the first state government facility specially designed for library purposes.

The State Library at Mid-Century and After

The acquisition funds of the State Library increased during the 1850s and 1860s, and many volumes were also acquired through gifts and exchanges. For example, by 1858 State Librarian C. J. Ihrie observed that acquisition funds had grown to $577.17, enabling the Library to purchase 177 volumes during the year. Further, 411 additional volumes had been donated to the state, including legislative acts of several states, statutes, codes, historical collections and colonial records. However, though improvements could be seen, the slow pace of growth was also noted. "Fifty-five years have elapsed since the New Jersey State Library had its origin. But a slow growth attended its advancing years, and, much like a tree planted on the margin of the Delaware, her silvery stream flowed gently and evenly by, implanting none of its life and moisture, and consequently the tree depended upon the rains and dews and occasional sprays for its growth, deriving little advantage from its situation on the bank of a mystic river."[13]

By 1861 Ihrie reported crowded conditions which made it difficult to expand the collection, there having been added in that year over a thousand items including miscellaneous books, statutes, law reports, pamphlets and documents.[14] In 1862 Ihrie noted that the number of visitors during the year exceeded 11,000, and also that "the registry of books used for promiscuous reading, and others for reference in the several courts of the state number four thousand one hundred and sixty-one copies, seven times greater than the year 1854."[15]

The State Librarian's constant reference to the increase in collection size apparently had its effect. In 1863 the legislature voted funds to alleviate the crowded conditions of the library and its architect drew up plans for expanded space. Some difficulty was encountered in defining the exact nature of the expansion, but after an exchange of views between the governor and the legislature, additional funds were made available and a southerly expansion of the capitol building was undertaken, making room available for a new library as well as increased space for the executive branch.

C. J. Ihrie remained State Librarian from 1853 until 1866. He was succeeded in 1867 by Clarence J. Mulford, who perhaps best summarized his three-year tenure in his first annual report: "Nothing of importance occurs at any time during the year that would give especial interest to one report over another. The business operations of the Library are rather monotonous, and to give a plain, full statement of its transactions is about all it would afford."[16] And plain statements he indeed gave, noting that by 1869 the total collection of the State Library had reached 17,098 volumes.[17] The legislature's Joint Committee on the State Library noted that the State Library should issue a printed catalog, none having been issued since 1853.

In 1871 Jeremiah Dally began a brief two-year tenure as State Librarian. He noted that the "Library Room" was finally being enlarged, some seven years after the legislature had voted funds for that purpose.[18] However, to begin is not necessarily to complete, and it was not until 1876 that this leisurely construction was brought to a successful conclusion.

James S. McDanolds succeeded Dally in 1872, and served until 1884. The record of the State Library during the last quarter of the 19th century is largely one of stability, gradual improvement of collections, and continuing concentration on the Library's role as a support to government, to the exclusion of any wider role in the development of libraries statewide.

As early as 1864 an annual stipend was voted for the State Librarian, replacing the per diem rate previously in effect. By 1873 this annual rate had reached $1500. In addition, the legislature authorized in 1885 a stipend of $1000 annually for the hiring of a permanent assistant for the State Library, having first been urged to do so in 1873. As with the expansion of library space, the wheels of progress respecting the State Library continued to grind exceedingly slow.

The method of appointing the State Librarian was changed in 1878, providing for the appointment of the State Librarian by a Commission composed of the Governor, the Chancellor, the Chief Justice of the Supreme Court, the Secretary of State, the State Treasurer and the State Comptroller.[19] In effect, this would eventually turn the State Librarian's position into a political appointment subject to the will of the Governor, as occurred in the 20th century, but this seems not to have disturbed the placid nature of the State Library operation in the latter part of the 19th century. Actually, one can reasonably suspect that the position had always been subject to the political process when State Librarians had been appointed by the legislature. The creation of an executive administration to oversee the appointment of the State Librarian probably did little more than shift the locus of power from the legislature to the chief executive.

The mission of the State Library appears to have remained unchanged during the late 19th century. The collection continued to grow until by the turn of the century it exceeded 50,000 volumes. This growth was promoted by a continuing increase in the funds available for this purpose. In 1878 $750 was appropriated by the legislature for collection development, a sum which grew to $1500 by 1881, and $3000 by 1889. This growth, of course, had the usual effect on library quarters, causing extreme crowding. State Librarian Morris R. Hamilton noted that it had been determined to devote the third floor of the "new fire-proof front of the State House" to the Library[20] but it was not until 1891 that the move was actually accomplished. The new quarters proved to be worth the wait, being provided with electric power as well as gas, a feat accomplished at the cost of some disruption while the Edison Electric Company installed its equipment.

By 1899 the State Library was once again calling attention to its lack of space, and by 1902 it proposed to address the problem by construction of a two-tier steel bookstack. However, investigation reflected in subsequent annual reports of the State Librarian determined that the walls and floor of the library area in the State House were not strong enough to accommodate the additional weight that the move would require. The expansion took place in 1913, when rooms on the third and fourth floors of the Capitol's new westerly extension were dedicated for library purposes.

Public Library Development in the Late 19th Century

Although the role of the State Library seemed unchanged in the late 19th century, societal changes were occurring which eventually would change the mission and shape of the Library. With the beginning of a shift in America from a rural to an urban economy creating a need for a more highly educated work force, and with a national ethos based on individual opportunity for improvement, the country required an educational system that would meet the needs of the age. This resulted in a system of universal public education, and accelerated the growth of public libraries and learned societies. Developments in New Jersey reflected the same pattern. In 1884 the state legislature passed "An Act for the Encouragement of Free Public Libraries in Cities," the most important comprehensive statute dealing with public libraries up to that time.[21] This statute laid the groundwork for much of the growth that occurred in New Jersey in public libraries, and it exerts a continuing influence to the present day.

Little sense of this growing activity is reflected in the annual reports of the State Librarians of the period.

The isolation of the State Library from the changing events in the library world is reflected in an annual report of State Librarian Hamilton. During the mid–1890s a great deal of statewide interest had been generated in the possible creation of a "traveling library"

that would bring books to people in rural areas. Some of this speculation had centered on the possibility of delegating such responsibility to the State Library. Hamilton commented, "It is a great satisfaction to us to know that the 'traveling library' question has been
referred to a special commission of the Legislature, as the State Library is hereby relieved from any complication with the speculative
issue, and can maintain its referential status without the danger of
being made a medium of general circulation to which its books are
not adapted."[22] Traveling libraries were clearly not on Hamilton's
agenda!

Despite the State Librarian's opposition, the fledgling New Jersey
Library Association joined with the New Jersey Federation of
Women's Clubs in 1898 to help pass a bill creating a system of "traveling libraries" to be administered by the State Library.[23] Perhaps
the shock proved too great for Mr. Hamilton, for he chose that year
to retire. Nor did the State Librarian's brand of leadership pass un-
noticed within the library profession. Commented the *Library Journal* upon his retirement, "In New Jersey the retirement of the state
librarian finds justification, for the former incumbent in his 15 years
tenure of office had kept aloof from library progress and had maintained the library in a condition of masterly inactivity."[24]

In one respect, the State Library did respond to the changing
times. While the State Librarian might oppose the agency's assuming any role in providing service to rural areas, increasingly the State
Library was acting as a direct service institution to the general public, particularly to students. During the late 1890s the State Librarian on several occasions noted growing use by students from state
colleges and business schools, and even by high school students
from the area. By 1897, he was reporting that 9,000 students had
used the Library during the previous year, and in a strikingly modern vein, students had to be denied the use of pen and ink during
their visits due to mutilation of the collection.[25]

The Era of the Public Library Commission

The principal and almost exclusive concern of the State Library during its first hundred years was to serve state government, primarily
the legislature and the judiciary. While the state government had
taken a number of actions to promote the establishment of libraries
throughout the state, there was little or no involvement of the State
Library with the gradually increasing number of libraries throughout New Jersey. While this might have been acceptable in earlier
days before the advent of universal public education, by the latter

part of the 19th century pressure began to build for a more active stance by state government concerning the cultural and educational needs of the citizenry. This concern led professionals in many fields to join together to pursue mutual interests.

One such group was the New Jersey Library Association, whose formation in 1890 fostered the rapid growth of new libraries. Discussion in the Association led in just a few years to the realization that some state agency was needed to assist in the development of public libraries statewide, and that the State Library, with its orientation toward the legal and legislative needs of the state government, was unlikely to meet this need. Two years after the creation of a "traveling library" in the State Library, a move which led to little concrete action, many interested parties, including the Association, called for a new state agency to deal with public library issues. In 1900 an "Act to Promote the Establishment and Efficiency of Free Public Libraries" resulted. A Public Library Commission was established, and a focus was provided for the long-term development of public libraries in all parts of New Jersey. The second major cornerstone of the present State Library was laid.[26]

The first five-member Commission was appointed by Governor Voorhees in 1900. This included, among others, the Librarian of Princeton University, Dr. Ernest C. Richardson, and the Librarian of the Newark Public Library, Dr. Frank P. Hill. The initial charge to the Commission was to stimulate the establishment of public libraries in New Jersey, to offer advice regarding their organization, support and operation, and to aid in their service to local communities.

After a few years of operation it became obvious that the State Library's "traveling library" service was not performing as had been hoped, only 15 of 62 traveling collections were in use. In 1904, by agreement of the State Library and the Public Library Commission, the "traveling library" was transferred to the Commission, a move which in the coming years helped to focus the Commission's attention on the large, unserved rural areas of New Jersey. One of the functions of the Commission-run "traveling library" was to place books within easy reach of the residents of New Jersey, however small the community in which they might live. They did this by establishing small collections of 50 books, packing them in a self-contained book case, and lending them upon application from ten individual citizens, and from local clubs, granges, and educational associations.

One of the original traveling collections established by the Commission was a small collection placed at the New Jersey State Prison for the use of female prisoners, an early example of the broad scope of services supported by the new agency.[27] Over the years the Commission's early involvement in institutional library service grew, extending to state correctional facilities and to such institutions as a home for disabled veterans and their wives and a home for the mentally impaired. Parallel to the widening scope of the Public Library Commission came the recognition of the need for a permanent, professional librarian to administer the programs of the Commission. Enter Sarah Byrd Askew!

New Jersey has been fortunate at several junctures in its library history to have attracted extraordinarily gifted individuals to serve in leadership positions in the State Library and its predecessors; leaders who have proven sensitive to the needs that confronted them, and hardy enough to serve long terms in office, while remaining alert to the shifting library needs of the state. Sara B. Askew was the first of these figures. Her presence dominated the New Jersey library scene for the 37 years during which she served as Secretary-Librarian of the Public Library Commission, from 1905 until her death in 1942. The 1909 annual report of the Commission announced the loss of Miss Askew's services due to her move to the State Library, but despite this concern the move did not seem to have had the effect the Commission feared, for Miss Askew continued to be listed in subsequent reports as the Commission's principal administrator which post she continued to hold until her death in 1942.

In addition to its advisory functions with respect to the establishment and operation of public libraries, and the direct operational functions occasioned by the transfer of the "traveling library," the Commission's responsibilities grew in other ways with the passage of time. In 1909 a system of special loans was inaugurated to enable small libraries to meet study and reference needs, and to furnish some books to students in districts without libraries. In addition, a system of interlibrary loans was begun.

In 1913, an event of far-reaching significance occurred. Dr. Calvin N. Kendall, the State Commissioner of Education, proposed that the Public Library Commission take over the administration of state aid to school libraries. He believed that this would be preferable to having the Department of Public Instruction set up a library department to administer the program, duplicating some of the functions of the Public Library Commission. In 1913 the legislature made the Commissioner a member of the Public Library Commission, and in 1914 it give the Commission jurisdiction over school libraries.[28] This close connection between the Commission and the "education establishment" of the state, and the Commission's supervision of school libraries, may well have been a significant factor when three decades later the State Library was merged with the Public Library Commission and placed in the Department of Education.

In 1920 "An Act to Provide for the Establishment and Maintenance of Free County Libraries" made possible the creation of the Burlington County Library, the state's first county library, and the other county libraries that were established later in many of New Jersey's (then) less populated counties.[29] The initial impetus for this legislation came from organizations in Burlington County that asked the Public Library Commission to conduct a study of the library situation in the county. The study itself and the law which followed were the product of the Commission and, more particularly, the work of Sarah Byrd Askew.

Some aspects of the County Library Law have created problems over the years, designed as it was to serve the needs of the more simple, rural New Jersey of 75 years ago. Nevertheless, the establishment of county libraries was a great step forward in library service in New Jersey in the 1920s, and has proven a major asset to public library service in New Jersey in the 1990s. From early accounts, it is clear that the Commission intended to press for the establishment of county libraries in almost all of the counties in New Jersey. "With the program as now marked out the Commission hopes to have a county library established in every county except Hudson, within ten years."[30] This was later revised to exclude Essex County. These two counties were considered to be too densely populated and urbanized to warrant county libraries.

Two other facts need to be noted in assessing the accomplishments of the Commission during its early days. By the mid–19th century, only 57 public libraries had been formed in New Jersey.[31] By 1901, 102 libraries reported to the Public Library Commission. "Fifty-two of the 102 libraries reporting are free, and thirty-eight subscription. . . ."[32] By 1911, 214 public libraries were reporting to the Commission.[33]

The Commission was equally successful in its direct services. In 1912 it circulated 39,750 books through 282 traveling collections.[34] By 1920, the Commission noted that 354,000 books had been circulated through 1,572 traveling collections.[35] By 1926 some 3,007 traveling collections containing 150,450 books accounted for 930,280 books circulated to the public.[36]

Another program of note was initiated immediately after the arrival of Miss Askew on the scene. Upon entering the service of the Commission in 1905 Miss Askew began almost immediately to plan the first of what came to be an annual series of library education summer institutes, designed to provide a basic level of training for working librarians. The first institutes took place in Asbury Park in 1906. Basic though these institutes may have been, they were the earliest comprehensive attempt to provide organized training for librarians working in New Jersey's smaller libraries, and they provided a forward-looking, continuing operation during the entire life of the Commission. In addition, the Commission sponsored many other extension courses throughout the years to supplement the training available through the summer institutes.

In the 1920s the Commission began a program to develop industrial libraries. Its 1924 annual report notes that seven such libraries were established during the year, and seven more were reported in 1925. "The Oxford Street Company pays two-thirds of the cost of running the Oxford Free Library; the Whitall Tatum Company contributes largely to the support of the Millville Library; the Taylor-Wharton Company supports the High Bridge Library."[37]

The Crisis of the 1930s

In 1930, the year after the crash of the stock market and well into the Depression, the Public Library Commission took stock, showing little reaction in its annual report report to the ominous financial climate.

This is the thirtieth year of active work òn the part of the commission. In these thirty years the number of libraries in New Jersey has increased from eighty-nine (89) public, private, and institutional libraries, and eighteen (18) high school libraries, to 325 local public libraries, 10 county libraries, 173 high school libraries, 2 university libraries and 9 college and seminary libraries, besides the State Library, the New Jersey Historical Society Library and the collection of the Public Library Commission. Of the public libraries in this state in 1900 only 46 were free. Of the 325 libraries at present in existence in this state only 2 are subscription libraries.[38]

Reaction to the financial crisis was not long in coming, and annual reports for the remainder of the decade are replete with references to hard times. "With the need of cutting budgets this Commission has been called in by many communities to advise as to how this paring might be done without ruining the service."[39] On the kind of advice the Commission gave on these occasions it remained silent. On its own plight resulting from the crisis, it was more forthcoming: "With a good collection of books up to June 1932, it has been possible to render some aid to almost all those who have imperative needs but it has been necessary to give the books on hand extremely hard wear, which has resulted in many of them being worn out from constant use. . . . We enter the year 1933–1934 with a greatly depleted stock of books and few recent additions."[40] By 1936 the Commission was able to report some improvement in the general library situation, while noting that public library budgets on average were still some twelve percent under comparable budgets in 1929.[41] Only gradually did public library budgets assume some semblance of normality.

Under the leadership of Miss Askew, the Commission continued to exert its influence on the development of library service in New Jersey. It supported the formation of new libraries and extended new programs through the development of institutional service. It strengthened service through existing libraries by providing advice and material assistance through supplementary collection support, and augmenting school services statewide through both its advisory services and its provision of collections to supplement local resources. From its beginning in 1900 until it was merged to form a consolidated State Library in 1945, the influence and achievements of the Public Library Commission were far-reaching. For those in our own time who have come to believe that government can never do anything right, even a brief look at the saga of the Public Library Commission should prove instructive. Seldom has influence been exercised by any institution, public or private, that has been more profoundly right.

One positive occurance in the fortunes of the State Library must be noted during this period. In 1931 it moved from its quarters in the Capitol to the first floor of the new State House Annex.

The Consolidation of 1945

In 1945 a number of library and archival/historical activities were drawn together under a Division of the State Library, Archives, and History of the State Department of Education. The modern State Library was born. The emergence of this omnibus organization was anything but sudden. For several years, the possibility of combining the state government's library activities in one organization had surfaced sporadically and almost as quickly dissipated.

If there was any central obstacle to consolidation, it probably lay in the organic differences between the State Library and the Public Library Commission. The State Library had always been a direct service organization which provided services to legislators, jurists and other state employees. It was governed by a Commission made up of the Governor, the Chief Justice, the Secretary of State, the

State Comptroller, the State Treasurer and the Attorney General. Most of these individuals changed with new administrations, as did the State Librarian. In a word it was highly political, and over the years men of varying talents occupied the office of State Librarian. State Librarian James E. Downes described the situation in a message to the State Library Commission at the time of his resignation from office in 1943: "Apparently the position of State Librarian has been looked upon as an unimportant job that could be given to any 'deserving' party worker as a 'reward' without any consideration of his qualifications for the job, or interest in it."[42] By contrast, the Public Library Commission was apolitical, although its members were appointed by the Governor. Its leader, Sarah Byrd Askew, had served for thirty-seven years. It is perhaps not coincidental that the merger and reorganization was only achieved three years after Miss Askew's death.

Perhaps the overriding reason for the consolidation of library functions was the general move toward consolidation of state agencies. A proposal to reorganize the departments of state government had been defeated by the voters in the early 1940s. But when a new State Constitution was adopted in 1947, provisions for a reorganization of state agencies were submitted to the legislature and passed. Among the new measures introduced was the State Library reorganization bill, authorizing the consolidation of the existing State Library, the Public Records Office, the Law Library and the Public Library Commission into a new expanded State Library.

In a letter to Governor Charles Edison, December 2, 1942,[43] State Librarian Downes outlined some of the reasons for his support of consolidation, noting that it would enhance the prestige and influence of the combined agency and should result in an increase in efficiency, with more effective use of personnel. At the same time, he cautioned against consolidation until, among other things, "the State Library is taken out of politics." This observation, of course, was being made by a State Librarian who was part of the very process against which he cautioned, marking James E. Downes as one concerned with the welfare of the State Library, and detached enough to view it with some perspective. This was a most unusual and admirable man!

Establishing the New State Agency

The law creating the Division of the State Library, Archives and History in the Department of Education was passed on March 26, 1945.[44] It mandated that the State Librarian must, among other things, "have had at least one year of training in a school of library science accredited by the American Library Association and at least four years of library experience in a responsible administrative capacity."

The new agency was composed of four bureaus: the Bureau of Archives and History, the Bureau of Law and Legislative Reference, the Public and School Library Services Bureau, and the Bureau of General Reference. In addition to setting minimum qualifications for the position of State Librarian, the law also mandated that the head of the Bureau of Law and Legislative Reference must have both a law degree and a year of library training, that the heads of the Public and School Library Services Bureau and the Bureau of General Reference must have a year of library school training, and that the head of the Bureau of Archives and History must be a college graduate with special training or experience in historical and archival work. An era of politics at the State Library was being brought to a halt and a new standard of job qualifications for administrative appointments was being introduced.

In March 1947, under the consolidation law, Roger H. McDonough, Librarian of the New Brunswick Public Library, was chosen to head the new agency, and he proved worth waiting for. He provided a quality of leadership until his retirement in 1975 that the State Library had never had before. As with Miss Askew before him, McDonough has been one of those pivotal forces in New Jersey library history that combined force of personality and professional and governmental skills with longevity in office. In both cases, these qualities accounted for the extraordinary progress made during their terms in office.

The old Public Library Commission and State Library Commission were replaced in the new law by an Advisory Council of the Division of the State Library, Archives and History. The Advisory Council was composed of the Commissioner of Education ex officio and seven members appointed by the Governor for five-year terms. Thus, control passed from statutory commissions under the old laws to the Department of Education under the new, with advice from an advisory council.[45]

In addition to the problems inherent in any reorganization (territorial and jurisdictional questions, and unfamiliarity of staff with one another, etc.), some unique problems faced the new State Librarian. The Public Library Commission, newly converted into the Public and School Library Services Bureau, had had one strong leader for 37 years until 1942, and two successive heads thereafter, over the next five years. The need to establish a strong identity and direction was pronounced. This was particularly true in issues of library organization relating to cooperative endeavors. Nationally, this was a period when librarians all over the country were asking searching questions about how to organize library service in the post-war era.

Inevitably, McDonough turned much of his early attention to restructuring the Public and School Library Services Bureau. He created the positions of Public Library Services Supervisor and School Library Services Supervisor, appointing Janet Zimmerman (later Janet Zimmerman McKinlay) to the former and Jane B. Hobson to the latter. In 1949 McKinlay was appointed Bureau Head and did much to restore the luster to the Bureau previously enjoyed by the Public Library Commission under Sarah Byrd Askew.

As Head of the Bureau of Law and Legislative Reference, McDonough appointed Margaret E. Coonan. Coonan possessed both legal and library credentials, and her addition to the staff added substantially to both its prestige and performance. Under her successor, Herta Prager, the Bureau continued to provide increasingly sophisticated services to the state government, the legal profession and the public.

The functions of the old Public Record Office were assumed by the State Library's Bureau of Archives and History, under its first Head, Thomas Amelia. The Bureau's first professional librarian/archivist was Kenneth W. Richards. As its activities expanded during the 1950s and 1960s the Bureau established itself as a modern State Archives, with increasingly professionalized services in the preservation, storage and recording of archival collections, a records management and microfilming program, the publication of historical documents such as the colonial laws, and regulation of and assistance to county and municipal archives. As part of the records management program legislation was enacted giving the Bureau control over all public records—of state, county and local government. Under this law, no records created in the course of conducting public business could be destroyed without the approval of the Archives Bureau. But for this program, thousands of public documents would have been lost to posterity. On his death in 1975 Richards was succeeded by William C. Wright, during whose tenure the records management collections were relocated from warehouses to a new facility shared by the Library for the Blind and Handicapped.

One of the most important steps taken after the consolidation was the creation of the Office of Legislative Research Services, which was established by McDonough, and soon came to be headed by Samuel Alito. As the work of the office expanded it became indispensable to the operations of the legislature, which now had a systematic and sophisticated source of information for the making of laws for the first time in its history. As McDonough had anticipated, its success led the legislature to transfer the office to its own jurisdiction in 1964. Thus, the State Library was at the center of a historic change that helped to enhance the role of the legislature in the state government. In the past three decades the successor to the Library's Office of Legislative Research Services has become a critically important component of the legislative staff.

Other steps were taken to coordinate the activities of the new, expanded agency. During 1947–48 technical processing services were centralized, with ordering and cataloging consolidated for all units of the Library. A cataloging backlog inherited from preconsolidation days continued to plague the operation for several years. Substantial efforts were also made to integrate the collections of the various units to permit maximum operating efficiency.

The State Librarian's annual report for 1950–51 reflects the kinds of issues that seemed most pressing in those early days of reorganization.[46] Among the more important, McDonough noted the need for construction of a new State Library building and records center, the need to explore interim steps until construction could take place, the advisability of creating a graduate school of library studies at Rutgers University, and the need to establish a program of state aid to promote the growth of regional library service.

Many of these requests for action have long since been met. A building has been constructed to house the State Archives and the State Library. A graduate library school was established at Rutgers University. And state aid for regional library service forms a cornerstone for library programs in New Jersey.

The State Library Past Mid-Century

Much of the history of the New Jersey State Library during the past 45 years has been intimately connected with federal aid legislation— the Library Services Act (LSA), later the Library Services and Construction Act (LSCA), and the Elementary and Secondary Education Act (ESEA)—and with successive programs of state aid designed to encourage the improvement of local libraries and the development of area and regional services. The effects of federal action on the libraries of New Jersey will be considered in some detail in chapter six, while the impact of successive efforts by state government with respect to libraries will be considered in chapter five. Our purpose here is not to look at these statutes in detail but rather to look more broadly, in passing, at the effects of these initiatives, and also to view the State Library in its planning, organizing and administrative role with respect to statewide library development. The activist role assumed by the consolidated State Library of the 1950s and beyond, stimulated by federal and state legislation, continued to propel the institution in the same kind of key role it had always assumed in its days as the Public Library Commission; even its role as information resource to state government was transformed by a more energetic stance.

Planning for Statewide Library Development: The 1950s and 1960s

The modest seed planted in the State Librarian's annual report of 1950–51 began to sprout in the years following. In 1953–54 the State Library staff served as consultants in the design of a master plan for the development of public library service in New Jersey prepared by the New Jersey Library Association's Library Development Committee, and titled *Books for the People of New Jersey*. The report called on the people of the state to supply financial aid to public libraries, considering such factors as equalization, per capita grants and incentive grants aimed at establishing larger units of service. Many of the ideas in this report were incorporated in the report of the Commission to Study Library Service, established two years later by the legislature, titled *Better Libraries for New Jersey*, and later enacted into legislation. This "State Library Aid Act of 1959" established the principle of state aid as a major factor in statewide public library development. The State Library provided much of the professional expertise that led to the legislation.

In 1956, with the passage of the federal Library Services Act, the Public and School Library Services Bureau of the State Library was charged with the responsibility of formulating a program to use the new federal funds appropriated under the Act. As part of its responsibilities after the passage of both the federal and state laws, the State Library entered a new era of both planning and administering activities begun under the provisions of the acts. This is a responsibility that persists down to the present day.

The decade of the 1960s was a period of unparalleled growth for libraries. With major legislative initiatives, both federal and state, and with rapid growth in local libraries, the State Library was a vital element in a service system that was experiencing explosive growth. It was directly responsible for administering ambitious service programs deriving from federal and state legislation. With its traditional role as advisor and consultant carried down from its days as the Public Library Commission, it also found itself intimately connected with the local library scene.

As in the 1950s, when the New Jersey Library Association began to look at issues of library development in the state in the mid–1960s it turned once more to the State Library as a resource to enable the Association to examine the issues and to craft new solutions. Staff of the State Library were closely involved in supporting the planning effort. This led to the publication in 1964 of a comprehensive analysis of library needs in New Jersey, *Libraries for the People of New Jersey; or Knowledge for All*. This effort was a product of the leadership of Mary Gaver and Lowell Martin, co-chairs of the New Jersey Library Association's Library Development Committee, and was supported by the staff of the State Library. Gaver and Martin were two of the most accomplished and prominent librarians in America.

This effort led to the new "State Library Aid Act of 1967." After its passage the State Library became involved in planning for implementation of the Act and in its administration. While the State Library (more particularly the Public Library Commission) had always had some responsibility for administering state programs, with the advent of new state and federal legislation from the 1950s on its regulatory function began to assume increasing importance.

The legislation did two major things. While the "State Aid Act of 1959" had established the principle of per capita state aid to local public libraries, the actual amount of money was small. The new law substantially increased the amount of money going to local libraries. Secondly, it created a pyramidal three-level service structure: the local level, which formed the base of the structure; the area center level, to which local libraries and/or patrons could resort if the local library could not meet their needs; and a research level, capable of supplying the most sophisticated needs for service. This concept of direct state aid for local library support and a shared network structure supplementing local efforts, represented a giant step forward from the modest initial state aid of 1959.

In 1960 legislation authorized the state to borrow funds from the Teacher's Pension and Annuity Fund for the construction of new buildings for the State Library and State Museum. A new State Library building was dedicated on September 26, 1965, as part of a Cultural Complex which also included a new state museum. This made it possible to house all of the elements of the State Library together for the first time in many years, and to incorporate for the first time the collection of the Public Library Commission. However, the assignment of all units to the State Library building lasted only until the end of 1966, when a newly created Library for the Blind and Handicapped was located in rented quarters. A Special Services Bureau was created to administer both the Library for the Blind and Handicapped and institutional library services.

In 1966 the legislature also established the New Jersey Historical Commission and placed it in the Division of the State Library, where it was housed until its relocation to another building in 1975.

The Decade of the 1970s

If the 1960s represented a period of unparalleled growth for New Jersey libraries, the 1970s demonstrated that prosperity and growth are often transitory. Fed by a continuing war in Vietnam, and by runaway oil prices, the rate of inflation rose, while the idea of California's Proposition 13, limiting the size of local government expenditures, spread throughout the country. The size of local budgets was severely restricted at a time when rising prices found local government least able to cope. In New Jersey budgetary restrictions took the form of the adoption by the legislature of municipal "caps," which limited the size of annual budget increases in local, state and school budgets from year to year. The legislature provided an escape mechanism by exempting "capital" expenses from the limitation, thereby encouraging municipalities to list as "capital" a variety of expenditures never before so defined. In this respect at least, by adding interest payments to ordinary operating costs, the cost of government was increased under the guise of lowering it. As prices rose and the economy slowed (economists sometimes referred to this general economic condition as "stagflation"), library budgets as well as other governmental expenditures came under increasing pressure. It is against this background that the efforts of the State Library in the 1970s must be viewed. Given all of the difficulties facing libraries during much of the 1970s, it is all the more remarkable that steady progress continued to be made in the State Library, as well as in New Jersey libraries generally.

During the early 1970s the State Library continued to adapt its organization, shifting gears to reflect changes in the library world, to experiment with new technology, and to remain alert to the need to constantly evaluate and examine the effects of new programs on service goals. In 1971 the Bureau of Public and School Library Service was transformed into the Bureau of Library Development, and its functions were broadened to include the Library for the Blind and Handicapped. During the late 1960s and early 1970s, support for the implementation of emerging technologies was evidenced by, among other things, the development of the micro-automated catalog project using microfilm to make bibliographic records of the State Library and the Newark Public Library catalogs available to libraries throughout New Jersey, and by utilization of OCLC by the State Library.

Early in the 1970s librarians began to evaluate progress under the State Aid Act of 1967, and to consider ways in which it might be improved. This effort proceeded once more through the work of the Library Development Committee of the New Jersey Library Association with the assistance of the State Library staff, and lasted for much of the decade. This did not occur because the 1967 legislation had not achieved its purposes; during the early 1970s per capita state aid to local libraries represented close to 20 percent of local library budgets (a figure which has sharply declined since). Rather, librarians saw that there were still issues that the 1967 legislation had not adequately addressed.

Among such issues was the belief that the areas designated as the second level of service might be too small (some twenty-five area centers had been designated under the plan); that the areas designated had no adequate check on their power to choose the services they wished to deliver, since they were only required to set up "advisory" boards to provide their constituencies with a voice in determining policy; and that most areas designated by the state essentially dealt with public library issues interests, with little concern for school or special library services. From 1972 to 1977 these and other issues were studied. In 1977, with the strong endorsement of the library community and the State Library, the legislature's County and Municipal Government Study Commission was asked to look at the state's involvement in library development and to recommend new initiatives if needed. The Commission's report was reviewed by the profession, and gradually a new program emerged, much of which was enacted into legislation by the mid–1980s.

The new legislation continued the existing program of direct per capita aid to local municipalities, but it altered the other elements in the 1967 program by replacing the second-level area libraries with six multi-type regions. As well as improved funding for network services, the new structure featured independent regional governing boards with substantial powers of self-governance, subject to the review of the State Librarian.

In the midst of this period Roger McDonough retired as State Librarian in the fall of 1975. As in the case of Sarah Byrd Askew, the retirement of a respected leader who had served a long term in office created a vacuum at a critical time. As occurred earlier, it took three years until a permanent successor was appointed.

On this occasion the delay was caused by a move to upgrade the position of State Librarian from that of a Division Head in the State Education Department to an Assistant Commissioner of Education. The move was strongly endorsed by the library profession. In the process, the status of the position was also changed from the classi-

fied to unclassified service within the civil service system. Instead
of filling the position by civil service examination, the new Assistant
Commissioner would now be appointed by, and serve at the pleasure of, the Commissioner of Education. In retrospect, it appears
that little was gained by this move to upgrade the status of the State
Librarian. The State Librarian now reported to a Deputy Commissioner of Education rather than directly to the Commissioner, and
even less attention was paid to the State Library by the Department
than was true formerly.

The new State Librarian, Barbara Weaver, was New Jersey's first
woman State Librarian. She was appointed in 1978, after a three-
year period during which David Palmer, Assistant State Librarian,
ably served in an acting capacity. Ms. Weaver was hardly settled in
when a move was made to change the status of the State Library,
taking it out of the Education Department and placing it in a proposed new Department of Cultural Affairs. Librarians reacted nega-
tively, believing that libraries were best placed in the Education Department, with a closely related mission. It is possible that some
minds might have been changed had anyone approached the library
community with the proposal before it was introduced in the legislature. However, the primary sponsor of the move was the Senate
President, the second most powerful man in New Jersey government, and he appeared to have little interest in persuasion. When
the Senator was chided on this score by the New Jersey Library
Association leadership, his response was terse: "You'll move, and
you'll learn to like it!" Librarians did neither, and created such a
stir that the State Library was left out of the new plan. Without the
State Library the new department lacked substance, and the plan
had to be abandoned.

In other encounters involving the State Library, librarians were
less successful in achieving their ends. In the early 1980s the New
Jersey Historical Commission was moved from the State Library to
the Department of State. When a new building combining a records
storage center with the Library for the Blind and Handicapped was
opened in 1982, management of the records storage facility and the
State Archives were also transferred to the Department of State,
where the State Museum and the State Council on the Arts were
also moved from the Education Department.

The State Library, Today and Tomorrow

There were times during the mid–1980s when it appeared that the
library progress of the 1960s might return. The passage of the new

multitype regional library legislation led to improved funding for library cooperative ventures, and the per capita aid formula was improved despite the Department of Education's active opposition. But this progress proved illusory. The library world in New Jersey and throughout the country quickly returned to the decline of the 1970s. The general reduction of government has affected libraries as surely as it has every public agency.

The change in fortunes occurred at a time when the State Library once again entered a period of transition with the retirement of Barbara Weaver in 1991 and her replacement by Louise Minervino in 1992. Weaver's reign, by New Jersey standards, was short, but its impact was pronounced, at least in the short run, with the structure for library cooperation being substantially changed during her term in office. The State Library had once more offered effective leadership at the state level.

The opportunities for the State Library to display statewide leadership have declined in recent years. From 1988 to 1994 the staff of the Library declined by 37 percent, from 148 to 93. Moreover, the staff of the Bureau of Library Development declined by 60 percent, from 25 to ten. Staff reductions have occurred primarily through resort to seniority, which has little relevance to staff skills or specialization. In addition, special incentives were given to senior staff to encourage early retirement, which has cost state government, the State Library included, some of its most capable and experienced people. Under such conditions, a sharp falloff in effectiveness was inevitable. At the present time, the State Library can hardly be staffed during the five days a week that it is open, and with further cuts still a possibility, the present limited schedule could face further reductions.

Perhaps even more dismaying than the cuts in the State Library's service capacity was the increasing difficulty experienced by the Library, and by successive State Librarians, with the Education Department leadership. Immersed in the many problems facing the public education system, successive Commissioners of Education gave little time or encouragement to libraries. Given such circumstances, many librarians came to believe that removing the State Library to a more congenial climate would be in the long-range interests of the agency, a belief that the Education Department appeared to share. In 1996 the State Library was transferred to Thomas A. Edison State College, New Jersey's external degree institution. Although the library community was largely ignored in the early exploration of the feasibility of such a move, librarians became receptive to the idea, doubtless reacting to the Department's lack of interest in retaining the State Library.

Parallel to the decline of the State Library's resources and its marginal position within the Education Department have come serious questions relating to the effectiveness of the Library's leadership. This issue made newspaper headlines in 1995 with the removal from office of the State Librarian by the Education Department. Treating it as a personnel matter, the Department declined to comment publicly on the reasons for the dismissal. Minervino charged that she had been fired for refusing to support the Department's policy designed to cut statewide regional library funding. The reaction of librarians was muted, apparently reflecting disaffection between the former State Librarian and the library community, even though the cause of dismissal may have been her defense of library interests. Shortly after the dismissal the Education Department filled the position on an interim basis by appointing John H. Livingstone as Acting State Librarian, an appointment which has now been made permanent. This action was clearly related to the State Library's pending move, and was intended to allow a permanent appointment to be made once the move had been completed.

The fate of the State Library will relate closely to the future of government generally, particularly at the state level. There is a popular perception in this country that government can be run at equal or improved efficiency, at less cost. While we have proven that government can be run more cheaply, we have yet to learn what this will cost us in effectiveness. If the State Library or the other libraries in New Jersey are any gauge, the loss in effectiveness will be substantial. What will be the reaction of the people when it becomes evident that some things don't run very well under the new constraints? For the State Library the equation is simple. If the State Library continues to run at the present level, it will have only limited significance, either as a statewide leader or within state government, as many state libraries used to operate before the advent of LSA and LSCA. It is only if state government recognizes that the leadership role of a state library in the life of a library community is unique and irreplaceable, and determines to make its funding decisions based on achieving a worthwhile mission, rather than solely on the basis of cost, that any significant State Library progress will again become possible. One can only hope that the state government will study the record of the State Library carefully, for surely, over the two hundred years of its existence, the taxpayers of New Jersey have never had a better bargain.

Notes

1. New Jersey Legislature. General Assembly. Votes and Proceedings. Friday, March 18, 1796.

2. New Jersey Legislature. General Assembly. Votes and Proceedings. Friday, March 11, 1796.

3. I am indebted to Mary Alice Quigley and her unpublished thesis *The Eighteenth Century Origins of the New Jersey State Library*, c.1978, a work that has been of great assistance in reviewing the early activity of the state legislature's collection development, identifying some 60 printed and 8 manuscript volumes which were part of the collection.

4. *Votes and Proceedings of the Twenty-eighth General Assembly of the State of New Jersey* (Trenton, N.J.: Wilson and Blackwell, 1804), 169.

5. *Ibid*: 166–170.

6. "An Act for the Better Preservation of the Books and Papers Belonging to the Legislature of this State," dated November 16, 1822, in *A Compilation of the Public Laws of the State of New Jersey* (Camden, N.J.: J. Harrison, 1833), 22.

7. "An Act to Provide for the Gradual Increase of the State Library." Passed by the Assembly December 31, 1824.

8. *Acts of the Fifty-ninth General Assembly of the State of New Jersey* (Trenton, N.J.: Joseph Justice, 1835), 153.

9. *Acts of the Seventy-ninth Legislature of the State of New Jersey* (Trenton, N.J.: Phillips and Boswell, 1855), 498–9.

10. *Acts of the Sixty-ninth Legislature of the State of New Jersey* (Trenton, N.J.: Phillips and Boswell, 1845), 226–8.

11. *Acts of the Seventy-second Legislature of the State of New Jersey* (Trenton, N.J.: Phillips and Boswell, 1848), 259–60.

12. *Acts of the Seventy-seventh Legislature of the State of New Jersey* (Somerville, N.J.: Donaldson and Brokaw, 1853), 485.

13. *State Librarians Report to the Legislature of New Jersey for the Year 1858*. No imprint data, no paging. Annual reports of successive State Librarians are housed in the collection of the New Jersey State Library.

14. *Report of the State Librarian for the Year 1861*.

15. *Report of the State Librarian for the Year 1862*.

16. *Report of the State Librarian for the Year 1867*.

17. *Report of the State Librarian for the Year 1869*.

18. *Report of the State Librarian for the Year 1871*.

19. *Acts of the One Hundred and Second Legislature of the State of New Jersey* (Elizabeth, N.J.: Drake and Cook, 1878), 225–8.

20. *Report of the State Librarian for the Year 1887*.

21. *Acts of the One Hundred and Eighth Legislature of the State of New Jersey* (Camden, N.J.: Sinnicksin Chew, 1884), 81–2.

22. *Report of the State Librarian for the Year 1896*.

23. *Acts of the One Hundred and Twenty-second Legislature of the State of New Jersey* (Trenton, N.J.: MacCrellish and Quigley, 1898), 415.

24. *Library Journal*, February, 1899, 60.

25. *Report of the State Librarian for the Year 1896*.

26. *Acts of the One Hundred and Twenty-fourth Legislature of the State of New Jersey* (Trenton, N.J.: MacCrellish and Quigley,1900), 95–7.

27. *Fifth Annual Report of the Public Library Commission of New Jersey* (Paterson, N.J.: News Printing Co., 1905), 5, 6. Most annual reports of the

Commission issued subsequently were unpublished reports directed to the current governor and are to be found in the collection of the New Jersey State Library and/or the New Jersey State Archives.

28. *Acts of the One Hundred and Thirty-eighth Legislature of the State of New Jersey* (Union Hill, N.J.: Dispatch Pub. Co., 1914), 346–7.

29. *Acts of the One Hundred and Forty-fourth Legislature of the State of New Jersey* (Trenton, N.J.: MacCrellish and Quigley, 1920), 257–9.

30. *Report of the Public Library Commission of the State of New Jersey, 1926–7*, 3.

31. Howard Larison Hughes, *Public Libraries in New Jersey, 1750–1850* (Trenton, N.J.: New Jersey Library Association, 1965).

32. *Second Report of the Public Library Commission of the State of New Jersey* (Trenton, N.J.: John J. Murphy Pub. Co., 1901), 6.

33. *Twelfth Annual Report of the Public Library Commission of the State of New Jersey, 1911* (Trenton, N.J.: State Gazette Pub. Co., 1912), 13.

34. *Thirteenth Annual Report of the Public Library Commission of the State of New Jersey, 1912* (Trenton, N.J.: State Gazette Pub. Co., 1913), 5–6.

35. *Twenty-first Annual Report of the Public Library Commission of the State of New Jersey, 1920* (Trenton, N.J.: State of New Jersey, 1920), 20.

36. *Twenty-sixth Annual Report of the Public Library Commission of the State of New Jersey, 1925–6.* (Typewritten copies of the annual reports of the Commission from 1924 on, are to be found in the collection of the New Jersey State Archives, currently housed in the State Library Building in Trenton).

37. *Twenty-fifth Annual Report of the Public Library Commission of the State of New Jersey, 1924–5*, 7.

38. *Thirtieth Annual Report of the Public Library Commission of the State of New Jersey, 1929–30*, 1.

39. *Thirty-second Annual Report of the Public Library Commission of the State of New Jersey, 1931–2*, 1.

40. *Thirty-third Annual Report of the Public Library Commission of the State of New Jersey, 1932–3*, 1.

41. *Thirty-seventh Annual Report of the Public Library Commission of the State of New Jersey, 1936–7*, 8.

42. Unpublished correspondence in the files of the New Jersey State Library.

43. Unpublished correspondence in the files of the New Jersey State Library.

44. *Acts of the One Hundred and Sixty-ninth Legislature of the State of New Jersey* (Trenton, N.J.: MacCrellish and Quigley, 1945), 132–7.

45. NJSA 18A:73–23.

46. Unpublished report in the files of the New Jersey State Library.

3

County Libraries

Claudia B. Sumler

Until comparatively recent times, libraries were established in New Jersey primarily in larger, more settled communities. Early library companies were formed in the larger communities of the day, in Trenton, Elizabeth and Burlington. This was logical when membership required annual subscription fees and a reasonable number of affluent members with an interest in learning were needed to support such a venture. As libraries of a more clearly public character appeared in New Jersey during the nineteenth century, sustaining their financial support continued to require the affluence and size of more settled communities. With the spread of universal public education and the increase of population in the more rural areas of New Jersey, there emerged in the last decade of the nineteenth century a concern for the education and enlightenment of people living outside of the larger urban centers, and a determination to give them some form of library service.

Before the turn of the century these efforts, undertaken by such groups as the State Grange and the State Federation of Women's Clubs, were directed at creating within the State Library a traveling library service designed to distribute collections of books to less settled areas of the state. Although such a service was created, the State Library was little interested in it and did little to achieve its purpose. This in turn led concerned groups to shift their focus to the creation of a totally new agency of government which would have as one of its primary interests the wider distribution of library materials in less settled areas. In 1900 the Public Library Commission was created.

In its first twenty years the Public Library Commission and its missionary head, Sarah B. Askew, concentrated much of their effort on creating a network of traveling collections which were scattered throughout the countryside, located in granges, schools, town halls, and private homes; indeed, everywhere that people congregated in rural New Jersey. Despite this effort, it was still clear that the service that could be provided in this manner was only token at best. Collections most often consisted of about fifty books, supplied with a carrying case, and exchanged periodically to freshen the stock to which the public had access. While the traveling collections provided a beginning, it was a modest one.

Against this background the movement for a more satisfactory solution began. Since so much of New Jersey in the early twentieth century was still composed of small isolated communities, it was apparent that the governmental level on which to base a system of local library service in rural areas was not the municipality, in which only a limited part of the total population lived, but rather the county, which included entire geographical regions in its jurisdiction. It was in that direction that the movement to go beyond traveling libraries to create a more comprehensive service began.

The County Library Law of 1920

In 1920 the Public Library Commission noted: "With the growing appreciation in the rural districts of the value of books has come an appreciation of trained supervision and the benefits of the services of a library specialist. From this is developing the County Library idea. The many county organizations that have aided in distributing books for the Commission and have been aided by the Commission in their work, desire a county librarian to work with them."[1]

On April 7, 1920 "An Act to provide for the establishment and maintenance of county free libraries" was passed by the legislature and shortly thereafter signed into law.[2] The law provided: "There shall be established in each county of this State by the board of chosen freeholders thereof a free public library to be known as The Free County Library. Such library shall be established for such subdivisions of said counties as do not maintain free public libraries."[3] The legislature intended to provide a practical method for all communities in New Jersey to have access to a free public library—either a municipal free library for larger communities or a county free library for all other communities which, for whatever reason, were unable to create a municipal free library.

The act further provided that county free libraries were to be created by public referendum, the board of freeholders being required to submit the question to the public at the written request of not less than three hundred voters. A board of freeholders, upon passage of a referendum by the voters, was permitted to contract with any existing library in the county to provide countywide library service. If the freeholders did not move to contract for service within sixty days, they were required to appoint a "County Library Commission" of five members. The board of freeholders was to provide an annual budget of not less than one-fifth of a mill on all real and personal property in each community served by the county library for the maintenance of the free county library. Municipal free libraries might apply to the county library commission for membership in the county library, which would then require them to pay for the maintenance of the library.

The impact of this legislation has been enormous. County libraries have grown into one of the strongest forms of public libraries in the state. Providing a mechanism to permit the organization of libraries in rural and less settled areas proved to be the catalyst that made it possible to create the network of public libraries that now serves virtually every resident of the state. However, there were several features of the new legislation that would raise significant problems in future years.

The act was initially silent about what would happen if a community served by a county library subsequently organized a free municipal library. Would the community in such an event be required to pay a municipal library tax *and* a county library tax? This question was raised almost immediately, and in 1921 an Attorney General's Opinion stated that the establishment of a municipal library permitted a municipality to withdraw from a county library. A 1923 Supreme Court decision established that "association" or non-municipal libraries were not considered eligible for withdrawal and must remain members of the county system. Thus the fundamental nature of county libraries was set at an early period and this has affected them ever since. While the ruling that permitted withdrawal from a county system by communities establishing new municipal libraries had only a minimal impact in rural 1920s New Jersey, much later, with the increasing urbanization of the state, the temptation to withdraw by growing municipalities would pose serious questions for county libraries, since withdrawal meant the loss of revenues.

As in the case of municipal free libraries, the new law required a minimum library tax to be levied for county free libraries, one-fifth of a mill, somewhat less than the one-third of a mill required for support of municipal libraries. This lower level of mandated support, coupled with the larger area to be served by county libraries, made public support more difficult to achieve than in more compact service areas. The effect for many years was to keep support of county libraries low. Contributing to this, as well, was the perception that the mission of the county library was to provide books and reference service, but not to create large central libraries, such as those of municipal libraries.

The County Library Act of 1920 noted in passing that each County Library Commission should adopt rules for the establishment and upkeep of the library, but it said little about what such rules might include. This omission was partially rectified in 1922; an amendment to the law enumerated some of the powers of the library commissioners, including the power to purchase supplies and equipment and incur the expenses necessary to carry out the provisions of the act.[4] This question of the powers of library commissioners has been a problem throughout the years, with the powers granted to county library commissioners falling somewhat short of those granted to municipal library trustees, particularly as they relate to the employment of personnel.

Early Success

The first county library was established[5] in Burlington County in 1921 through the efforts of county residents and the cooperation of the Librarian for the Public Library Commission, Sarah B. Askew. By 1926, libraries were established in Atlantic, Camden, Cape May, Monmouth, Morris and Ocean counties. In addition to the provision of general reading for the public and the services of trained librarians, one of the primary features of these libraries was the provision of school library services, a strong selling point for those counties which had not yet established county libraries. One of the consequences of the creation of county libraries appears also to have been the creation of more small "association" libraries. "The four counties which have been operating for from two to four years have more than justified the expectations of those advocating the move. A number of small towns in each county, which have not felt that they could raise sufficient money to support a library, have started small association libraries with a nominal contribution from the town because they were assured of the use of county books and supervision of the county librarian."[6]

The Monmouth County Library was typical of these early county libraries, with its location in a small room in the basement of the courthouse. Established in 1923, the headquarters facility was "meant to be only an office with storage space for books. It was not intended to be a circulating library."[7] In 1923 the library had seventy-eight active stations established in various localities. The arrival of books was greeted with such enthusiasm that sometimes the librarian was unable to complete the route because the new books were taken from the truck before all the scheduled stops were reached.[8]

Another example of what was intended in county library service was provided by the Atlantic County Library. Organized in 1926, the Library's first director was Jane Brown, who came to the job with credentials from Western Reserve University and the Atlanta Library School, as well as experience in organizing Army and Navy libraries. Offices were set up in an old fire house, and the collection was soon on the road. A Ford automobile equipped with shelves visited library branches or stations which contained deposit collections. Branches were distinguished from stations by their size and by the support that they received from the county library. Stations tended to be very small and operated with volunteer help. Locations were often stores, public buildings or even private homes. Branches tended to be in spaces completely dedicated to library use and had financial support from the county library tax. By the end of 1926 branches had been established in Absecon, Hammonton, Linwood and Northfield. Books were also placed in fifty-seven grade schools and in the high schools. A books-by-mail program was available to county residents who did not live near the book truck route. Interlibrary loan service was also available.

Other early county library histories confirm the emphasis that was given to placing the collection in various rural communities. Although trucks were commonly used, automobiles were also pressed into service, sometimes to the detriment of the vehicles. In the first annual report of the Morris County Library, Director Edith Smith noted: "The rough roads, over which this car must travel, have twisted the body so that one of the doors frequently opens on the road. It is difficult for the driver to discover this at once and several books have been lost on the way, but as far as we can determine, they have all been returned to us." Hunterdon County Library's first annual report notes that the librarian traveled over 5,000 miles to one hundred and twenty-six stations. It is difficult to imagine how any library service beyond delivery and retrieval of books could have been provided in those early years.

By 1930 additional county libraries had been established in Hunterdon, Mercer, Somerset, Sussex and Warren counties. With mandated funding set at a level below that for municipal libraries (which perhaps reflected minimal expectations for facilities and services), service usually consisted of a small headquarters building, designed to warehouse the traveling collection and with some capabilities for reference service. Collections were expected to be located in schools, spaces in public buildings, or in private homes, all at no expense to the county library budget. Yet, minimal as this model may have been, in their own terms the early county libraries appeared to be successful following it until the Depression caused serious erosion in services. In fact, they were so successful that the Public Library Commission looked forward to future progress. "With the program as now mapped out the Commission hopes to have a county library established in every county except Hudson, within ten years. The exception is made of Hudson because it is entirely composed of cities which are served by municipal libraries."[9] The State Commission's annual reports of this period are replete with comments about new counties on the verge of opting for county libraries: "From Middlesex, Gloucester, Bergen, and Somerset counties have come requests that campaigns of education for county libraries be started in those counties. . . ."[10] And again: "A campaign for a county library in Somerset County is under way and Sussex, Warren, and Middlesex counties have asked for aid in presenting it [county library proposals] to their people."[11] While many of these efforts came to fruition, in either the long or short term, the unsettling years of the Depression and World War II had arrived. Libraries, among many other services, were held hostage until larger national issues could be resolved.

Depression and War

While progress in the creation of new county libraries had been rapid in the 1920s, given generally favorable economic conditions and the desire of people in rural locations for improved access to books and knowledge, the beginning of the Depression brought much of this activity to a halt. In 1933 the Public Library Commission reported: "The economic situation has prevented the establishment of more county libraries. Salem and Sussex Counties are very anxious for this time to come. . . ."[12] In 1937 the Commission wrote: "We now have eleven county libraries. Five counties were expecting to vote on county libraries but economic conditions became so bad they were not able to do so. Middlesex, Passaic, and Sussex Counties have begun to agitate the matter again but cannot take the final step until this Commission is able to work with them in getting the matter before the people. . . . We are not able to do this with the present cut in our appropriation."[13] Yet, despite difficulties in creating new county libraries, progress in the existing county systems had been substantial. "The figures which follow show the extent of the work which is being done under many difficulties.

Number of County Libraries	11
Total Population Served	601,104
Total High Schools Served	50
Total Elementary and Grammar Schools Served	644
Number of Library Stations serving the public	646
Local Libraries and reading rooms in County Systems	95 "[14]

Early in the Depression the Atlantic County Library saw increased use as people turned to library services for recreation and assistance in self-education. Increased demand for children's services led to a separate children's department being formed in 1930. By 1932 the library began to feel the impact of the Depression when it received a 53 percent budget cut and had to suspend almost all purchases. Hours were severely limited and children were told to borrow their books from the school library. One year later county library services were suspended, with only the librarian remaining on staff as part-time caretaker.

By 1937 any county overlooking New York City was considered an unlikely prospect for county library development because of its urban demographics. Continuing changes in the relationship of county libraries to municipal libraries were recognized when counties began expressing concern about the proliferation of exempt districts which were not contributing to the support of the county library.

County libraries which had weathered the Depression often had to cope with cutbacks during World War II. The Cape May County Library faced the prospect that it might have to close due to the lack of coal, and increased paper costs eroded book purchasing power.

In Ocean County the Depression had increased the use of the county library, which managed to stay open. By 1935 it was serving thirty-six schools, four libraries, and one hundred and fifteen stations. During the war gasoline rationing brought about a decline in library book circulation and led to the consolidation of many stations.[15] Despite budget concerns, county libraries not only worked to serve the public but took on added responsibilities in the wartime effort. County libraries in coastal areas like Ocean and Atlantic counties made materials available to the Coast Guard. Dorothy Van Gorder, Director of the Somerset County Library, organized a book drive to provide a basic collection to the Veterans' Hospital at Lyons. [16] By the end of World War II county libraries, along with other public libraries in New Jersey, were poised at the edge of a period of expansion that would increase their numbers and change the fundamental nature of the service they would provide to an eager public.

The Post-War World

The end of World War II initiated profound changes in all aspects of society, libraries included. The pursuit of the American dream never seemed as possible as it did in the post-war decades, and for many the dream included moving to less populated areas where land and housing seemed plentiful and cheap. Even rural counties like Sussex and Cape May saw phenomenal growth occur.

Some county libraries did not show rapid growth in their service areas during this period. Some of these counties had shown growth earlier, and several had suffered from the withdrawal of local communities from the county system as they formed their own municipal libraries, reducing the number of people served by the county library even as the county's population continued to grow. On the whole, however, substantial growth in population served by the county library was the rule.

As people moved steadily into the less settled areas of the state, their aspirations reached beyond a larger home with a larger yard. Higher education became an attainable goal as veterans benefited from the federal government's GI Bill of Rights and new colleges began to spring up everywhere. What these upwardly mobile adults were achieving for themselves they also wanted for their children. Greater expectations of the local school system also included greater expectations of public libraries, as a supplement to their children's

Population Served by County Libraries[17]

	1958	1982
Atlantic	88,180	148,888
Burlington	208,000	296,529
Camden	233,924	206,914
Cape May	35,713	71,713
Hunterdon	38,746	79,459
Mercer	60,245	118,614
Monmouth	202,790	299,100
Morris	198,464	214,065
Ocean	77,916	318,113
Somerset	114,458	107,115
Sussex	34,286	104,113
Warren	26,162	51,204

education. Many of these adults migrating from older communities to suburban and rural areas were used to receiving a high quality of public library service, and they expected their new communities to provide a reasonable level of library service as well.

The County Library Dilemma

In a 1966 study of the Camden County Library, consultants Harold Roth and Theodore Hines observed the changing expectations in library service since the early 1900s: "If we continue to view libraries as providing some access to the literary treasures of the past, light reading for ladies, and mystery and detective stories for the tired husband, as well as a few children's books, the local municipal library in a smaller community may well serve such needs. If the library is viewed as providing an access point for the kind of materials needed for intelligent citizenship and participation in community, business, industrial, and educational affairs for the world of today, the smaller municipal library certainly cannot do so unaided."[18]

In fact, as time passed, the original premise of county libraries to create a basic level of service in unserved areas began to lead to the destabilization of the county system. If a county library was "to assist in the orderly growth of library services throughout the county area, it must help in the establishment of new libraries and provide services where there are none."[19] Much of this service was provided through small, independent "association" libraries which county libraries assisted in providing local service, and through modest "central" libraries. With rapid population growth in previously rural areas, these initially modest central headquarters of county libraries became the centers best able to provide not only reading materials but also a broad range of reference service, not only for their core constituency but for other libraries as well. Demands to improve this level of service mounted.

In addition, with population growth independent communities began to feel that they were large enough to support their "own" library (particularly as the service level had begun to improve with some help from the county library), and some of these began to withdraw from county libraries. In the very act of promoting the establishment of new libraries and the improvement of library services offered in all of the library agencies belonging to the county, the county library often began to nurture a sense of self-sufficiency which tended eventually to raise questions of community withdrawal from the county library. In some cases, the very act of improving reference and information services in central libraries helped to alienate communities located at some distance from a central library; the feeling in such cases was that the remote central library offered little service while utilizing a disproportionate share of available resources.

Thus, as county libraries moved to meet library needs, they began, in some cases, to stimulate the desire of some communities to establish their own municipal libraries and withdraw from the county library system. If successful, these moves would lead to a loss of county library revenue, and in turn would decrease the tax revenue available to continue support of the communities that chose to remain.

The 1960s and Beyond

With the passage of time the changes in county libraries were profound. Increased strengthening of the central facilities of county libraries led to a shift in direct use of county library facilities in favor of the central library. Increased visits to the headquarters building to borrow a growing range of materials, rather than relying on library "stations," bookmobile stops, school collections, and even the use of independent "association" libraries, profoundly altered the original concept of the county library. In essence, the changing character of modern life had changed the character of the county library: changing times demanded a changing institution, and the institution indeed began to change rapidly.

No longer were library users content with small, rotating collections located in the corners of municipal buildings or in small town stores or homes. Increased use meant an increased need for space. By 1954 the Ocean County headquarters library had moved several times, seeking quarters large enough to provide a complete range of library services, a pattern that could be found in many county libraries. In addition, Ocean County had branches in Island Heights, Brick Township, Tuckerton and Long Beach Island, which was the first county library branch in New Jersey when it opened in 1960.[20]

Ocean County was not the only system to experience a post-war boom as population expanded and expectations for library service grew. In the 1960s many county libraries were designated "area libraries" under the state's new cooperative library program, charged with providing a wide range of reference services. In Monmouth County plans progressed to build a facility capable of housing the type of collection necessary to meet an enhanced need for reference services, and in 1968 the library's Eastern Regional Branch was opened. Under County Library Director John Livingstone, the next phases of the plan ensured that additional libraries would be built, including a new headquarters library which would not only meet the need for an in-depth reference collection but also provide expanded meeting room and program space for the cultural and educational programs the public sought.[21]

Many county library headquarters were initially located in the county seat, often in the county courthouse. Where the county seat was large enough to support a municipal library as well a curious phenomenon occurred. The county headquarters would be located in a local community it could not serve, alongside a municipal library; in some places the two would be separated only by a short three-minute walk, as was the case in Warren County. Thus the county library was cut off from its most natural patrons, its nearest neighbors, while serving those who lived in more remote communities which paid to support the county library. Although the Somerset County Library system grew during the years it operated out of county office space in Somerville, efforts to combine the Somerville municipal library and the county library system were fruitless. When the county library system moved into its own headquarters building, it moved out of the county seat to Bridgewater.[22] As part of the move it was agreed that the county library would served as the local library for residents of Bridgewater, avoiding any repetition of the situation in Somerville.

After World War II the use of the Camden County Library declined as users began to expect more in-depth service. Operating out of the courthouse in Camden, the county library was not easily reached by most of its constituents and was of little interest to the residents of Camden City, who had their own municipal library. Once more there was the curious situation of a county headquarters library located in a city it could not serve, which had its own municipal library. Once more there was a county system which received no tax support from its largest community, whose tax revenue supported its own municipal library. Over the next few years, several communities withdrew from the county system, believing that they could offer more complete library service on their own. It was not until the late 1960s that the County Library Commission recognized the necessity to move out of Camden City. With the reorganization of the Camden County Library Commission and the appointment of Nina Ladof as director, library operations were finally moved from the courthouse basement to a more central location in Voorhees, a member community.[23]

By the 1970s many of the county libraries were moving into substantial headquarters buildings, each designed to serve as a main library for the system as well as a central administrative headquarters. In Atlantic County headquarters space remained limited (once more relegated to the county courthouse), and the County Library Commission continuously lobbied for a large central library in Mays Landing. A new director, Joseph Green, convinced the Commission that in a predominantly rural area a distributed branch system would provide broader coverage.

In fact, whether or not a system developed a large central facility, service through branch libraries of county library systems fast became a basic goal throughout the state. The Sussex County Library reflects this trend. There was a ten-year gap between the main library's construction in 1956 and the construction of a second building, a branch, in 1966, but then new branches appeared with regularity for the next several years. The Mercer County Library also reflects this pattern during much of the 1970s and 1980s, with rental of branch space followed by expansion through construction of branches and location of a new central headquarters in rehabilitated space. Currently engaged in a new cycle of updating, the Mercer County Library is currently expanding all of its branches and its headquarters library, under its long-time director, Martin Winar. Not only has expansion of all of these county library facilities throughout the state improved services generally; it has also served to retain communities that might otherwise have withdrawn from county library systems.

The growth of such complex library systems was not envisioned when the legislature passed the original law authorizing funding of one-fifth of a mill. County libraries were meant to rely on donated space and in-kind services with volunteer staff. The demands for professional services from a trained staff in buildings designed for library purposes led to increases in the library tax rate that many municipalities regard as a loss of control. In the post-war years many county libraries suffered from the efforts of municipalities to pull out of county library systems and develop local libraries; the county libraries, meanwhile, struggled to meet the needs of the communities that remained in the system.

County Library Funding and Growing Stability

Over the years attempts were made to stabilize the county library financial base, with generally limited success. In 1957 legislation was passed to set a minimum expenditure for county libraries at 1/15 of a mill on county net apportionment valuation (designed to reflect the actual valuation of real property). This minimum based on the valuation of communities that were part of the county system did little to discourage withdrawals. In 1954 Governor Robert Meyner appointed a commission, which published the first major state-sponsored study on library service in New Jersey, *Better Libraries for New Jersey*.[24] The report recommended, among other things, that exempt areas in counties served by county libraries should be incorporated into county library systems to provide more efficient service. This approach was incorporated in the first State Library Aid Law, passed in 1959, which provided incentives for municipalities to remain members of county libraries, and encouraged federation of city and county libraries.

Despite these measures, fourteen communities withdrew from county libraries between 1958 and 1968. In 1967 a new state aid law was passed, providing, among other things, that municipalities which supported a local association library would share state aid earned on the basis of community population with the county library. The law provided little real incentive for local communities to remain in a county library system.

There were also attempts to tailor funding and services to meet the needs and politics of particular counties. One early attempt was the establishment of a Tri-County Services Center for Salem, Gloucester and Cumberland counties, utilizing newly available federal funds.[25] Although this experiment never quite achieved all that it intended, it did lead to the creation of the Cumberland County Library.

Although Morris County did not grow as rapidly in the post-war years as the more rural counties in New Jersey, it did have a highly educated, white-collar population. A thirty-thousand-square-foot main library was opened in Whippany as the headquarters for the system, offering a more sophisticated level of reference and information service than had previously been possible. However, the tax base declined as municipalities withdrew from the county system to establish their own local libraries. Nonetheless, the services of the county library improved despite these withdrawals, and residents of exempt communities began to press for access to the improving information resources of the county library.

In 1977, special state legislation was passed for Morris County designating two levels of county library service. One level provided local library services to member communities that paid for them in the form of a county library tax. A second level offered reference and information services to all communities in the county. In 1985 additional legislation was passed defining the methods for funding these two levels of service. While the special legislation did not settle all outstanding issues relating to the Morris County Library, the library grew into one of the most impressive in the state, a position challenged in recent years by serious cutbacks in funding.

Significant developments relating to county libraries occurred in the late 1970s as a result of the work of the state government's County and Municipal Government Study Commission. Its report, *The Development of Libraries and Networks*, published in 1980, noted that the structure of county libraries did indeed lead to an unstable base of support; services were impeded by a lack of formal relationships with association libraries, and exempt communities, through their municipal libraries, demanded network services that strained the ability of county libraries to provide services to their member communities. In short, the structure and service roles of county libraries had created an ongoing process of withdrawal by municipalities from county library systems during the 1970s. The loss of communities from county systems meant the loss of tax revenues, thus limiting the services that could be offered to remaining members, and triggering the potential loss of other members. The continuing concern over potential loss of revenue forced many county libraries to make important decisions based on political considerations rather than on considerations of library service.

The County and Municipal Government Study Commission's recommendations attempted to balance the need of county libraries for financial stability with the prerogatives of local communities to form their own libraries should they so desire. In the "County Library Reorganization Law of 1981," resulting from the work of the Commission, provisions were made for the establishment of a county library study commission to review alternative options for county library development. These options included branch development, tax sharing options, and expanded options for contractual agreements. Of these new alternatives, the most significant was the accelerated development of county branch libraries. If the nature of county libraries has been shifting dramatically in recent years, one basic reason is certainly the movement away from stations and association libraries as local service units and toward the establishment of branches, a movement materially assisted by the county reorganization legislation.

A second law which had a significant impact on county libraries was passed in 1986. This provided that a municipality could not withdraw from a county library system for two years after the passage of a local referendum authorizing such a move. This law provided county libraries with some opportunity for long-range planning. Before its passage a municipality could place the question of withdrawal from a county library on the ballot in November, and if it were passed, the municipal library would be established by the following January. While this measure helped to promote greater stability in county libraries, the major reasons for the growing stability were the positive actions of the county libraries themselves, the growth of county library branches, and the growing impact of technology.

One of the most significant recent influences on all libraries, and a positive force for county libraries, has been the technological revolution in the last quarter of the century. Computers linked by telecommunications have enabled county libraries to provide access to their entire collection for all branches. Recent developments in networking have also enabled county libraries to offer sophisticated services to branches, no matter how small, so that the resources of the entire system are easily available to anyone in the service area. Although these services are expensive to install and maintain, the larger unit of service of the county library combined with a common administrative home permits county libraries to meet the needs of their member communities in a way that has not been practical in small municipalities.

Despite concerns over possible withdrawal by member communities, the value of the larger unit of service has led to the continued growth of county library systems. County libraries throughout the state have been at the forefront of expanded and innovative library services. Each county library has developed its own unique characteristics to meet the needs of its jurisdiction. Morris and Cumberland counties offer county library service under legislation quite different from the law enacted in 1920. Atlantic, Mercer, Morris and Sussex county libraries have become county departments, with the library commissions relegated to advisory status, which to some observers is a cause for concern.

No matter how they are organized, however, many of the county libraries have expanded branches, and increased funding, have been among the first to implement the newest technology, have seen use expand in great numbers, and have become highly visible institutions in their counties. These institutions, which were once planned as an interim step in the development of municipal libraries in New Jersey, have become a viable alternative to supporting individual small libraries in each local community. They now make up the backbone of public library service for a large percentage of the population. In the face of rapidly changing technology, the economy of scale provided by county libraries offers the potential for them to maintain a leadership role in the state.

County Libraries: Present and Future

County libraries currently face two major issues: the stability of their base of support, that is, the continued participation of member communities in the library system, and the increasing pressure from the public to have immediate access to the public library of their choice. These problems notwithstanding, the history of the past decade has been a period of unparalled success for county libraries.

1. TABLE
County Library Statistics, 1984, 1994[26]

	Population	Budget	Collection	Circulation
Atlantic County				
1984	155,086	$1,702,844	221,773	496,275
1994	169,390	3,912,909	359,107	745,316
Burlington				
1984	301,203	2,397,576	475,901	753,007
1994	312,366	5,185,275	824,646	1,530,593
Camden				
1984	212,470	1,650,891	352,700	552,422
1994	232,529	3,657,681	327,866	976,622
Cape May				
1984	73,974	1,234,626	287,759	310,691
1994	81,297	3,260,823	319,497	349,577
Cumberland				
1984	134,002	557,448	151,422	134,002
1994	64,662	899,448	181,700	90,527
Gloucester				
1984	103,505	475,088	112,820	93,155
1994	82,134	1,506,338	212,727	139,628
Hunterdon				
1984	82,088	1,223,932	222,242	426,426
1994	102,341	2,846,103	390,943	757,323
Mercer				
1984	107,015	3,382,744	368,132	663,493
1994	123,207	6,069,177	489,131	1,281,353
Monmouth				
1984	306,502	3,120,190	830,620	1,624,461
1994	352,908	7,266,376	1,150,480	2,329,193

Morris				
1984	217,944	3,166,726	518,707	414,094
1994	428,157	3,348,188	248,331	385,341
Ocean				
1984	330,148	3,565,598	544,744	1,386,622
1994	391,471	12,503,584	688,989	3,327,504
Somerset				
1984	108,479	1,994,929	400,287	737,657
1994	130,037	5,136,461	534,452	1,209,344
Sussex				
1984	105,245	1,221,894	265,217	505,176
1994	119,416	2,535,202	306,899	561,255
Warren				
1984	48,539	526,648	99,990	126,201
1994	57,471	2,241,493	159,195	494,251

Still, the challenges remain. As the resources and services of the county libraries have grown, the loss of any community means the possible loss of a significant portion of basic funding. The reduced funds do not simply mean eliminating services to a particular community, but a reduction in services to the system as a whole. The remaining member communities are faced with what may be a significant increase in their tax rate in order to maintain the level of service currently provided. The decision of any member community to withdraw and establish independent municipal library service has a permanent, detrimental impact on every member community in the county library system. The repercussions can even be felt beyond the county library's immediate membership, since so many county libraries play important roles in the state regional networks, and any weakening of the county library tends to weaken the level of regional services that can be provided.

The technological advances that have affected every aspect of people's lives have been a major element enabling county libraries to provide maximum services for the most effective use of the tax dollar. Sharing resources with other libraries becomes easier with each new breakthrough in the world of computers and telecommunications. Such advances have also increased public expectations of what libraries can provide.

Today public library users expect to get information and material when and where they want it. They have become increasingly frustrated by restrictions placed on access to libraries based on jurisdictional boundaries. Not only does the public wish to use the library most convenient to their home or office; they are demanding access via their home computers, which enable them to connect to a variety of library databases. When they locate what they want, they want it immediately, and do not want to be told that they must go to their local library, request an interlibrary loan, and wait a week to ten days for a book or journal.

Yet county libraries have a need to preserve the very jurisdictional structure that sometimes frustrates non-residents, since their financial base must be secure if they are to offer any level of service at all. Clearly, technological progress proceeds along its own line of development, and this progress often has little to do with existing methods of public financing.

How county libraries resolve these issues involving technological and organizational development and often incompatible patterns of public financing will lay the foundation for the next chapter in the history of New Jersey county libraries.

Notes

1. *Twentieth and Twenty-first Annual Reports of the Public Library Commission of New Jersey, 1919–1920* (Trenton, N.J.: State of New Jersey, 1920), 25–26.

2. *Chapter 122, Laws of 1920.* State of New Jersey.

3. *Ibid:* 257–258.

4. *Chapter 92, Laws of 1922.* State of New Jersey.

5. *Twenty-second Annual Report of the Public Library Commission of New Jersey, 1921* (Trenton, N.J.: State of New Jersey, 1921), 12. The Commission noted that the referendum was approved by three-fourths of those voting.

6. *Twenty-fifth Annual Report of the Public Library Commission of New Jersey* (Trenton, N.J.: State of New Jersey), 3. Reports of the Public Library Commission subsequent to 1923 exist in typewritten form only and are located in the Archives of the State of New Jersey in the State Library Building.

7. *Monmouth County Library, A History: 1922–1985.* Compiled by Anna N. Suhl and Doris K. Handzo, n.p., 1986, 4.

8. *Ibid:* 7.

9. *Twenty-seventh Annual Report of the Public Library Commission of New Jersey 1926–1927* (Trenton, N.J.: State of New Jersey), 3.

10. *Ibid:* 3.

11. *Ibid:* 2.

12. *Thirty-third Annual Report of the Public Library Commission of New Jersey, 1932–1933,* 4.

13. *Thirty-seventh Annual Report of the Public Library Commission of New Jersey, 1936–1937,* 3.

14. *Thirty-fifth Annual Report of the Public Library Commission of New Jersey, 1934–1935*, 3.

15. Lacey, Jean C., *History of the Ocean County Library* (This paper was written in 1976 in partial fulfillment of a class requirement at Glassboro State College), 17, 18.

16. *Somerset County Library*, 9. This is apparently a transcript of a taped interview with the first director of the Somerset County Library. Dorothy Van Gorder, *Somerset County Library, 1930–1962*. No date of publication.

17. Statistics are drawn from *Public Library Statistics* published by the State Library in 1958 and 1982. The chart does not include figures for Cumberland or Gloucester counties where county libraries were established after 1958. Camden County statistics for the year 1958 were drawn from the 1959 report, since the Camden County Library did not file a population served estimate for 1958.

18. Harold L. Roth and Theodore C. Hines, *Library Service for Camden County* (East Orange, N.J.: Rothines Associates, 1966), 16.

19. *Ibid:* 19.

20. Lacey, 22.

21. *Monmouth County Library . . .* , 27–31.

22. *Somerset County Library*, 20.

23. *Camden County Library System, Strategic Plan, 1994–1998* (Voorhees, N.J.: Camden County Library, 1993), 9–10.

24. See Chapter 5 for a discussion of the Commission's recommendations and the background that led to its report.

25. See Chapter 6 for a discussion of the Tri-County project.

26. *Analyses of New Jersey Public Library Statistics, 1984* (Trenton, N.J.: New Jersey State Library, 1985), 42, 44, 46. *Analyses of New Jersey Public Library Statistics, 1994* (Trenton, N.J.: New Jersey State Library, 1995), 42, 44, 46.

4

The Newark Public Library

Bruce E. Ford

The Newark Public Library was established by referendum in 1888 and opened its doors in 1889. Library service in the city did not begin with the establishment of a free public library, however. Its antecedents can be traced to colonial times.[1] The public library acquired its first building from its immediate precursor, the Newark Library Association;[2] and—at least for a decade—books acquired from the association constituted a major part of its collection.

Frank P. Hill served as librarian[3] from 1889 to 1901. His renowned successor, John Cotton Dana, frequently receives credit for accomplishments that were, in fact, Hill's. He organized the institution solidly. Its new acquisitions were fully cataloged on the day that the library opened, and within a few years the books it had acquired from the Newark Library Association were also cataloged and classified. He established the "Newark Charging System," a method of circulation control used with only slight modification in most American public libraries until the advent of automation. Under his leadership the library in 1892 granted the public unrestricted access to all stacks except those housing fiction. "The Newark Public Library is one of the three large libraries where this boon is granted," he observed. "The others are Minneapolis and Cleveland."[4] During the library's first year of operation he established a "Bureau of Information":

> . . . a department of our library that may be looked upon as one of its leading features. It is the duty of the attendant to answer, or try to answer, all questions; give assistance to readers and students; where possible to guide the reading of the young, and in general, to see that no one leaves the library in a dissatisfied frame of mind.[5]

From the start the library cooperated actively with the schools of the city. The first *Annual Report* indicates that teachers brought classes to visit the library[6] and that Reference Department assistants compiled book lists for their use.[7] "Traveling libraries" were first installed in schools in 1901. "One classical and one scientific library were provided for the high school," reported Clara Whitehall Hunt, the assistant in charge of work with children, "and four general libraries of fifty books each for the grammar grades."[8]

During Hill's tenure the library also made an initial effort at outreach, establishing delivery stations at numerous points throughout Newark,[9] placing collections of twenty volumes in fire houses, compiling lists of books about timely topics and publishing them in newspapers, distributing relevant booklists to manufacturing concerns, and allowing free use of a lecture hall for university extension work.[10] When the library opened in 1889 its collections already included books in languages other than English.[11] By 1901 they included French, German, Italian, Polish, and Lithuanian.[12]

The library's collections and program of service quickly outgrew its first quarters. In 1892 Hill called for the construction of a new building.[13] The trustees held a design competition to select the architect, and the Philadelphia firm of Kellogg and Rankin submitted the winning design. The new structure, located on Washington Street and designed in the style of an Italian Renaissance "palazzo," was dedicated in 1901. The exterior was Indiana limestone, and the three-level interior court of graceful arches was of Tennessee marble. The grand staircase rose through the center of the court from the first to the second story.

The building itself consisted of a basement and four floors above ground. The main library adult reading rooms, catalogue and collection areas were on the second floor, with 22-foot ceilings in major rooms, and two galleries off the center section. The chief architectural feature of this floor was the large monumental reading room which extended the entire length of the front of the building facing Washington Street, with a large operating fireplace at each end. The third floor was intended primarily for offices and support services, and the fourth floor provided space for meetings, concerts and exhibits.

Frank Hill resigned as librarian in 1901, and the trustees appointed Beatrice Winser, who had joined the staff in 1889 and served as assistant librarian since 1894, to serve as acting librarian.

John Cotton Dana (1856–1929) was an influential figure in American intellectual and cultural life, particularly as an innovator and promoter of libraries and museums. In 1895 he was elected president of the American Library Association. After administering libraries in Colorado and Massachusetts, he became the director of the Newark Public Library in January, 1902. He spent the rest of his life there, building what came to be regarded as the preeminent American public library of the time.

An important product of his fertile mind was the establishment of the Newark Museum, which he began in the library in 1903 with one of the earliest exhibitions of American art. He was a prodigious writer and speaker on libraries and museums, had a lifelong interest in printing and publishing, and was active in a wide range of public affairs.

Dana's first innovation appears to have been the establishment of a pay-duplicate collection, about which he wrote,

> Owing to the constantly increasing demand for the latest novel, a demand which no library can afford to supply, it was decided to try here an experiment which has been successful in many other cities. Duplicates or extra copies of popular novels are bought and placed in a special bookcase to be lent at one cent per day . . .[14]

During his first year as librarian he also established a picture collection, which is still in existence and heavily used. Of this Kate Louise Roberts, an assistant in the Reference Department, wrote:

> . . . Many thousands of illustrations, taken from periodicals of France, Germany, England, and America, have been sorted into several hundred groups by topics and placed in manila folders. Their use by students and teachers has increased encouragingly. The collection begins to meet the needs of the school room by supplying interesting illustrations for history, mythology, geography, nature study, and other subjects.[15]

A program of bibliographic instruction for eighth graders was introduced in 1904.[16]

In 1906 the library became a depository for U.S. government publications and patents.[17]

Dana's unwillingness to be constrained by convention was manifested in his decision to move the Reference Departments to the Delivery Room, where circulating materials were located.[18] That decision has affected the organization of the library ever since. The same personnel who have assisted the public with the use of reference materials have helped patrons select and locate circulating materials.[19] And circulating subject collections have been located as close to corresponding reference collections as possible.

Dana replaced the *Library News*, the newsletter started by Hill, with *The Newarker*, a publication that related the work of the library to the life of the city.[20]

In 1904 the library's first branch was established in rented quarters on Academy Street. Heavy use by businessmen prompted Dana to transform it into a "business branch" stocked with directories and other information sources especially useful to them. This was the first publicly supported business library in the United States[21] and a model for many established elsewhere. Through an arrangement with the Clark Thread Company, a library that the company had run for its employees became the public library's second branch in 1905. Six branches, all housed in rented quarters, were established within a few years, but they were all closed in 1918 because the city's appropriation had not kept pace with rising costs. The Business Branch alone remained in operation. During the decade following World War I eight branches were established in city-owned buildings designed expressly for their use, and the Business Branch moved to a permanent city-owned site at 34 Commerce Street.

Dana broke new ground in library advertising and public relations. He successfully promoted the use of the library by segments of the population that had previously used it very little, including entrepreneurs, tradesmen, and immigrants who spoke little English. Strategically placed billboards bearing the text, "Who knows? Your library knows. Ask it," brought the institution's information services to the attention of those who saw the library as little more than a repository for novels. He persuaded merchants to display library advertisements in shop windows. He adopted the strategy of drawing working-class parents into the library through their children. Moving picture trailers were used to reach children not attracted through school visits.[22]

His commitment to promotion and a lifelong interest in printing prompted him to acquire a small printing press for the library. The quality of the promotional materials, book lists and other publications produced on this press set a standard still worthy of emulation.

Dana was a consummate politician. He won approbation from almost all the varied constituencies holding power in the city and thereby insured financial support for the library's expanding program of service. Since his time the city has continued to support the library generously, even if not always adequately.

Throughout his tenure as librarian he concerned himself primarily with external relations and with major questions of policy, leaving the administration of the library's routine affairs to the assistant librarian, Beatrice Winser. Winser had sole charge of the recruitment, training and deployment of personnel. She was also responsible for management of the physical plant. Upon Dana's death in 1929, she was chosen as his successor. Marguerite Gates, head of the Lending Department, succeeded Winser as assistant librarian.

Two additions to the main library building were completed in 1931: a smaller area providing work space for the staff, and a sorely needed stack elevator; and a larger area accommodating reference materials and seating for the public. These additions were utilitarian in design and devoid of the architectural detail evident in most parts of the original structure.

Because of her predecessor's fame, Winser's accomplishments are often overlooked. The stock market crash of 1929 occurred within two months of her appointment as librarian, and the Great Depression that followed brought both unprecedented demand for library materials and services and declining financial support. Under her leadership the library succeeded in meeting the demand. The book collection doubled in size and circulation reached an all-time high, even though hours had to be reduced, bookmobile service—just introduced—had to be eliminated,[23] and the deterioration of the main building necessitated both the shifting of departments and the temporary relocation of the Art and Music Department and the Children's Room to leased quarters in the Newark Museum.

Winser was an iron-handed micro-manager. She left behind hundreds of "Notices" to the staff, covering not only clerical procedures but every aspect of staff dress and deportment. She did, however, maintain personal contact with employees at all levels, and, whether because of her authoritarianism or in spite of it, she secured their cooperation.

In 1931 she introduced the Dickman Charging System—a mechanically assisted variant of Hill's original Newark Charging System, which speeded book charging and eliminated transcription errors but also lessened the library's control over delinquent borrowers.[24]

In 1938 she established a New Jersey collection, which eventually developed into the New Jersey Reference Division. In 1942 she established the War Information Center at the library "to provide information and materials about new agencies, regulations, and appointments as well as job training manuals to industries and groups in the city and surrounding areas."[25]

In the same year Winser tendered her resignation, charging the trustees with interference in the administration of the library. She firmly believed that the function of trustees was "not to do the job but to get it done."[26] Three decades earlier, when she had served on the Newark Board of Education, she had resigned because of the board's refusal to delegate what she considered sufficient administrative authority to the superintendent of schools.[27] Her resignation from the library bitterly divided the staff. Some employees applauded her for resisting what they viewed as politically-motivated interference. Others believed that after a half-century of service she had come to view the library as her personal domain, to be managed according to her own prejudices, and that she had given the board just cause to monitor her decisions about personnel very closely.[28]

Marguerite Gates, the assistant librarian, resigned along with Winser but agreed to serve as acting librarian until a new librarian was appointed. Catherine Van Dyne, head of the Lending Department, assisted Gates in the administration of the library during the interim.

The appointment of John Boynton Kaiser as librarian in 1943 brought drastic change in the way the institution was managed. Until his arrival the administration of the library had been highly centralized. Winser had maintained personal contact with members of the staff at all levels, and matters as trivial as an employee's request for a schedule change had been referred to her. Kaiser delegated to the heads of departments many decisions that had formerly been reserved to the librarian or assistant librarian and established rather formal and distant relations with rank and file employees.

His greatest accomplishments lay in the field of staff development. Dana had been skeptical of professional credentials for library workers. He had argued that until libraries could offer higher pay, librarianship would attract only the mediocre, and that library schools could accomplish little with those students they could attract.[29] Winser had never hesitated to assign professional responsibilities to "assistants" who had not attended library school. During the 1930s the movement toward the establishment of professional credentials for librarians had gained considerable momentum, and Kaiser believed that those who exercised professional responsibilities ought to have professional training.

The salaries which the library paid were very low. The institution had weathered the Depression partly at the expense of the staff. In 1932, for example, staff salaries had been reduced by 15 percent. With the outbreak of World War II wages in general had begun to rise dramatically, and the library's pay scale had not kept pace with changes in the economy.

Kaiser's tasks were to differentiate "assistants" who did professional work from those whose work was confined to clerical tasks, to encourage those who did professional work to obtain appropriate professional credentials, and to raise the salaries of all employees, providing appropriate salary differentials for professional librarians. He accomplished all these tasks within a few years. The position classification that he established for the library distinguished "librarians" from "library assistants," and soon after its adoption the title of the institution's chief executive officer was changed from "librarian" to "director."

After the war Kaiser was able to turn his attention to the main library building, which was overcrowded and in disrepair. He delegated responsibility for renovation of the building to his assistant director, James E. Bryan.

The renovation carried out under Bryan's direction created space for 200,000 more books and provided seating for 400 patrons—double the number that could be accommodated previously.[30] It provided space for the Art and Music Department and the Children's Room, which had been temporarily housed at the Newark Museum. It made possible an arrangement of library departments that was logical and convenient. It dramatically improved lighting, heating and ventilation. It was carried out with more solicitude for the architectural integrity of the building than most renovations of the period; but historic preservation values held little sway in the early 1950s, and from a present day perspective it seems heavy-handed. A monumental center staircase was removed from the central cortile. Handsome coffered ceilings were covered with acoustical tile and fluorescent lights were hung throughout the building. Blond-finished desks were placed in virtually every room, including the cortile.

The reorganization of the Lending and Reference Department accompanied the renovation. The Department was divided into five subject divisions: Science and Technology, Social Science and Labor, New Jersey, Popular Reading, and General Reference.[31]

The Depression and the war had curtailed library publishing. *The Power of Print*,[32] a four-year report covering the years 1942–1945, was published in 1946. In contrast to the staid reports published earlier, this publication included graphs and cartoons as well as anecdotes illustrating the many kinds of service that the library had provided to patrons, particularly during the war. Another report, *At Your Service*,[33] covering the years 1943–1957, was published at the time of Kaiser's retirement in 1958. *NPL News*, a library newsletter intended primarily for staff, was published for several years, as was *Personnel Reporter*, which explained Civil Service regulations and library personnel policy to the staff. The booklists that had previously been published irregularly were replaced by several new bulletins published regularly: *Business Literature, Technology in Print, Labor in Print,* and *Education in Print*.[34]

Upon Kaiser's retirement in 1958, James E. Bryan became director. At the same time Kaiser's other assistant director, J. Bernard

Schein, who had been in charge of personnel and technical services, was given the title of Deputy Director.

Bryan's appointment occurred a few months after the launching of the space satellite Sputnik, an event that many Americans viewed with alarm, supposing that it proved that the Soviet Union had surpassed the United States in scientific acumen. The public indicted American schools for lack of rigor, especially in the fields of science and mathematics. School curricula were overhauled. More challenging courses at all levels—from elementary school through college—sent students to libraries in record numbers. At the same time television was reducing the demand for light fiction. For the first time in the history of the institution, fiction accounted for only 25 percent of the adult circulation.[35] Studies conducted in the library revealed that the questions answered by reference librarians were growing more complex and that answering them often required the use of periodicals and primary sources.[36] The demand for science and technology materials soared.[37] The library altered its collection development practices to meet the new demands.

No other public library in New Jersey had comparable resources. During Christmas and Spring vacations, college students, many from the suburbs, filled the building beyond its capacity and overtaxed the staff. Individuals from all over New Jersey used the library's telephone reference services regularly.

Bryan had an interest in improving library service to all New Jersey residents. He also recognized that the Newark Public Library was in fact a statewide resource that was supported almost exclusively by the city of Newark. Consequently, he participated in the establishment of a cooperative library network in New Jersey. This network brought official recognition of the Newark Public Library's statewide role. Along with the libraries of Rutgers and Princeton universities and the State Library, the Newark Public Library was funded by the state—albeit minimally—for functioning as a research library. It was also compensated for serving as the Metropolitan Reference Center for northern New Jersey and as the Area Library for adjacent municipalities. Accordingly, an Interlibrary Services Division was established in 1968.[38] The library also began producing a bi-weekly list of its acquisitions for distribution to Area Libraries throughout New Jersey. In 1971 the card catalog was microfilmed, and copies of it were similarly distributed.

The library responded to demographic change in the city by making an intensive effort to acquire materials in all disciplines relating to African-American experience. To help other New Jersey libraries with the identification and acquisition of these materials, it began the regular publication of the *Black Studies List*.

Bryan retired unexpectedly in 1972 because of a family illness.[39] J. Bernard Schein, the deputy director, succeeded him. William Urban, the head of the Lending and Reference Department, became the assistant director.

Schein had begun his professional career as a branch librarian, and his primary interest appears to have been in community library services. Under his leadership the library opened two storefront "sub-branches" in neighborhoods not well served by existing branches. Library employees traveled to parks and public housing complexes in a van called the "Roving Reader" and presented programs—some involving music and storytelling—in an effort to encourage use of the library. Other efforts at promotion included radio announcements and bumper stickers identifying the Newark Public Library as "The Best Bargain in Town."

Upon Schein's retirement in 1977, William Urban, who was nearing retirement age himself, became director, and John R. Abram, head of the Lending and Reference Department, became assistant director.

Computer technology entered the library during Urban's brief tenure. The State Library was eager for the Newark Public Library to become an OCLC[40] member so that other New Jersey libraries would have electronic access to its holdings, and it offered to absorb start-up costs through a state grant. Urban appointed a staff committee to study the advantages and disadvantages of OCLC membership. The committee reported that the advantages were significant and that any attendant difficulties could be overcome. At Urban's urging the trustees accepted the grant, and in 1979 the library began cataloging on OCLC.

Upon Urban's retirement, Abram was appointed acting director and the search for a permanent replacement began. This led in 1979 to the appointment of Thomas J. Alrutz as the library's eighth director.

Alrutz brought a fresh perspective to the institution. His grasp of issues in librarianship was impressive. He was very active in professional organizations and kept abreast of the literature. He tried to foster innovation through staff development. To encourage staff participation in professional conferences he persuaded the board to appropriate money for staff travel and continuing education; and many more employees began to attend the annual conferences of the American Library Association and the New Jersey Library Association. In-service training sessions covering such topics as intercultural relations, merchandising, and security were held in the library.

Alrutz supported automation initiatives. Under his leadership the library obtained two Library Services and Construction Act

(LSCA) federal grants for retrospective conversion of its records to machine-readable form. In 1985 the card catalog was frozen and supplanted by a Computer Output Microfiche catalog. This catalog was understood from the beginning as a stop-gap, pending the development of an online catalog. The use of online sources for reference work also began during his directorship.

He encouraged a review of the library's cataloging and classification practices. With the publication of the Library of Congress catalog of printed cards[41] in the 1940s, most large libraries had abandoned idiosyncratic local cataloging practices in favor of L.C. practice, incurring short-term costs to achieve long-term savings from standardization. The Newark Public Library had not. The library had ignored three revisions of the Dewey Decimal Classification. With the passing of time cataloging and classification had grown increasingly labor-intensive, because the discrepancies between L.C. practice and Newark practice had grown wider, and L.C. copy required an increasing amount of modification to be brought into conformity with Newark practice. In some points Newark practice was not only idiosyncratic but indefensible. Virtually all materials about African-Americans, for example, were classified in 326, the number proper to slavery as a political institution. Economies from the use of OCLC could not be realized if copy had to be edited extensively. With full support from Alrutz, the newly appointed head of the Catalog Department made radical changes and the library embraced standardization wholeheartedly.

The establishment of a Job Information Center in the Education Division met an obvious public need and generated activity in an under-utilized division of the library.

Alrutz was greatly concerned about the percentage of the library's budget devoted to salaries. He believed that the library was overstaffed and that inflated personnel costs were partially attributable to an unnecessary proliferation of service desks. A budget crisis in 1982, which required the layoff of 82 "provisional" employees,[42] resulted in a permanent reduction of personnel expenditures, since not all who had been laid off were re-hired. In the matter of consolidation he considered many ideas but implemented only one: the merger of the Art and Music divisions.[43]

Alrutz perceived a need to change the library's organization plan, which had altered very little since Kaiser's time. He believed that far too many managers reported directly to him and that another administrative "layer" was needed. He moved cautiously, and the plan that he eventually introduced was, by his own assessment, less than ideal;[44] but it did reduce to three the number of people reporting directly to the director.

Alrutz was eager to delegate increased responsibility to middle managers. His ideas about participative management were, however, at odds with entrenched institutional culture. When Kaiser had decentralized the administration of the library in the 1940s, he had delegated authority over *routine* matters to department heads; but the kind of responsibility that Alrutz wanted them to assume was broader. Confusion and disagreement about the amount of authority they were to exercise persisted throughout his tenure.

Despite his ability and dedication, his success in mobilizing the staff for change was limited, and he failed to communicate effectively with the trustees. He resigned in 1987.

The trustees were convinced that the library had administrative problems which ought to be examined by a management consultant during the search for a new director. Consequently, they engaged Thomas A. Banker, who had recently resigned from his position as Assistant Business Administrator of the city of Newark, to serve as interim administrator of the library. Emily J. Matonti, head of the General Reference and Collections Department,[45] was designated as his first assistant. Banker met with Alrutz for several days. The two communicated amicably and Banker adopted a number of Alrutz's goals as his own.

In consultation with members of the administrative staff Banker reviewed the allocation of space in the main library building and the library's organization chart. He re-located "popular" collections to the first floor. He also oversaw the restoration of the Popular Reading Room on the second floor, which was re-opened as "Centennial Hall"[46] and thereafter used for programs and receptions. He devised an organization chart that divided the library into seven departments, each overseen by an assistant director. One of these was the new Development Department, which was to assume responsibility for fund-raising and public relations.

When his twice-renewed contract expired in 1988, Banker left the library. Charles F. Cummings was appointed acting director, and Bruce E. Ford was designated as his first assistant. The two oversaw the implementation of some of Banker's plans as the trustees' search for a new director proceeded.

Concurrent with the series of reorganizations and the expansion of outreach services was the growth of the special subject collections, which have done much to make Newark an important research library. These included the Art and Music Division, the Special Collections Division, the Rare Books Division, and the New Jersey Division.

The Art and Music Division made particularly impressive progress under two successive administrators, Julia Sabine and William

Dane. The Division's holdings include reference books, a picture collection, indexes to works of art and music, information files, periodicals, slides, musical scores, recordings and songs.

The Special Collections Division has collections of prints, photographs, posters, artists' books, illustrated books, greeting and post cards, portfolios of plates, autographs, book plates, trade cards and catalogs, and materials relating to the history of the library and the career of John Cotton Dana.

The Rare Books Division contains bound medieval manuscripts, incunabula, 16th–18th-century imprints, works published by the 19th-century Arts and Crafts Movement, illustrated books, Bruce Rogers imprints, 20th-century imprints of fine presses, works about the history of papermaking, and fine bindings.

The New Jersey Division has flourished for many years under the leadership of such outstanding administrators as Miriam Ball, Miriam Studley, Charles Cummings and its current head, Paul Pathwell. The Division's collections about the history and current affairs of the state and Newark include scholarly and popular books, newspapers, periodicals, maps, genealogies, laws and legal materials, photographs and other pictorial materials, archives and manuscripts, indexes, ephemeral publications, and videotapes.

In November 1988, Alex Boyd became the library's ninth director. His immediate priorities included improvement of staff morale, development of an "esprit de corps" in the administrative ranks, establishment of good relations with city government, improvement of the physical plant, more satisfactory accounting procedures, and improvement of security.

Within the first few months of his tenure he reorganized the Finance Department and removed the personnel office from its jurisdiction. He placed the maintenance staff, the engineers, the security guards, the carpenters, and the painters under the direction of the newly appointed assistant director for Personnel and Physical Plant. He refined Banker's allocation of staff.

Boyd established congenial relations with library unions.[47] He was rather liberal in approving promotions recommended by assistant directors. He recognized the importance of salaries in attracting competent employees to the library, and with the backing of the trustees he negotiated labor contracts that the unions considered favorable.

He saw to completion the renovation of the Springfield branch, which had begun during the interim, and then initiated the renovation of the Weequahic branch. Aware that the renovation of all the library's branches would take more than a decade, he instituted a program of refurbishment in those branches awaiting renovation. All were painted, carpeted and put into good repair.

He then turned his attention to the principal service areas of the main building. These were painted, carpeted, completely refurnished, and rescued from the aesthetic effects of the 1950s renovation. The renovation of the North Branch followed.

To meet the special needs of the ethnic groups that constituted the majority of Newark's population, he established the Sala Hispanoamericana and the African-American Room. The Sala houses all the library's Spanish-language materials. Although every subject collection in the library abounds in material relating to the African-American experience, the community has responded enthusiastically to the establishment of a multi-disciplinary collection of popular African-American materials.

A Special Services Room has been established to provide convenient access to services and materials needed by people with special needs. A Career Information Center, with facilities for resume writing, is housed in this room, along with materials for literacy instruction and for learning English as a second language as well as materials for use by the handicapped.

Under Boyd's leadership the library has made further progress in automation. A Dynix integrated library system was installed in 1990 and went into operation in 1991. An increasing number of electronic information sources have been acquired to supplement and supplant printed materials used in reference work.

Boyd, like Hill and Dana, has placed great emphasis on public programs and exhibitions. He views them not only as a means of encouraging the use of library materials but also as a legitimate educational activity in their own right.

Before coming to Newark he served as the Chicago Public Library's development officer, and he has remained intensely interested in the work of the Development Department in Newark. This Department has been responsible for the publication of *The Second Century*, the library's award-winning newsletter, as well as *A Century of Service*, a brochure commemorating the library's centennial. Many of the promotional pieces the department has produced have won awards, including the American Library Association's John Cotton Dana Award.

The Development Department has been successful in obtaining grant support for the library's program of service. Of all the grants received, the most noteworthy is a $550,000 N.T.I.A. (National Telecommunication and Information) grant, which will support expansion of the automation program and enable the library to provide access to the Internet at the branches as well as the main library.

Boyd's accomplishments cannot yet be summarized. His work has just begun. It seems clear, however, that he is creative, courageous, and committed to the ideals of service that have guided the library throughout its history.

Over the years the Newark Public Library has experienced many changes caused by panics, depressions, political events, wars and population shifts which have altered its direction. The library has also experimented with a variety of collection and staff organizations, and has developed, dropped and refined its specialized services as funds and personnel dictated.

In all of these shifting local and area conditions, the library has moved with considerable vigor to maintain and improve its services, stretching its efforts in times of poor funding and expanding in better times.

Because of its unique position in serving a large metropolitan area with substantial manufacturing, research and development, banking, insurance, medical educational and cultural requirements, the city fathers, boards of trustees, administration and staff have had to be discerning and creative; the greater Newark area has responded and provided an excellent environment for a human services institution like the Newark Public Library to develop and progress.

Notes

1. Julia Sabine, "Antecedents of Trustees of the Free Public Library, Made to the Honorable, the Board of Aldermen of the City of Newark, N.J." *The Newark Public Library. A Study of Books and Readers in Newark, 1666–1889* (Ph.D dissertation, University of Chicago, 1946).

2. The Newark Library Association, a stock company, operated a subscription library. Subscribers supported the erection of "Library Hall" which eventually became the home of the public library.

3. Until the 1930s the title "librarian" was used to designate the head of an institution. Later it came to be used for any library school graduate, and heads of libraries assumed the title "director."

4. *Fourth Annual Report of the Board of Trustees of the Free Public Library, Made to the Honorable, the Board of Aldermen of the City of Newark, N.J.* (Newark, N.J.: 1892), 40.

5. *First and Second Annual Reports of the Board of Trustees of the Free Public Library, Made to the Honorable, the Board of Aldermen of the City of Newark, N.J.* (Newark, N.J.: 1889 & 1890), 9.

6. *Ibid*: 16–17.

7. *Ibid*: 17–18.

8. *Report of the Librarian of the Newark, N.J. Free Public Library, 1889–1901* (Newark, N.J.: 1901), 17.

9. *Third Annual Report of the Board of Trustees of the Free Public Li-*

brary, Made to the Honorable, the Board of Aldermen of the City of Newark, N.J. (Newark, N.J.: 1891), 16.

10. *Report of the Librarian . . . 1889–1901*, 33.

11. Beatrice Winser, who in 1894 became assistant librarian, was engaged as a French and German cataloger in 1889. See *Beatrice Winsor, 1869–1947* (Newark, N.J.: 1948), 4.

12. *Report of the Librarian . . . 1889–1901*, 33.

13. *Fourth Annual Report of the Board of Trustees . . .* , 43–45.

14. *Fourteenth Annual Report of the Board of Trustees of the Free Public Library, Made to the Honorable, the Board of Aldermen of the City of Newark, N.J.* (Newark, N.J.: 1902), 17.

15. *Fifteenth Annual Report of the Board of Trustees of the Free Public Library, Made to the Honorable, the Board of Aldermen of the City of Newark, N.J.* (Newark, N.J.: 1903), 31.

16. *Sixteenth Annual Report of the Board of Trustees of the Free Public Library, Made to the Honorable, the Board of Aldermen of the City of Newark, N.J.* (Newark, N.J.: 1904), 20–21.

17. *Eighteenth Annual Report of the Board of Trustees of the Free Public Library, Made to the Honorable, the Board of Aldermen of the City of Newark, N.J.* (Newark, N.J.: 1906), 12.

18. *Fifteenth Annual Report of the Board of Trustees . . .* , 30.

19. Catherine Van Dyne, "The Organization and Work of the Lending Department, the Newark Public Library." *Library Quarterly* XI: 1, January, 1941, 69–84.

20. Kingdon, Frank, *John Cotton Dana, A Life* (Newark, N.J. The Public Library and Museum, 1940), 91.

21. The "Business Branch" was renamed the "Business Library" in 1944. Its name was changed to the Newark Public Library Business Information Center in 1989 when the library director, Alex Boyd, discovered that some who used the facility were not aware of its connection with the Newark Public Library.

22. *Ibid*: 13.

23. Julia Sabine, "Winser, Beatrice (1869–1947)," *Dictionary of American Library Biography*, Ed. Bohdan S. Wynar (Littleton, Colo.: Libraries Unlimited 1978), 567.

24. The Dickman system eliminated the use of a "reader's card," which indicated to staff that a borrower had outstanding loans and made it easy to prevent delinquents from borrowing more books.

25. Sabine. *Beatrice Winser . . .* , 567.

26. *Beatrice Winser, 1869–1947*, 5.

27. *Ibid*: 5.

28. Several Irish-surnamed trustees had been appointed to the board in 1941 and, according to Helen DeVita, Julia Sabine, and Miriam Studley, who had been library employees at the time. Winsor's dispute with the board concerned an Irish-surnamed employee. Several months after her resignation, Winsor wrote in a letter (found in the files of the Newark Museum), "the Catholic Church has seized the public library just as it seized the public schools."

29. Letter to the editor of the *Library Journal*, 49, (10): 492 (May 15,

1924) Reprinted in Carl A. Hanson, *Librarian At Large: Selected Writings of John Cotton Dana* (Washington, D.C.: Special Libraries Association, 1991), 102–103.

30. James E. Bryan, *History of the Newark Public Library.* Unpublished typescript, undated, no paging.

31. Renamed (more accurately) "Humanities" in 1974.

32. Compiled by Alexander L. Crosby and Carols S. Simon (Newark, 1946).

33. Written and designed by Alexander L. Crosby (Newark, 1958).

34. *At Your Service*, 6.

35. Bryan, *History of the Newark Public Library.*

36. *Ibid.*

37. *Ibid.*

38. *Ibid.*

39. Writer's personal recollection of a conversation with Bryan.

40. OCLC (originally "Ohio College Library Center"; later "Online Computer Library Center") is a consortium that maintains the largest bibliographic data base in the world. The data base is used for cataloging, bibliographic searching, and resource sharing. When a library catalogs an item on OCLC its ownership of the item cataloged is recorded in the data base, which functions as a union catalog for the nation.

41. *A Catalog of Books Represented by Library of Congress Printed Cards Issued to July 30, 1942* (Ann Arbor, Mich.: Edwards Bros., 1942–1946).

42. i.e., those who did not have permanent Civil Service appointments.

43. The Art and Music Department had always been a single administrative entity. The consolidation was physical, not administrative.

44. Writer's recollection of numerous conversations with Alrutz.

45. The Lending and Reference Department was renamed the General Reference and Collections Department when Alrutz's reorganization plan was adopted.

46. 1988 was, of course, the centennial of the establishment of the library.

47. Relations between the unions and Banker and Ford had been stormy.

5

Library System Development

Robert Fortenbaugh

Library system development in New Jersey began before World War II. When reviewing the record of that development one is struck by both the longevity of the many different concepts and plans that were discussed and the length of time often needed to bring them to fruition. Some of those concepts were proposed at least twenty years before the enabling legislation and accompanying regulations could be enacted.

In 1935 the Committee on Library Planning of the New Jersey Library Association recommended that the libraries of the state join in improving their services so that New Jersey could join with other states in providing comprehensive nationwide information services. During the Second World War the Association's Regional Planning Committee, which included staff members of the State Library (a cooperative relationship that was to continue for decades), was charged with designing a program for the future development of library service in New Jersey. The program's intent was to strengthen existing services and to find a means of providing assistance to areas without library service. The committee recommended a series of plans that included steps to encourage county and municipal libraries to join together to provide service wherever possible. In 1945 the Association surveyed its membership on the committee's proposals for cooperative county library services. Based upon the overwhelmingly positive results of the survey, the committee formulated legislation that would authorize the establishment of joint county libraries.[1]

A conference of committee chairmen of the New Jersey Library Association who were concerned with statewide planning was held in the fall of 1946. The committee noted that "what we in this State need most is the personnel to organize, direct, and supervise demonstrations to show how the services of existing libraries or agencies can be strengthened or extended and made more efficient by the addition of trained and capable personnel."[2]

By 1948 the Regional Planning Committee had collected statistics of libraries by county on salaries, volumes held, circulation and aid funds received, and in 1950 it had developed a plan for statewide services for the State Library.[3] The plan reviewed the state of library service in New Jersey in the late 1940s and suggested a structure of three federations and four regions as a potential solution. In 1951 the Regional Planning Committee began working on a plan for "complete and adequate modern library service for all the people of New Jersey."[4] The committee's *Proposed Program for Library Development in New Jersey*, submitted in 1952, recommended library service units composed of federations and four regional or multi-county libraries.

In 1953 the Library Development Committee (successor to the Regional Planning Committee), chaired by Mary V. Gaver, produced a three-volume study, *Library Service for the People of New Jersey*. It presented information about population served, number of library units, types of libraries and sources of income, expenditures, use of materials, personnel, etc. The second volume included a statement of minimum standards, while the third dealt with the Bureau of Public and School Library Services at the State Library.[5]

The Commission to Study Library Services in New Jersey

In a move that was to have far-reaching consequences the Library Development Committee sought the establishment of a joint gubernatorial-legislative commission to study and report on the prospects for state funding for New Jersey libraries. When the Commission to Study Library Services in New Jersey was created and held hearings in 1954, the NJLA's testimony was given by James E. Bryan, Director of the Newark Public Library, and by Professor Mary V. Gaver and Dr. Lowell A. Martin of Rutgers University. They addressed the points in the Association's master plan to improve library service and utilized excerpts from *Library Service for the People of New Jersey*. They highlighted the need to provide more services and funding for libraries. Gaver's testimony in particular emphasized the inadequacies of the current county library funding structure. She speculated on the viability of libraries whose service areas might be too small for long-term stability without support from a countywide system. She also expressed doubts about the ability of some of the smaller counties to serve their public effectively without regionalization or consolidation.

In response to the Commission's activity, a plan for a long-range program of library development in New Jersey was prepared in 1955 by a Special Regional Planning Committee of the New Jersey Library Association. The plan included four regional libraries and called for further study of existing library conditions. There also was public discussion about libraries outside the library community. A 1955 report of the New Jersey State Chamber of Commerce's Library Subcommittee reviewed the NJLA's master plan for improving library services in New Jersey. It endorsed the recommendations for educating more librarians and for additional funding for the State Library for the purpose of providing better services to local libraries on a cooperative basis.

The Commission to Study Library Services in New Jersey completed its work and released its report, *Better Libraries for New Jersey*, to the Governor and the Legislature in January 1956.[6] The report concluded, among other things, that 200,000 residents lacked any library service and an estimated one-half of the state's residents had inadequate service. Other deficiencies cited were too few books and other materials, insufficient trained staff, too small library units, and out-of-date facilities.[7] The Commission recommended a State Library aid program with authorization up to $2 million in annual awards, equalization aid, county library establishment grants, strengthening of the certification law requiring professional librarians in municipalities of 10,000 or more in population, an emergency aid fund, and an increase in the budget of the Rutgers University Graduate School of Library Service. The Commission also recommended increased support of the State Library's Bureau of Public and School Library Services and the establishment of a deposit and exchange library at the State Library.[8]

The year 1956 is a milestone in the development of library cooperation in New Jersey. Statutes were enacted authorizing the organization of library cooperatives among public libraries, particularly federations of municipal and county libraries. In addition Congress enacted the Library Services Act (LSA), the first acknowledgment of a federal role in directly encouraging and assisting national library development. Later that year the State Library issued a report on New Jersey's plan for the use of LSA funds.

A report on New Jersey's plan for the use of the Federal Library Services Act was prepared by the New Jersey State Library in 1956. The report addressed some of the problems that had been identified in *Better Libraries for New Jersey*.

The State Aid Act of 1959

As a direct result of the recommendations contained in *Better Libraries for New Jersey*, legislation was enacted late in 1959 concerning state aid for certain public libraries and providing an appropriation. The State Library Aid Act of 1959 provided four types of state aid: 1) minimum aid of either five cents per capita or 35 cents per capita; 2) equalization aid for smaller municipalities; 3) county library, county-wide federation, or county-wide joint library establishment grants; and 4) emergency aid. These provisions had all been recommended in *Better Libraries for New Jersey*. The establishment grant program was later amended in 1962 to include regional libraries. Portions of the program were designed to encourage the participation of libraries in federations.

The first disbursements of state aid were only $400,000, but the precedent of the state's agreeing to share in the cost of supporting its municipal and county libraries as part of the state's overall educational plan was finally in place. With the creation of the Rutgers University Graduate School of Library Service, mandatory professional librarian certification, and the initial State Aid Act, the 1950s had proven to be a highly productive period, the culmination of two decades of collaborative work by many people.

The 1960s

The 1960s were also to prove one of the most productive periods for New Jersey libraries. To the growing ability of professionals in the field to analyze library conditions and plan effectively were added the growing leadership ability and resources of the State Library, the presence of two such creative forces as Mary Gaver and Lowell Martin at the Rutgers Library School, and the growing willingness of government to experiment with new cooperative endeavors. Encouraged by the accomplishments of the previous decade, the state's library community pushed ahead with an even more ambitious program that would tie all types of libraries into a single system.

To obtain data for planning this program the Library Development Committee surveyed the libraries of the state in 1962–63. The survey included public, school, college, university and special libraries, and the State Library. Separate reports summarized the findings about the types and amounts of services offered by each category of library. These reports were then summarized in a statement presented to the New Jersey Library Association's executive board and the library community.[9] Three general findings were presented and they formed the basis for many of the recommendations found in the later Martin-Gaver report:

1. When the data about New Jersey library resources were analyzed by broad geographic regions, the lack of adequate library service in the three non-urban areas of the state was clear.
2. Bringing public, school and college libraries throughout the state up to national standards of minimum adequacy was an essential step for library development. The inadequacy of resources in New Jersey was so general that no total plan for development could hope to achieve strong service unless the individual units were considerably strengthened.
3. No library is an island. Libraries throughout the state supplement their resources with the resources of other libraries and of other types of libraries.[10]

   The report also cited the need for comprehensive statewide planning of library service and for the improvement of book resources. In addition, it addressed the shortage of professionally qualified librarians, the need for improved services to stimulate learning, and increased reference services.[11]

The report made four recommendations for continuing the analysis of the library situation in New Jersey, and it proposed a plan for library development in the state. The recommendations specified: 1) that the Library Development Committee be authorized to prepare a comprehensive library plan that would propose a network of libraries of all types in the state; 2) that a consultant be engaged to assist the Library Development Committee in further study of the findings; 3) that an advisory committee be appointed to work with the consultant; and 4) that the State Library continue to gather statistics for the evaluation of library services in the state.

In preparation for their later report, and as an aid to evaluate the data obtained in the 1963 Library Development Committee survey, Gaver and Martin in 1963 prepared a draft statement of standards for library service in New Jersey. The proposed standards covered four broad groups of readers: 1) elementary children; 2) secondary students; 3) college and university students and faculty; and 4) citizens in general. The standards as approved by the Library Development Committee in December 1963 represented minimum levels of library service. It was stressed that they were not future goals, but minimum levels needed immediately.[12] The committee issued two draft versions of the *Plan for Library Service in New Jersey*, the first in March 1964. The purpose of the plan was to link different jurisdictions and library units in New Jersey into a coordinated statewide program that would enable the state to achieve wider use of resources and ensure that all residents would have access to those resources. The committee's second draft issued in May 1964, covered standards of service and how well libraries met these standards. It also outlined the principles of a plan to bring "adequate library resources to all New Jersey readers and to do so by means of a coordinated program over the State."[13]

The minimum standards involved three levels of service providers: 1) local public libraries, elementary and secondary school libraries and college libraries; 2) area libraries; and 3) specialized research libraries. The plan also stressed networking as integral to effective resource sharing. It was presented at a general session of the New Jersey Library Association's 1964 Spring Conference.

Libraries for the People of New Jersey

The culmination of all of these activities by NJLA's Library Development Committee and the State Library was the landmark report, *Libraries for the People of New Jersey; or Knowledge for All,* issued in November 1964. Written by Lowell A. Martin and Mary V. Gaver, co-chairs of the Library Development Committee, the report outlined a plan for a three-tiered program of service for all the citizens and libraries of the state. It provided for a system of local libraries, area services, and statewide resource libraries, stating that "besides a structure for gaining access to specialized collections, there should also be a hierarchy of specialized reference service in New Jersey."[14]

The first level, local libraries, included community, municipal and county libraries, elementary and secondary school media centers, and college libraries that provided direct service to people. The 22 area libraries would be designated from the pool of strong public libraries, which would be provided state funding to expand their services and strengthen their collections. They would serve their traditional local clientele, as well as patrons on a region-wide basis. The Newark Public Library, the strongest public library in the state, was designated to play a special role in the system. It would be an area library and also serve to "backstop the area reference libraries throughout the whole northern part of the state by the establishment of the Metropolitan Reference Center of Northern New Jersey."[15] The enabling legislation was still several years away from adoption, but by using 1964 LSCA monies the State Library was able to award grants to fifteen of the stronger public libraries as area libraries. The use of the federal monies was possible because the revision of LSA in 1964 had removed the "rural" limitations. An additional grant of $100,000 was given to Newark for its role as the Metropolitan Reference Center.

The third level of service consisted of statewide specialized and research resources, with Princeton and Rutgers universities and the State Library joining the Newark Public Library at the top of the pyramid. The plan called for coordinated planning in building reference resources and the means for providing access to those resources. In addition, provisions were made for the use of the collections, interlibrary loan, and duplication of materials. The plan proposed that a Reference and Referral Center be established at the State Library to coordinate requests from local and area libraries. It also recommended additional personnel for the State Library and the expansion of its interlibrary loan service. Also suggested was expansion of its consulting services and the strengthening of its role in the administration of financial aid and of planning and research. The need for the State Library to provide leadership in planning the development of state resources was stressed.

As with any report, problems in the implementation of recommendations arose. A review subcommittee was established by the Library Development Committee for the purpose of hearing complaints, questions and recommendations in connection with the area library plan. They dealt particularly with petitions of libraries to serve as area libraries or to be served by a particular area library. There was also some discussion as to the roles of the Library Development Committee and the State Library vis-à-vis the responsibility for implementing the plan. Roger McDonough, Director of the State Library, stated that "it has been of help to the State Library to have the Library Development Committee lay out the plan for New Jersey." At the same time, he pointed out that the question of "who wears what hat is a continuing problem." The committee replied that "its recommendations are recommendations only; the State Library has the authority and responsibility to make the decisions."[16]

The many years of discussion and planning finally culminated with the signing of the New Jersey State Library Aid Act in 1967 by Governor Richard J. Hughes. Introduced by Senator Mathew Feldman of Bergen County, the legislation provided a structure and funding for the 1964 plan of the three-tiered system of local, area, and research libraries. The law provided graduated state aid payments, which gave communities an incentive to increase their local expenditures for libraries. The law also changed the method of funding county libraries by providing aid directly to counties and the municipalities. Typically, the state's financial position was not good, so that the authorized level of appropriation of $7.8 million was not met immediately. The precedent of inadequate appropriations to fund the formula set in 1968–69 continued into the 1990s, except for several consecutive years in the late 1980s and once during the 1970s.

The law also expanded the amount given for emergency and incentive grants. The grants were to be used for existing or proposed federations, contractual services, or other cooperative projects. The legislation also defined the new terms of area library and research library center service, and provided permanent funding for each type of library.

At almost the same time, the State Library received a major report by Nelson Associates regarding county library services in the state. *A Regional System Reorganization Plan for New Jersey County Libraries* had been commissioned in 1966 "to evaluate the role of the county library in the emerging New Jersey library pattern and to recommend appropriate changes which will contribute to improved library service throughout the state."[17] After examining the current situation, the authors concluded "that the inherent problems which have faced the county libraries cannot be overcome by any short-term measures . . . the main thrust of our report is directed to library needs on a regional, rather than a county-wide basis."[18] The report's recommendations included regional libraries to be formed by local and county initiative, a regional governing body, the transferral of county library assets to the regional libraries, a redistribution of the funding with the state assuming a major portion of the costs, and necessary administrative regulations.

In a 1968 report prepared for the State Library, consultant Joseph Eisner presented suggestions for implementing the interlibrary recommendations proposed in the Martin-Gaver report. The recommendations included cooperative activities among area libraries, and between area libraries and research libraries, and the role that the State Library should assume in this networking structure.[19]

In February 1969 the Library Development Committee requested that the State Library "fund and start to organize an evaluation of the statewide library plan, structure as well as services, using such expertise as there is available on the Library Development Committee."[20] In a series of papers delivered at a symposium marking the dedication of the new building of the Rutgers Graduate School of Library Service in April 1969, the Martin-Gaver plan was the primary topic of discussion. While New Jersey was praised for the scope of the plan, the lack of funding for the activities recommended by the plan was criticized, and suggestions were made for the personnel and service enhancements it had proposed.

The 1970s

In 1972 a group of public libraries in Morris and Union counties agreed to establish the Morris-Union Federation of Libraries for the purpose of reciprocal library services among six communities— Berkeley Heights, Chatham, Madison, Morristown, New Providence and Summit. MUF extended into Somerset County with the addition of Bernards Township in 1978. A unique feature of the federation was the agreement to share the responsibility for certain collection specialization among the various members. In the mid–1990s the MUF libraries were still providing these enhanced collections in twelve different subject areas. The program eventually expanded to include academic libraries in Morris County—The College of St. Elizabeth, Drew University, and Fairleigh Dickinson University-Madison.

Planning for the future of the state library network continued into 1974. The Library Development Committee under the chairmanship of Kenneth F. McPherson, Director of the Morris County Library, formulated a new proposal for improving library services. Three alternative approaches were presented with recommendations for changes in the 1967 structure. The alternatives were: 1) continuing the current area system consisting of up to 26 areas; 2) creation of 18 intermediate regions; or 3) a program of a larger region concept consisting of six regions.[21]

These ideas were considered at a series of four regional institutes, co-sponsored by the New Jersey Library Association, the New Jersey State Media Association, and the New Jersey State Library, held during 1974. The programs dealt with school media centers, statewide library planning, and the future of library development in the state. The panels were composed of representatives of local and state governments, Rutgers, school media centers, and local library officials. At the January 1975 meeting of the Library Development Committee it was reported that the three alternative plans would be presented to NJLA members in the Association's journal, *New Jersey Libraries.*

When it appeared in the March issue the plans were summarized in table form, and included the basis of regions, governance, administration, responsibilities, funding sources and methods, and the role of the State Library.

During 1975 the Library Development Committee reviewed the

state's existing library development program. As discussion proceeded, it became evident that the process would be enhanced by a sharper delineation of goals than had been previously developed. A subcommittee on "Goals for a New Jersey Library Development Program" was established. The resulting documents were titled *Interim Goals for a New Jersey Library Development Program (1975)* and *Program of Action in Support of Interim Goals for a New Jersey Library Network Program (1975)*.

The goals stressed equal and free access to libraries and information services by all citizens of New Jersey. Twenty-minute travel time to a library was considered the maximum for proper and effective service. It also stated that every local library that met the state criteria should receive state funding to assist local programs. Provision was made for the inclusion of school and academic libraries. Every municipality would be required to provide minimum local tax support for library services based on the state equalized valuation, a goal that was not achieved until 1985. Another goal was that all library resources in the state be integrated into a coordinated system of library service. The network would be supported by state funds and, where possible, by federal and private funding. The *Program of Action* included recommendations for specific appropriations to support the proposed local services. It also specified support for the improvement of service at intermediate and highly specialized libraries, as well as for systems development and research.

All of these planning and study activities gained urgency as state aid funding was reduced by 27 percent in the 1975/76 fiscal year. It became increasingly important to choose a course of action that resulted in the most effective use of the state funds available. Assistance in making this critical choice came from several sources. The results of a 1975 questionnaire sent by the State Library to all libraries in New Jersey were reported in *New Jersey Libraries*. The intent of the survey was to evaluate the quality and effectiveness of area library services and to gather planning data for the future of the area library program. The survey showed that the libraries were generally pleased with the service offered by the area libraries, but that problems existed with regard to publicity, the provision of workshops and training sessions, and the relationship of the advisory council to the area library. Another conclusion was that, while public and academic libraries were relatively involved in the area library structure, school and special libraries seemed to be outside the structure.[22]

Further assistance came from a study in 1976 by the Gallup Organization which was prepared for the State Library in response to the Library Services and Construction Act requirement for a long-range plan based upon a needs-assessment statement and documentation. The Gallup report, *The Use and Attitudes Toward Libraries in New Jersey*, included a survey of patron use of public libraries and recommendations for future use of the data and the need for other studies. Among its many conclusions were:

1. That "the needs of most New Jersey adults can best be met by a 'two-faceted' approach: a) Develop full resource reference centers in areas where there are concentrations of business firms with many white collar employees, and there are many young adults"; and b) "Develop and strengthen neighborhood libraries to include services that supplement the traditional book borrowing and children's services."[23] The report emphasized the distinction between full- and limited-resource libraries, the primary difference being the extent of reference resources.
2. "An important consideration is that the accessibility of a range of services through neighborhood libraries is probably essential if the public library system is to satisfy the interests of non-users in these services."[24]
3. Special efforts were necessary if public libraries were to attract more users and use of the full range of services that the libraries offered. Meeting the needs of adults fifty and older also required special attention.
4. A program designed to develop awareness of the full range of public library services among the school-age population is likely to have a significant long-term payoff.

The report also recommended further research into the motivation of library users, clarifying the difference between research and information-seeking users, and a needs assessment of black and Spanish-speaking persons.

In September 1976 the Library Development Committee received a letter requesting its endorsement of the development of a Bergen-Passaic Regional Library System. The committee was asked to recommend to the State Library the funding of a pilot project using LSCA monies to establish the system. This idea was viewed as feasible because it built on the existing smaller systems in the two counties and was considered a good example of the potential for cooperation among libraries.

With $50,000 from the Bergen County Board of Chosen Freeholders and $25,000 in LSCA funds, the Bergen County Cooperative Library System (BCCLS) began in 1979. The Passaic libraries, originally part of the proposal, were no longer included because Passaic County officials chose not to provide funding. On the other hand, Bergen County had three existing public library interlibrary systems prior to the formation of BCCLS, serving the Mid-Bergen, North Bergen and South Bergen areas. BCCLS had been formed to further that resource sharing through reciprocal borrowing on a county-wide basis.

In 1985, 21 of the system members created an additional not-for-profit corporation, the BCCLS Computer Consortium, to provide for automated circulation and cataloging. In 1990 the two entities were consolidated into a single unit. By 1996 BCCLS was providing services to 70 public libraries and 19 school districts. It was providing Internet access, online indexing and text from the *Bergen Record*, magazine data bases, and a net lender reimbursement program. The system had grown to include public library members in Passaic, Hudson and Essex Counties and was handling in excess of seven million circulation transactions per year with reciprocal lending representing approximately one out of every six circulations.

The *Interim Goals* were revised in 1977 to reflect the importance of school and academic libraries, as well as to provide more details on the concept of networking and library cooperation. The first version of *Networks for Knowledge: Mobilizing Libraries for the People of New Jersey* was issued in the summer of 1977.[25] It reviewed the progress of the State Library development program from 1967 to 1977 and finalized elements that had been introduced earlier in the Library Development Committee's report on *Interim Goals*. It noted the positive effect of the 1967 legislation in bringing public libraries into full compliance with the minimum criteria. The number had doubled between 1968 and 1974. It also included an equalization aid proposal, a recommendation that all K–12 students have library access within their school building, academic library integration into the state plan, and, as always, more state funding.

The final report issued by the Library Development Committee in 1978 contained recommendations intended to identify problems, provide a framework for further discussion, and contribute to the continuing study of the New Jersey library network. Funding programs, integration of a coordinated state network of services into a national network, availability of more specialized materials, and comprehensive, easy-to-reach services were among its many recommendations.

The New State Plan for Library Development

A Statewide Planning Group was appointed by the State Librarian in June 1979 to achieve a consensus on the direction in which library development should proceed and to delineate a process for the achievement of its goals. The advisory group consisted of the state's selected delegates to the White House Conference on Library and Information Services and representatives of the major library associations in the state. The Group's report, *A Developing State Plan for Library Services*, placed "clear responsibility upon the State Library, the profession, and library users throughout the State, to monitor and evaluate library services of all types . . . and to perfect the means of delivery of quality services within the limits of cost-effectiveness."[26] The report proposed an Access/Networking structure that was soon embodied in legislation.

Just five months later, the County and Municipal Government Study Commission issued its report, *The Development of Libraries and Networks*. This was another crucial element in the the next great step forward for the libraries of New Jersey.[27] The Study Commission was created in the 1960s by the Legislature to examine various public services in which the State was a participant in order to make recommendations to the Legislature for the improvement of those services. Working with a large advisory committee of professional librarians from all types of institutions, the Commission (known popularly as the "Musto" Commission, after its long-time chairman, Senator William Musto of Hudson County) concluded that a major revision of the State's role in assisting libraries was necessary. The widespread support demonstrated in these various proposals for redesigning the library network led Senator Feldman to introduce a bill in 1982 that would establish and maintain a statewide multitype library network.

With the landmark legislation signed by Governor Thomas H. Kean in January 1984, a multitype network was now possible. Based on the oft-proposed regional concept of service areas dating back to the early 1950s, the six regional library cooperatives (RLCs) encouraged the voluntary membership of all the academic, institutional, public, school, and special libraries in their areas. The legislation stated: "The Legislature finds and declares that promoting cooperation among the various types of libraries in New Jersey will provide this State's residents with full and equal access to library materials and programs not currently available within their communities; that increased cooperation and access will help control the cost of maintaining local libraries while providing for improved services; that establishing a library network can be best accomplished by assisting libraries to form cooperatives on a regional basis and by having the Division of the State Library . . . promote, coordinate and fund such cooperative efforts."[28] The legislation guaranteed four basic services: reference, interlibrary loan, material delivery, and citation/

location. Additional services or programs could be included by any cooperative that decided they were appropriate.

The previous network had relied primarily on the strengths of certain public libraries and the statewide service libraries, but it did not effectively utilize the resources of the many other types of libraries, nor did it allow for adequate interaction with other public libraries. It also did not encourage broad participation by all of the state's libraries. To further the cooperative nature of the RLCs, the responsibility of selecting service providers in each region and for determining the amount of funding given to each service provider was vested in the executive board of each RLC. The State Library no longer distributed networking funds to designated public libraries using a rigid formula.

Six regions were recommended to the State Librarian by the Statewide Planning Group the day after Governor Kean signed the legislation. Through the early 1980s draft policies and procedures had been developed which utilized population, population density, number and types of libraries, information resources, and area as factors in designing possible RLC service boundaries. In 1983 an additional consideration was adopted: no county would be split between two regions. The six regions resulting from the group's study made as equitable as possible the distribution of library resources and population but not geographical area. RLC 6 in South Jersey covered 43 percent of the state; the RLC serving Essex and Hudson counties only two percent.

In 1984 each region established an Interim Planning Committee (IPC) whose duties included electing officers, identifying all libraries and their resources, formulating a service plan and a first-year budget, drafting by-laws, and preparing for incorporation. The members of each IPC were appointed by the State Librarian and included librarians and lay representatives from all types of libraries. Each IPC was assigned a two-person team from the consultant staff of the State Library's Library Development Bureau. In October 1984 an interim Library Network Review Board (LNRB) was appointed by State Librarian Barbara Weaver. Its charge was to recommend to the State Librarian by June 1985: an organizational structure for the LNRB, draft bylaws, and plans for inter-regional, interstate and national cooperative programs and services.

The first RLC to establish itself was Region 4 (Union and Middlesex counties) in the spring of 1985. Region 2 (Bergen and Passaic counties) was officially established in June, and Region 5 (Mercer, Monmouth, Ocean) and Region 3 (Essex, Hudson) were established in October. In January 1986 Region 6 (Atlantic, Burlington, Camden, Cape May, Cumberland, Gloucester and Salem counties) was established, followed a week later by the last of the new RLCs, Region 1 (Hunterdon, Morris, Somerset, Sussex, and Warren counties).

Before the RLCs became operational the old network of area libraries and state contract libraries remained in place, providing services as they had since the mid–1960s. The Interlibrary Loan (ILL) Access Center for libraries without direct access to OCLC began operation in September 1985, fully funded from the statewide services portion of the network appropriation. Funding for the statewide contract libraries of the Princeton University Library, the Newark Public Library, Rutgers University Libraries, and the State Library was now drawn from the network appropriation as well. By the late 1980s the New Jersey Institute of Technology (NJIT) and the University of Medicine and Dentistry of New Jersey (UMDNJ) had been added as ILL and photocopy service contractors for the network. When the RLCs began letting contracts for the required services, many of the former area libraries were among the contractors; but as the years passed and the funding became tighter, all of the RLCs gradually reduced the number of contracting libraries.

In the state budget for FY 1991 the network appropriation was cut 16 percent, as was the Per Capita State Aid program. Despite the reduction, the RLCs were able to maintain the majority of existing services. Many of the regions dispensed with or reduced their walk-in reference contracts (a service not required by the network legislation). The open-borrowing program was a casualty in Region 3, Comet delivery schedules (a statewide contract delivery service provided in all regions of New Jersey) were reduced in some cases, and in most cases operational expenses were frozen.

In 1993 State Librarian Louise Minervino proposed, as a means of addressing the continued under-funding of the network, that regional service areas be reorganized. This was done in an attempt to reduce network administrative costs and to consolidate services. Many alternatives were examined during the summer. They ranged from splitting some regions by county and assigning each component county to another region, to merging whole regions with one another. Because of the nature of the RLCs' incorporation, it was determined that mergers were the least problematic solution. Region 1 merged with Region 2 to form the Highlands Regional Library Cooperative. Region 3 merged with Region 4 to form the INFOLINK Regional Library Cooperative. The other two regions remained unchanged in their service areas but were renamed; Region 5 became the Central Jersey Regional Library Cooperative and Region 6 became the South Jersey Regional Library Cooperative.

Many challenges face the Network, but the first ten years have demonstrated flexibility, resiliency and a cooperative spirit which had proven, thus far, equal to the tasks. The Network has continued to provide services, leadership and support to the member libraries in response to the ever-changing information technologies.

Notes

1. New Jersey Library Association, Regional Planning Committee, *minutes, September 28, 1945.*

2. New Jersey Library Association, conference, October 23, 1946, *Library Development Program*, 1.

3. Leigh, Robert D. *Suggested State-Wide Plan.* 1950. (No publisher, no place of publication).

4. New Jersey Library Association, Regional Planning Committee, Report, 1951.

5. New Jersey Library Association, Library Development Committee, *Library Service for the People of New Jersey* (Trenton, N.J.: 1953–54. 3 v.).

6. New Jersey Commission to Study Library Services in New Jersey. *Better Libraries for New Jersey* (Trenton, N.J.: State of New Jersey, January, 1956).

7. Ibid: 11.

8. Ibid: 12–13.

9. New Jersey Library Association, Library Development Committee, *Preliminary Report,* 1963.

10. Ibid: 6.

11. Ibid: 12–14.

12. New Jersey Library Association, Library Development Committee, *Standards for Library Services in New Jersey,* 1963.

13. New Jersey Library Association, Library Development Committee, *Draft Plan for Library Service* (March 1964, part 4), 2.

14. New Jersey Library Association, Library Development Committee. *Libraries for the People of New Jersey or Knowledge for All,* (New Jersey Library Association, 1964), 30.

15. Ibid: 51.

16. New Jersey Library Association, Library Development Committee. *minutes, meeting, 1965,* 2.

17. Nelson Associates, Inc. *A Regional System Reorganization Plan for New Jersey County Libraries* (New York, N.Y.: April 1967), 1.

18. Ibid: cover letter.

19. Joseph Eisner, *Suggested Recommendations for Interlibrary Cooperation in the State of New Jersey* (Plainview, N.Y.: published by the author, 1968).

20. New Jersey Library Association, Library Development Committee, *minutes, February 28, 1969,* 2.

21. New Jersey Library Association, Library Development Committee. *Examination of Three Avenues of Development for Libraries in New Jersey* (No imprint. 1975).

22. Henry Michniewski, "Area Library Evaluation." *New Jersey Libraries* v.9, #4, April 1975.

23. The Gallup Organization. *The Use and Attitudes Toward Libraries in New Jersey* (New Jersey State Library, Department of Education, Trenton, NJ, January 30, 1976), S–14.

24. Ibid: S–15.

25. New Jersey Library Association, Library Development Committee. *Networks for Knowledge: Mobilizing Libraries for the People of New Jersey* (Summer, 1977. Revised 1978).

26. New Jersey State Library. *A Developing State Plan for Library Services.* (Trenton, N.J. January 1980).

27. New Jersey. County and Municipal Government Study Commission. *The Development of Libraries and Networks: Prospective Roles and Responsibilities* (Trenton, NJ.: June 1980).

28. New Jersey. Laws of 1983, ch. 486, section 2.

6

Federal Funding

Henry Michniewski
&
Wenda G. Rottweiler

Library buildings; new construction, additions, renovations; library services; interlibrary loans, automation, services for the disadvantaged—the legacies of federal funding to New Jersey's libraries are numerous and lasting. Those familiar with library service in New Jersey can "attest to the innovative programs given life"[1] through federal dollars. Before 1956 many public libraries were funded at subsistence levels, most of them by local taxes, private philanthropy or some combination thereof. There was little if any place in budgets for many essential services, let alone for experimental programs. The passage of the federal Library Services Act of 1956, followed by the Library Services and Construction Act, permitted the State Library to organize programs which increased cooperation and efficiency among libraries and empowered local libraries to experiment with activities that would not have been undertaken without the availability of grant funds. The passage of federal legislation also lent impetus to the state's efforts to assist local libraries and encourage cooperation among libraries.

The Fight for Federal Funding

On June 19, 1956, during the annual conference of the American Library Association in Miami Beach, President Eisenhower signed the *Federal Library Services Act*, which had been a major ALA project for more than ten years. In signing the measure he said: "It represents an effort to stimulate the states and local communities to increase the library service available to rural Americans."[2]

Proposals for Federal legislation in support of public libraries had been included in the ALA's *A Plan for National Libraries* (1935) and had long been on its congressional agenda. In 1946 Congresswoman Emily Taft Douglas of Illinois, introduced the *Public Library Service Demonstration Bill*, whose purposes were:

> To provide a demonstration of adequate public library service to people now without it or inadequately served.
>
> To provide a means for studying the various methods of providing public library service primarily in rural areas, and for studying the effect of planning on an area basis upon the development of library service.[3]

Senator Lister Hill of Alabama sponsored a similar measure in the Senate. In spite of substantial obstacles, the *Library Services Demonstration Act* became law in 1949.[4]

Over the years, many bills to aid public libraries were introduced. Two major themes ran through these bills. One theme was demonstration, as featured in the 1949 law. The other theme was service to rural areas, as emphasized in the Hill, Douglas and Akin bill, *Public Library Services in Rural Areas*, enacted in 1951.

Federal legislation in support of public libraries was the major aim of ALA's State and Federal Relations Committee and its Washington office headed by Julia Bennett. ALA's efforts were strongly buttressed by the activities of members in the various states. In New Jersey, Roger McDonough, State Library Director, and Janet Zimmerman McKinlay, head of the Public and School Library Services Bureau, were among those leading the fight. Although at first there were many defeats and only minor victories, the tenacity of the library community in pursuing its goal was illustrated in a memorandum from the New York Federal-State Relations Committee: "Early bills for federal government assistance had failed but with consistently *decreasing* margins of opposition or indifference."[5]

These efforts culminated in 1956 in the passage of the *Library Services Act*, which authorized funds for five years "to promote the further extension [by the several states] of public library service to rural areas without such services or with inadequate services." "Rural areas" were defined as places, determined by the 1950 census, having populations of 10,000 or less. "Public library services" were those services provided free to all residents of a municipality and supported wholly or in part by public funds. School library services were excluded from the definition.

Under the law Congress could appropriate up to 7½ million dollars each year through 1961. New Jersey's share ranged from a minimum of $40,000 in 1957 to $107,803 in 1964 as the authorization was extended beyond the first five years.

Nationwide LSA and its subsequent incarnations had an immediate and significant impact on library service. "Countless bookmobiles appeared, there was substantial improvement in state libraries, and various library experiments, some inventive and exciting, were attempted."[6] In New Jersey this infusion of federal funds gave lifeblood to the many projects that libraries initiated.

The Library Services Act of 1956

New Jersey's Library Services Act (LSA) funds were administered by the State Department of Education through the Public and School Library Services Bureau of the State Library. The state received the following amounts under the Library Services Act program:

Fiscal Year	Amount
1957	$ 40,000
1958	$ 74,163
1959	$ 85,783
1960	$ 97,403
1961	$103,153
1962	$102,000
1963	$109,459
1964	$107,803

It is estimated that through 1963, 70 percent of the funds were spent in support of the Tri-County Library Demonstration Project. The remainder of the federal funds were used to augment the Public and School Library Services Bureau's personnel and materials budgets[7] and to support several smaller projects. One such project was the series of workshops in 1964 on the use of reference materials for libraries in communities with populations under 10,000, which featured Hannah Severns and Doreitha R. Madden as speakers. Libraries that participated in the workshops were allowed to select $100.00 worth of reference materials. A federal grant of $7,000 was given to Rutgers University for formulating and disseminating a plan for library services.

In order to qualify for the federal money New Jersey had to expend almost twice the amount of the grant in state and local funds for the same purposes, according to the state plan submitted to the Federal government. The identification of these "matching funds" was a difficult task. Edith Estabrooks, the Tri-County Regional Librarian, prepared an extraordinarily detailed formula to identify the matching expenditures. For example, the 1962 report of expenditures devotes 61 pages to the documentation of the matching formula. The contortions practiced to match annual federal grants of $10,000 or less came to be viewed by State Library staff with amusement in later years, when the federal grants exceeded a million dollars.

Tri-County Project, Cumberland, Salem and Gloucester Counties

Studies and findings by the New Jersey Library Association's Library Development Committee and by the State Library led Janet McKinlay and State Library officials to recommend that federal funds might be put to best use in New Jersey by "a concentration or a demonstration of library service in Cumberland, Gloucester and Salem counties."[8] Clearly, the southwestern corner of the state could benefit considerably by an improvement of library services. The area met the "rural" requirement of the federal act. Approximately 80 percent of the people could be so designated, and nearly 35 percent of the rural population received no free public library services of any kind. The remainder were served by 19 libraries supported, on average, by less than 35 cents per capita annually. In addition, the three counties were undergoing industrial development and their population was shifting and expanding.[9]

The State Library was also guided in its decision by the report of the legislative Commission to Study Library Services in New Jersey, *Better Libraries for New Jersey*, issued in January 1956. This report emphasized the importance of improving library services and the need to equalize services across the state. The proposed plan for the use of federal funds stated:

> ... it therefore appears reasonable and advisable to select these three counties as the area to be served by a regional library services center operated as a branch of the New Jersey State Library.
>
> It is anticipated that such a demonstration center would prove its value during the first five years and that library service would be continued in this area upon the termination of federal aid as one of following:
> 1. a multi or tri-county operation
> 2. Several independent county systems
> 3. a regional branch of the State Library.[10]

The decision to establish the Tri-County Library Service Center was made in 1956, and the next year and a half was spent in developing plans, seeking a site for the center, hiring staff, selecting a book-mobile, purchasing books, and promoting the project throughout the counties.[11]

Edith E. Estabrooks was appointed Regional Librarian in January 1957. Her energy, professionalism and interpersonal skills were to-tally devoted to the development and improvement of the Service Center and accounted for much of its success.[12]

Perhaps the most perceptible evidence of the new Tri-County Service Center was the brand-new bookmobile launched in Febru-ary 1958. Twenty-eight feet long, with a 2,000-volume capacity and built at the cost of $13,672, it was under the competent control of the bookmobile librarian, Robert Staples. It became a familiar and welcome sight on the roads of the three counties.[13]

Estabrooks and Staples worked tirelessly to promote and publi-cize the Center and its services. By the middle of 1958 the Center housed 9,000 volumes and had a circulation of 27,000. However, in 1959, the first full year of operation, the total circulation was 101,000. McKinlay took some pride in this: "The Center's demon-stration program is just a sample of what the people in the area could enjoy on a permanent basis through a larger unit of service supported at a reasonable rate from public funds."[14]

During 1959 the services of Tri-County were fully developed. The staff included three professionals (Dorothy Thompson joined the staff in January) and three paraprofessionals. Their goals were:

To provide public library materials to existing public libraries
To provide a bookmobile service in an area where there were no local libraries
To provide consulting and technical assistance to existing libraries
To encourage cooperation among existing libraries
To persuade people of the advantages of cooperation and the need for public library services.[15]

There was mounting concern in the three-county area over the future of the Center after June 1961, when the scheduled cutoff of federal funds would occur. Estabrooks and the staff of the Public and School Library Services Bureau prepared a proposal under which the Center would be funded by a combination of federal, state and county monies, with the counties gradually assuming a greater share over a five-year period. The apparent crisis ended when the Library Services Act was extended, on August 31, 1960 for a five-year period.

Although the fiscal crisis which would have occurred upon the termination of LSCA had ceased to be an issue, the State Library was committed to withdrawal of federal funds from the Tri-County operation "because other areas in New Jersey need and deserve federal-state assistance."[16] So, on May 13, 1960, Roger H. McDonough sought approval from the Commissioner of Education "to take whatever action is needed to terminate the federal phase . . . and to inaugurate a locally supported regional library services center[17] effective December 31, 1962.

New legislation permitting the establishment of regional and multi-county libraries was enacted during the summer of 1962, and the State Library was ready with several proposals in hand for various service area combinations, including support of a Bridgeton/Cumberland area, a Cumberland/Salem area and a Salem/Cumberland/Gloucester area.

During the summer and fall of 1962, McKinlay and McDonough lobbied hard to garner county freeholder support for some kind of cooperative regional library center in southern New Jersey. There was great disappointment when the Bridgeton Public Library Board of Trustees rejected the proposal for the establishment of a city/county library. The Board cited legal technicalities which it felt would interfere with the establishment of such a library. The inequitable financial burden such a program would place on the townships was considered to be another roadblock.

McKinlay noted the negative attitudes of the freeholders in her Field Reports. A freeholder from Gloucester "mentioned that they have been 'stuck' with the state before. They didn't like state aid. The state was great on promises. The county wasn't great on going in with other counties on anything." A Salem freeholder indicated he wanted the headquarters, but wasn't favorably disposed toward establishing a library because the taxes were too high.[18] A Cumberland/Salem plan that had appeared to have popular support in Salem County was voted down by the freeholders 14 to 1 in March, 1963. A flavor of the attitude in opposition to Salem County participation is found in an editorial of a Salem County newspaper following the freeholder's vote: "The Salem County Board of Chosen Freeholders might be a bunch of 'farmers' but they recognize a 'bastard' and legitimately denying paternalism say 'thumbs down on a bookmobile' . . . that was well done and every . . . taxpayer in Salem County can say: 'thank God' and 'praise Allah.' "[19]

It appears that cost was a major factor in the rejection of a three-county regional library. Both Dorothy Thompson West and David West believed the projected budgets were excessive.[20] In fact, an early State Library plan suggested three possible budgets for the operation of the Tri-County Regional Library; $150,000, $250,000, $338,000.[21]

With the library building located in Cumberland County, the counties of Salem and Gloucester were not prepared to spend a significant amount of money for the Tri-County service. They only saw one tangible benefit—the bookmobile. In addition, there appeared to be an unwillingness to cooperate with other counties, perhaps because there had been little, if any, experience in multi-county cooperation. Governance was also a concern. Each of the Freeholder Boards wanted direct control of the operation of the library. Another important factor was the general distrust of state government. All of these combined to make the establishment of a regional library service for the three county area less than attractive.

Finally, on May 9, 1963, the Cumberland County freeholders accepted the State Library's proposal for the establishment of a county library. The Cumberland County Library was established on July 1, 1963. The proposal suggested a total budget of $85,000 with federal and state aid establishment grants being made available for three years. The Cumberland freeholders agreed to continue the employment of all the existing staff and accepted the position and classification plan suggested by the State.[22]

Reflecting on the Tri-County Library experience, Robert Staples characterized it as a "first class operation." It had a "superior book collection" that was developed, in part, with assistance from Professor Margaret Monroe of the Rutgers Library School and from the Rutgers Extension Agency. The center was also blessed with an energetic and highly competent staff. Staples felt that the state never firmly communicated its intent to withdraw after a period of time. Representatives of the three counties thought that "the State would continue forever."[23] This conflict over who would fund what and when would be a recurring theme of federally funded demonstration projects in New Jersey.

The effort of the State Library to use federal money to establish a "larger unit of service" in an area of the state which was in desperate need of such services was visionary, and the demonstration was executed at a high level of competence. Unfortunately, it is unlikely that the service would have remained viable without a continuing high level of financial support from state/federal sources. However, this experience of the first federally funded library project in New Jersey highlighted possible future obstacles and underscored areas for potential successes. These lessons would inform the State Library planning staff well in the years ahead.

The Library Services and Construction Act

P.L. 88–269

On February 11, 1964, President Lyndon Baines Johnson signed the Library Services and Construction Act. This amendment to the Library Services Act removed the rural population limit of 10,000; increased the amount authorized for public library services to $25,000,000 per year, and for the first time for this purpose authorized $30,000,000 for fiscal year 1965 for the construction of public library facilities. Under this legislation New Jersey would receive $1,690,000 of which $940,000 was earmarked for the construction of public library buildings and $750,000 for public library services.

Although the fully authorized amounts under this legislation were paltry compared with other federal budget items such as military hardware, they were extremely significant and impressive sums for the public library community.

In addition to dropping the rural requirement from LSA and permitting funding of library construction, LSCA also broadened the federal government's influence on libraries by adding several Titles. Over the last 32 years of LSCA, the act has grown to eight Titles, some of which have never been funded (Titles VII & VIII).

Currently existing titles include:

TITLE I:	Library Services
TITLE II:	Library Construction & Technology Enhancement
TITLE III:	Interlibrary Cooperation & Resource Sharing
TITLE IV:	Library Services for Indian Tribes & Hawaiian Natives
TITLE V:	Foreign Language Materials
TITLE VI:	Library Literacy Program
TITLE VII:	Evaluation & Assessment of Federally Funded Programs
TITLE VIII:	Library Learning Center Programs

As LSCA has evolved, there has been considerable overlapping of Title mandates. In New Jersey, some grants have been awarded both Titles I and III funds (although not necessarily at the same time) in order to benefit the greatest number of communities. Overall, it has been funding primarily allocated under Titles I, II and III, or some combination thereof, that has been responsible for most of the major contributions to libraries and library service in New Jersey.

After the passage of LSCA, New Jersey librarians worked hard to prepare for the disbursement of the incoming federal funds. In November, 1964, the Library Development Committee of the New Jersey Library Association (NJLA) issued a report that would shape the development of public libraries in New Jersey. *Libraries for the People of New Jersey or Knowledge for All* outlined an approach for the improvement of library service in New Jersey at three levels. Level one libraries were the local public, school and college libraries. Appropriate achievement standards were recommended for these libraries. It was also recommended that the state be divided into 22 areas to be provided backup reference and other services by the strongest public library in each given area. The report specifically identified 15 libraries that were ready to serve their areas with reference, interlibrary loan service, and other backup services. These "area" libraries were to be the second level of a "pyramid" leading "toward a genuine network of library service in the state." The third level would be Research Library Centers whose statewide research and referral resources would be coordinated and made available to the state's libraries by a Library Reference and Referral Center in the State Library.

Phasing in the Three-Level Plan

Area Libraries

The State Library decided to employ the federal money to begin to move NJLA's recommended plan forward. Area reference libraries were to be assisted in demonstrating the kind of services which might be developed with the full financial support pattern called for in the State Plan. More than two-thirds of LSCA funds available to New Jersey in 1965 went to fourteen libraries designated Area Reference Libraries, in grants ranging from $18,350 to $56,114. The formula for these grants provided a base grant plus an additional per capita amount. The Newark Public Library, which was designated the Metropolitan Reference Center of Northern New Jersey, received $100,000.

In 1968, after the passage of state legislation providing support of the "three-level" system, (Senate Bill 348 creating the three tier system was actually signed by Governor Richard J. Hughes on April 24, 1967), state funds began to be used to share in the cost of the Area Reference Libraries. By 1970, because of a threatened cutback in LSA funds and the long delay in the appropriation of the federal monies, it was decided to fund Area Libraries solely from State Library Aid sources. In that year the Newark Public Library received $150,000 in addition to its Area Library grant in order to expand its interlibrary loan services through the provision of foreign language and fine arts materials.

Developmental Libraries

Initially fourteen libraries were designated as Area Reference Libraries. Many areas in the state were without Area Libraries. Seeing it as "a major step forward in the implementation of the Area Library System" the state library selected 14 libraries to receive grants over a five-year period to enable them to develop sufficiently so that they might be designated as Area Reference Libraries. The program ran its planned course with seven of the developmental libraries actually receiving an area library designation.

Research Library Centers

Under the newly enacted state legislation, each Research Library was now entitled to receive an annual grant of $100,000 for the performance of special services as specified by contract with the state. The Research Libraries designated were the Newark Public Library, the Rutgers University Library, the Princeton University Library, and the New Jersey State Library. Beginning in 1968, LSCA Title III funds were combined with state aid to support this third level of service.

This use of federal money to initiate the activities of the three-level plan through Area Libraries, Developmental Libraries, Research Libraries, and the Metropolitan Regional Library was a well conceived and well executed effort that demonstrated the viability of this approach to the librarians of the state, the users of such libraries, and eventually, to the legislature. It brought about state financial support to the three-level approach by the demonstration of actual performance rather than by discussion of an unproven concept and laid the groundwork for New Jersey library service and cooperation for years to come.

In addition to support for the newly created three-level network, federal funds were used for a wide variety of other purposes.

Title I: Library Services

Over the years, many of the most familiar and popular library programs in New Jersey have been born of Title I funding. These have included services to the disadvantaged, reference services and workshops, the Library for the Blind and Handicapped, State Library operations, literacy programs, collection development projects, and automation assistance, just to name a few. The development of these praiseworthy services may be the most admirable contribution generated by federal library support. Without federal funding, many of the programs discussed below would never have been attempted, let alone have resulted in creative and successful programs which benefit all the citizens of New Jersey.

The State Library

Every year, a portion of Title I monies has gone to the administration of the State Plan and to strengthening the State Library Agency. These awards have helped to create the infrastructure that has enabled the State Library to coordinate the funding and implementation of library services in New Jersey. In addition, Title I support has funded library research activities, enabled the State Library to back up the statewide library network with the provision of interlibrary loan and telephone reference services, fund vehicular delivery of interlibrary loan items and further computerization projects.

Library Service to the Disadvantaged

The Outreach Services Program of the New Jersey State Library seeks to encourage and assist libraries in providing library services to those populations who are underserved or inadequately served and do not receive the full benefits of library service due to disadvantages related to handicap, race, sex, language, age, culture, economic deprivation, illiteracy, lack of education, geographic location, institutionalization, or other factors.[24]

In 1968 the state library co-sponsored a one-day conference, *The Potential Role of Libraries in the Model Cities Program.* The Model City Program was a federal effort to improve urban areas. In connection with this program, and generally in response to the problems delivering library services to the urban and rural poor, a grant program supporting non-traditional, experimental programs was initiated in 1969. This grant program would distribute more than 4.25 million dollars by the end of FY 1985.

Some of the earliest projects included

- development of a black history library in a housing project in Franklin Township
- development of two library centers with Spanish materials in apartment complexes in Lakewood

- launching of a minimobile offering library materials, story hours and film programs and establishment of a Spanish information center (Biblioteca Criolla) in Jersey City.

Other libraries trained parents to conduct story hours in their housing developments (Glassboro State College), placed racks of high interest/low reading difficulty paperback materials in a Human Resource Center (Atlantic Community College), and offered story tellers, films, teen discussion groups and home economics instruction from bookmobiles (Monmouth County). The quality of programs developed by New Jersey librarians was reflected in a 1977 publication of the U.S. Office of Education, *Library Programs Worth Knowing About* which highlighted excellent and creative library programs "stimulated by federal funds." Of the 61 programs described, five were from New Jersey.

In the 1970s, in addition to projects similar to those described above, other kinds of programs were initiated. Services to jails and prisons increased in Newark, Hackensack, Woodbridge, Burlington County and North Brunswick. Programs for library services to migrant worker camps could be found—most notably those of the Cumberland County Library. The concept that the poor should be aggressively provided with "survival information" and with some degree of advocacy was best illustrated by the NICHE (Neighborhood Information Center Helps Everyone) project in Montclair. Projects to assist the mentally handicapped or physically disabled were instituted in Gloucester City, East Orange, Montvale and Berkeley Heights.

In the early 1980s literacy improvement was given high priority by the State Library. The public libraries of Mercer County had, by that time, a well-developed literacy program. The libraries of the city of Camden and Camden County joined to develop a literacy project for Camden County. In central New Jersey, the Old Bridge Public Library administered a Basic Reading Literacy Project for 14 libraries of Middlesex County. The experience with that project revealed the need for a county-wide ESL (English as a Second Language) project. Both projects, but particularly the ESL program, continue to be heavily utilized.

The State Library also targeted for outreach another underserved special population—non-speakers of English. In FY 1991, the Newark Public Library received $250,000 to establish a Non-English Language Acquisitions Center, later called MultiMAC (Multilingual Materials Acquisitions Center), to help libraries select, acquire, catalog and publicize materials for the use of their non-English speaking clientele.[25] By 1993, continued federal funding of MultiMAC had enabled Newark Public Library to purchase and catalog more than 17,000 items in Chinese, Korean, Vietnamese, Russian, Haitian Creole, Hindi, Gujarati, and Spanish and to make them available for individual or bulk loan.[26]

Other recent projects have focused on services to the aged including homebound programs, acquisition of large-print materials, mini-libraries in senior citizen centers and on programs designed to strengthen urban libraries such as collection development and identification of special populations.

Institutional Library Services

On July 19, 1966 Title IVA was adopted as part of LSCA. This additional Title made federal funds available for the development of library services in state institutions. Also, in FY 1971, by P.L. 91–600, Titles IVA and IVB (Services to the Blind and Physically Handicapped) were consolidated under Title I (Library Services). Early grants were used for staff at the State Library and for demonstration programs such as those at Rahway State Prison (now East Jersey), New Jersey State Home for Boys (Jamesburg), and the New Jersey State Home for Girls (Trenton). However, because the problem of library services in state institutions was large and the amount of money available through LSCA was trivial, little progress was made. Improvement came from outside the library community beginning with the establishment of a state school district for institutions in 1972.

The new superintendent of this school district, Dr. Daniel Sullivan, saw the development of library services as essential for his education program. By June 30, 1973, six trained and experienced librarians were working in correctional institutions (previously there had been none) and correctional institution law library collections were under development.

Although library services in prisons continued to receive LSCA funds through the Garden State School District, other institutional programs were also undertaken. A bookmobile library service was provided to the state's four residential centers operated by the Division of Youth and Family Services and library services were provided at the New Jersey Home for Disabled Soldiers at Menlo Park through the Woodbridge Public Library.

In FY 1983, the State Library developed a unified contract block grant approach with the Department of Human Services. Under this approach, DHS was authorized to allocate portions of the grant of LSCA funds to the various mental health and mental retardation institutions administered by that agency. In 1984, for example,

LSCA funds were used to improve libraries in 14 day training centers, six development centers, three psychiatric hospitals and one residential training and research center.

In the mid-1980s LSCA grants made possible the establishment of videotape African American and Hispanic American studies collections at some institutions, and funded creative writing and poetry programs and career information centers at others.

While the goal of the State Library has been to persuade the various institutions, particularly at the state level, to provide adequate library services (and encourage local libraries to supplement library service at the local and county level), it has continued to enhance institutional library service through federal funding. Recent grants have gone toward assisting in the "establishment, provision, improvement or expansion of library services to persons in New Jersey state institutions who are without public library services and/or who do not receive the full benefits of library services due to disadvantages related to institutionalization."[27] Over the two-year period FY 1994–FY 1995, 11 institutional libraries were awarded grants totaling $91,577. These included Bergen County Day Training ($10,000), Forensic Psychiatric Hospital ($9,995), New Jersey State Prison ($10,000) and Warren Residential Group Center ($9,999).

The Library for the Blind and Handicapped

Funds for library services to the physically handicapped, which includes the blind and visually handicapped, became available at approximately the same time (FY 1966) that the New Jersey Library for the Blind and Physically Handicapped was established. Prior to this time, blind New Jersey residents had been receiving service from Philadelphia.

The Library for the Blind operates with a collection of over 400,000 books which have been specially produced in a variety of different formats—Braille, recorded disk or cassette, or large print. In FY 1976, $164,000 in federal funding propelled the establishment of a computerized circulation control system which enabled the Library to both monitor circulation and distribute materials according to readers' designated preferences. The Library also lends machines for use in conjunction with their media. In addition, one unit of the Library, Audiovision, uses more than 100 volunteers to broadcast local, daily newspapers over closed circuit radio.

Regional Film Centers

Sixteen-millimeter films were so expensive that only a few of the larger public libraries could develop a collection of any size. In the

1960s, some small and medium-size libraries banded together to form film circuits, jointly purchased films and passed them around among themselves. In this way a library might have available for a period of time (one to three months for example) a collection of 25 to 50 films to offer to their patrons. (Similar video and large print book circuits still exist.) There was, in the language of the time, a "felt need" for a statewide film service.

Five public libraries were found to have a collection of at least 250 16mm films. This was considered to be the minimum size for a library to be able to serve as a film center. These were the Camden Regional Film Center, the East Orange Public Library, the Hackensack Public Library, the Monmouth/Woodbridge Film Center (a cooperative arrangement between these two libraries) and the Morris County Library.

Most of the operating expenditures of the film centers were supported by LSCA funds, anywhere from $75,000 to $150,000 each from 1975–1980 (funding for East Orange, Hackensack and Camden began in 1974). By 1979, film circulation had risen to well over 100,000 state-wide. Circulation per print averaged 15–16 per year, exceeding by many times the national measurement for a successful film operation. A March 1979 survey of users found a satisfaction rate in excess of 90 percent. The largest groups of users were found to be libraries and teachers.

The Regional Film Centers were conceived of as demonstrations. That is, federal funds would support them for a few years until they proved their value and then financial support would be transferred to state sources. This idea foundered during the state budget crisis preceding the implementation of the income tax. Later the economic downturn and increasing reluctance of the governor and legislature to support library funding contributed to the project's demise. Although it was an active, well-used and well-administered program, the rise of other technologies, such as cable and videocassette, and the State Library's desire to employ the funds (over a half million dollars per year) for other purposes led to the decline and later dissolution of the program by the mid-1980s. But, in its time, federal funding of the Regional Film Centers enabled people throughout New Jersey to view films at library, school and institutional programs.

Other notable early Title I programs included the Recruitment and Scholarship Program of the late 1960s and early 1970s and Reference Training and Children and Young Adult Services workshops. The 1980s saw the end of the Regional Film Centers but the continuation of the Library for the Blind and Handicapped, grants for public library collection development and literacy programs. In the

1990s, federal funding granted under Title I enabled New Jersey libraries to benefit from two new programs which have become highly utilized additions to New Jersey library service. Newark Public Library developed MultiMac and East Brunswick Public Library was awarded $150,000 to initiate After Hours Toll Free Reference—NJ Nightline, to provide ready reference answers and/or referrals up until midnight seven days/week.[28]

Most recently, Title I monies have permitted New Jersey libraries to explore and take advantage of new technologies. Grants that expand access to the Internet have been a priority of the State Library. An outstanding Title I program in FY 1994 was the *Technology for Public Library Services* program. The purpose of this grant was to assist small public libraries in providing reference services using newer technologies. Twenty-one libraries received grants totaling $100,000.00

Title II: Construction

Probably the most visible impact of federal funding on New Jersey libraries was the accelerated construction of new library buildings. Ralph Gers reported that in the five years preceding 1965, an average of six public library construction projects was undertaken annually. Most of these were very small. Many were simple repairs to a building.[29] In the ensuing nine years of the Title II program, the number of projects more than doubled and their scale increased considerably.

In order to receive a grant of money, the applicants for LSCA Title II grants were required to comply with federal requirements as well those developed by the State Library. A minimum size requirement (square footage per population served) was instituted. This criterion was scrupulously adhered to throughout the years of the program. Priority was given to Area Libraries, thirteen of which were assisted in building new structures, additions or rehabilitations. Libraries that were least able to provide funds were also given high priority. This ability was measured by a ratio of population to state equalized valuation of property.

Each applicant, represented by the library director, a representative of the library board, the architect, a representative of local government and a library building consultant, if one had been engaged for the project, would meet at the State Library with the Construction Advisory Board for a detailed review of preliminary building plans. The purpose of the review was to improve the plan so that the resulting building would be a more efficient and effective library structure. As a result of this process, many plans were revised exten-

PROGRAMME

OPENING EXERCISES

FREE PUBLIC LIBRARY

NEWARK, N. J.

MARCH FOURTEENTH

1901

Photo 1. Program cover for the dedication of the Newark Public Library main building, 1901.

Photo 2. Free Public Library of Trenton, Charles Skelton Branch built in 1929.

Photo 3. Elizabeth Public Library, Main Building, E. L. Tilton and C. G. Poggi, Architects. Opened in 1912.

Photo 4. Elizabeth Public Library. New addition to 1912 building. Opened 1967, Levy and Anderson, architects.

Photo 5. Atlantic City Public Library, Main Building (old). A Carnegie Building opened in 1905 and designed by Albert R. Ross of New York.

Atlantic City Public Library

Photo 6. Atlantic City Public Library, main building (new) opened in 1985, Martin F. Blumberg PA/Greun Assoc., architect.

Photo 7. Clifton Memorial Library. Faridy Thorne Fraytak, architect. Many of New Jersey's newer libraries have been designed by this Trenton firm. Photo reprinted with permission Otto Baitz/Esto.

Photo 8. Walsh Library of Seton Hall University. Designed by M. Alfieri Co., Inc. and opened in 1994.

Photo 9. Burlington College County Library. Opened in 1996 and designed by G.B.Q.C. of Philadelphia.

Photo 10. Mendham Public Library in Morris County.

Photo 11. Ocean County Library Headquarters. Taken sometime before 1938. The county headquarters' libraries of Ocean and Burlington counties reflect the modest nature of services in the early days after their creation.

Photo 12. Burlington County Library Headquarters. Early headquarters.

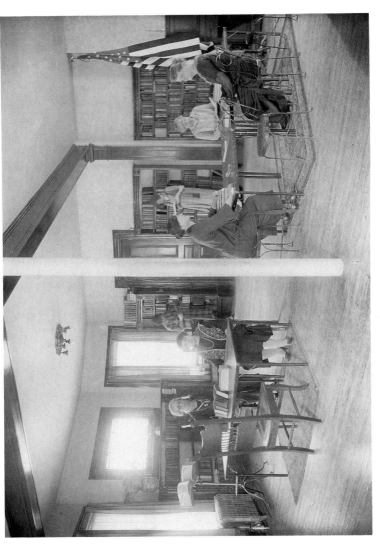

Photo 13. The Ocean Grove Branch of the Monmouth County Library.

Photo 14. Library School at the New Jersey College for Women. Book Week exhibit, 1930. Room 104, Recitation Hall showing the relation of the classroom to the office.

Photo 15. Glassboro Elementary School Library staffed during this period by a W. P. A. (Works Progress Administration) worker.

Photo 16. Florham Park Library, 1939.

Photo 17. The Atlantic County Library providing service to the Somer's Point Hospital. This 1948 photo pictures Fanny Tabor, County Library Director bringing service to hospital patients.

Photo 18. Elizabeth Public Library. View of the office and reference room from the reading room. This photo pre-dates the construction of the library's new addition in 1967.

Photo 19. Hanover County Library Station, Morris County Library.

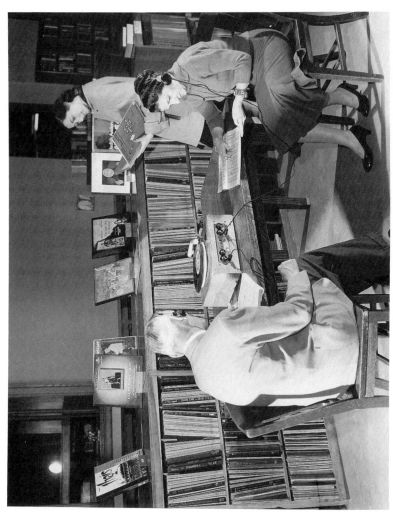

Photo 20. Elizabeth Public Library, 1958. Audio–visual area.

Photo 21. Matawan Public Library. Depression era photo of WPA assistants.

Photo 22. Burlington County bookmobile during the 1920s.

Photo 23. Somerset County "book car" serving the Watchung School, 1939.

Photo 24. Sussex County Library. Station in a store.

Photo 25. Roger H. McDonough, long-time director of the State Library and later
Legislative Advocate for the New Jersey Library Association.

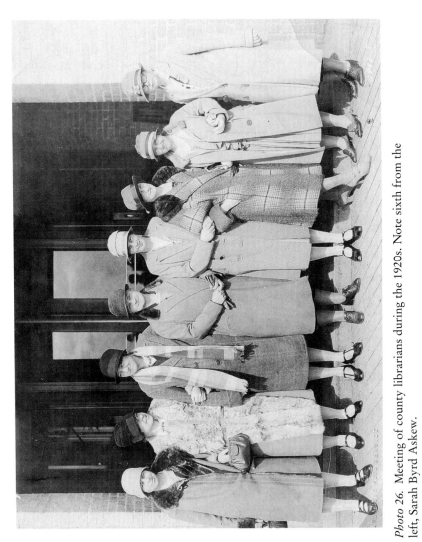

Photo 26. Meeting of county librarians during the 1920s. Note sixth from the left, Sarah Byrd Askew.

Photo 27. James E. Bryan, former director of the Newark Public Library, and president of the New Jersey Library Association and the American Library Association.

Photo 28. (From left to right) Charles Reid, Trustee of the Paramus Public Library, former Mayor of Paramus, member of the state assembly, and later Chairman of NCLIS (The National Commission on Library and Information Sciences); Neal Harlow, Dean of the Rutgers Library School; Ralph Shaw, co-founder of Scarecrow Press, former president of the American Library Association and the New Jersey Library Association; Janet McKinlay, former Head, Bureau of Public and School Library Services, New Jersey State Library.

Photo 29. Signing of State Aid to Libraries Bill, 1966. (Seated left to right):
Dr. Joseph Clayton, Acting Commissioner of Education; Governor Richard J.
Hughes; Harold J. Roth, President of NJLA and Director East Orange Public
Library. (Standing left to right): James E. Bryan, Director, Newark Public Library;
Professor Mary V. Gaver of Rutgers Library School and newly elected President of
the American Library Association; Veronica Cary, Director, Trenton Public Library;
Miriam Evans, Director, Ocean County Library; Senator Mathew Feldman, chief
sponsor of the legislation.

Photo 30. NJLA annual meeting at Atlantic City, 1962. Program participants. (From left to right): Mrs. A. E. Tatar of Summit; Jane McClure of the Summit Public Library; author Santha Rama Rau; Beatrice James, director of the Bergenfield Public Library; and Michael Harney of the Bayley Ellard School in Madison.

Photo 31. New Jersey Library Association Program. (From left to right): Monsignor William Noe Field of the Seton Hall University Library and Mayor Charles Reid, Mayor of Paramus.

Photo 32. Tri-County bookmobile demonstration supported by Library Services Act (LSA) funds. State Librarian Roger McDonough (center) and Tri-County Regional Librarian Edith Estabrooks (right) greet Mrs. Reeves (left), trustee of the Bridgeton Library.

sively and significantly. Although at times an acrimonious and painful experience, the review process resulted in much better library buildings being constructed in New Jersey.

Although the Construction Advisory Board performed a very valuable function, they did so late in the planning cycle, at a point when tentative approaches may have hardened into final decisions. In order to provide for the earlier intervention of informed opinion, the State Library established the Building Consultant Grant Program. A library board considering a building program was encouraged to hire a library building consultant and was provided LSCA funds for up to 50 percent of the cost of the consultant with a maximum grant of $1,000. Seventy-six of these consultant grants were awarded. Edwin Beckerman, Kenneth McPherson, James Bryan and Ben Grimm were prominent among the consultants.

The construction program lasted nine years from fiscal year 1965 through fiscal year 1974. (Fiscal year 1973 funds impounded by President Nixon were released for expenditure in 1974.) Seventy-four public library building projects were approved and seventy-two public library buildings. (Elizabeth and Newark received two grants each for their buildings.) A total of $5,478,538 was granted to New Jersey public libraries under this program. Most grants went to fund the construction of new buildings; however some additions were built, and there were a few substantial rehabilitations. It was not uncommon for a project to combine rehabilitation and an addition.

This was truly a "seed money" program. Many old plans were pulled out of dusty drawers and brought up to date as a result of the availability of federal funds. The five-and-a half million federal dollars in the program for New Jersey stimulated the expenditure of more than thirty-five million dollars in local funds for public library construction. Gers was not far off the mark when he asserted that ". . . for one reason or another, usually because of the insufficiency of federal funds, not all construction projects could be assisted. However, the planning required in order to submit an application undoubtably provided the impetus for eventual construction of the library."[30] About 60 percent of the applications received an LSCA grant. Perhaps half of the remainder moved forward without a grant.

This was a period of public library construction unparalleled in New Jersey's history. Some might suggest that Andrew Carnegie's philanthropy had a greater impact, but such is not the case. New Jersey received $1,066,935 in Carnegie grants which assisted in the construction of 34 library buildings,[31] as contrasted with the 72 libraries built or improved with federal funds.

Although New Jersey has continued to receive limited Title II funds since 1974, new construction has been limited and the awards have primarily gone to additions and physical plant upgrades—energy retrofits, handicapped access, roof replacements, etc. For instance, in FY 1985, $705,751 was awarded to ten libraries for "upgrading" projects and in FY 1990, the only Title II grant ($200,000) went to Old Bridge Public Library towards a new 45,000 square-foot facility[32]. LSCA Title II funds allocated for FYS 1993, 1994, 1995 were combined so that the greatest number of libraries could be funded. Eight libraries received grants totaling $1,361,745.00.[33] With the recent elimination of all funding for Title II and the lack of funding for library projects at the state level, New Jersey finds itself in the unenviable position, for the first time in many years, of having no funds available to assist local communities in library construction.

Title III: Interlibrary Cooperation and Resource Sharing

LSCA extended federal financial encouragement for library cooperation from rural public libraries designated under LSA to all public libraries. In FY 1966, LSCA was further expanded by the addition of Title III, which encouraged the support of cooperative activities among all types of libraries. Initial Title III funds supported third-level libraries, the Research Libraries. Later, key projects have included the development of the Micro Automated Catalog and the New Jersey Union List of Serials. In addition, Title III funds, in conjunction with Title I monies, have been instrumental in facilitating automation in New Jersey.

Mac/Com

Concern that fire and/or civil disruption might result in damage to the State Library card catalog led to its being microfilmed in 1969. The then head of the Bureau of Archives and History, Kenneth W. Richards, suggested that copies of this microfilm be deposited in the Area and Research libraries so that these libraries would have direct and immediate information about books and library materials owned by the State Library. Named MAC (Micro Automated Catalog) it was a simple, inexpensive and brilliant idea.[34] Soon Newark Public Library, the other major bibliographic and interlibrary loan source for Area Libraries, also had its catalog microfilmed and deposited with the Area Libraries. Microfiche (card film) replaced the MAC microfilm in 1979. The complete catalog of the State Library could now be carried in the inner pocket of a suit jacket. To those accustomed to drawers upon drawers filled with 3 x 5 catalog cards, this was phenomenal. In the early 1980s, computer technology permitted the merging of those parts of the collections of the State Library and the Newark Public Library which had been cataloged on OCLC to produce a computer/output/microfiche (COM) catalog. The sixth edition of the COM catalog contained 400,531 records, and the full catalog totaled 426 fiche. Seventy copies were distributed to Area and Research Libraries and to state government libraries to facilitate the interlibrary loan of materials. By August, 1985, the project had outgrown the two-library combination and only the State Library's holdings were included.

Newspapers on Film

The effort to preserve deteriorating New Jersey newspapers on microfilm was a small but fairly productive project. At the program's start, any type of library could microfilm deteriorating newspapers and the state would pick up two-thirds of the cost, with the cost split evenly between the State Library and the New Jersey Historical Commission. A copy of the resulting microfilm would be deposited with the State Library. Later, the State Library microfilmed the newspaper and gave one copy to the cooperating local library.

NJULS

"The New Jersey Union List of Serials is perhaps the most widely used single reference tool for resource sharing in New Jersey," wrote Keith Michael Fiels, program manager, in a report to the LSCA Advisory Council.[35] The NJULS provides information on over 70,000 periodical and serial holdings of over 70 New Jersey public, academic, special and institutional libraries.

Despite five annual grants of $105,635 each, originally provided to Rutgers University to expand and improve the serials holdings listings (1975–1980), the burden of maintaining this list became excessive and in 1982 the State Library assumed the cost. It was decided in 1983 to convert the existing list to OCLC and to decentralize maintenance. In FY 1994, the Atlantic County Library was awarded $35,000 to provide online access to the New Jersey Union List of Serials "in order to improve library network resource sharing of periodical articles for libraries who do not have online access to the database via OCLC Online Computer Library Center, Inc."[36]

OCLC Access Center

The MAC/COM projects facilitated interlibrary loan for the Area and Research libraries from the State Library and Newark Public Libraries and the NJULS program improved library resource sharing of periodical articles. In FY 1987, the State Library launched a program that would greatly enhance interlibrary loan services for New Jersey libraries. The Access Center allows non-OCLC New Jersey libraries to take advantage of the more than 15 million bibliographic records available on the OCLC electronic interlibrary loan system. This successful program has enabled small and medium libraries of all types to access materials from all over the country for their patrons.

NEDCC

During the 1980s, the State Library dispensed $10,000 annually to the Northeast Document Conservation Center. The Center provided advice and consultation to all types of libraries on the conservation of documents and other materials. It also sponsored workshops in New Jersey on conservation techniques, and provided surveys and consultations.

The State Library and Automation

After considerable debate during the mid- to late 1970s concerning library services and the emerging technologies, by the early 1980s the State Library decided to firmly commit LSCA funds to assist New Jersey's libraries in various automation projects. Initial emphasis was placed upon support of OCLC-based resource-sharing among different types of libraries and later committed to implementation/retrospective conversion grants. Identical automation consultant programs were developed under each Title to provide grants to libraries seeking to study the potential application of automation, and to develop detailed feasibility studies prior to implementation of automated circulation systems and/or online catalogs. In addition, since 1982, the State Library has awarded Retrospective Conversion Grants in order to encourage academic, institutional, public, school and special libraries to convert collections retrospectively to machine-readable form. As a result over 12 million records have been added to the statewide bibliographic database. These subsidies have expanded bibliographic control and access to the material resources of the state and have enhanced sharing of these resources among different types of libraries.[37]

The automated circulation systems and online public access catalogs (OPACS) that are springing up in New Jersey public libraries are a direct result of this federal support.

Current automation commitment is to Internet and database access. In FY 1995, the most noteworthy Title III program was Internet Access for Public & High School Libraries whose purpose was to increase electronic access to information through the use of specialized resource databases on the Internet. Thirty-nine public libraries received grants totaling $31,656. Seventy-six school media centers were awarded grants totaling $60,477.[38]

The Future of Federal Funding

In New Jersey, the seed money provided by the federal government grew into library buildings and programs that attempted to provide library service for all segments of society. It has "enhanced the many ways libraries contribute to the economic vitality and increased productivity of their communities" and broadened "horizons for youth, emerging minorities, immigrants and older people."[39]

Some projects failed, some were altered so as to have little resemblance to the original conception, and others continued as part of the library's normal program. But the overall effect has been manifest. At the national level,

> . . . although federal funding constitutes a minuscule portion of expenditures for local library service, LSCA would appear to have some impact. Paul Howard, the first director of the American Library Association's Washington office, testified before the Senate committee on Labor and Public Welfare in 1946 that 35 million Americans of a total population of 132 million did not have access to library service. Today, virtually every citizen in the United States has access to some manner of public library service. Many librarians credit LSCA for this achievement. Even some critics of LSCA concede that it has achieved its original purpose of expanding library service.[40]

This expansion of library service has been mirrored in New Jersey. The distance between the particulars of the rural Tri-County project and current Internet access programs is immense, yet the shared goal of broadening horizons through library service has remained the same.

The future of library funding, along with that of many other federally funded programs, is uncertain. In FY 1995, the last year of the 1990 reauthorization, LSCA Titles were funded at levels matching or topping the previous year's. This was a real victory, since the Clinton Administration and the House had reservations about funding the program at all. In 1995, the Senate passed P.L. 103–382 which authorized LSCA through FY 1996. Whether LSCA is reauthorized after that, absorbed into another act, rewritten in a Library Services and Technology Act, as now proposed, split into two or more laws, or eliminated altogether remains to be seen. What is clearly visible is the impact federal funding has had on the libraries of New Jersey. With only limited funding available at the state level, the loss of federal funds would certainly deal a severe blow to the efforts of New Jersey libraries to meet the many challenges the future will bring.

Notes

1. Betty Turock, "The New Case for Federal Library Support," *Library Journal*, 15, Feb. 1994: 126.

2. Public and School Library Service Bureau, *Annual Report* (Trenton, NJ: Department of Education, 1957), 2. The Public and School Library Services Bureau, renamed the Library Development Bureau, was a part of the Division of the State Library Archives and History, New Jersey Department of Education.

3. *Congressional Record*, March 12, 1946.

4. American Library Association, *Federal Relations News*, February 26, 1984.

5. American Library Association, State Federal Relations Committee, Memorandum, August, 1951.

6. Alice Gertzog and Edwin Beckerman, *Administration of the Public Library* (Metuchen: Scarecrow Press, 1994), 40.

7. Except when specifically noted, the data on LSA and the Tri-County project are derived from the annual reports of the Public and School Library Services Bureau and the later Library Development Bureau, and from the grants reports.

8. Public and School Library Service Bureau, *Annual Report 1954–1955* (Trenton, NJ: Department of Education, 1955), 16.

9. Public and School Library Service Bureau, *New Jersey Progress Report—Library Service Act 1957–58*, October 8, 1957: 2.

10. Public and School Library Service Bureau, *New Jersey's Proposed Plan for the Use of the Library Service Bill Fund* May 1956: 3.

11. Janet Z. McKinlay, Field Trip Report, July 26, 1956. LSA and Tri-County Project Papers, New Jersey State Library, Trenton.

12. Ann Voss, Personal interview conducted by Henry Michniewski, February, 1986; and Robert Staples, Telephone interview conducted by Henry Michniewski, February, 1986.

13. Public and School Library Services Bureau, *Annual Report* (Trenton, NJ: Department of Education, 1958): 46–48.

14. Janet Z. MacKinlay, *Press Release*, January 7, 1960.

15. Edith Estabrooks, "Regional Libraries Serve Rural Areas," *New Jersey Municipalities*, February, 1959: 1–4.
16. Public and School Library Services Bureau, *Basic Facts About the Proposed Regional Library*. Memorandum, October 8, 1962.
17. Roger H. McDonough, Memorandum to Commissioner Frederick Raubinger and the State Board of Education, May 13, 1960.
18. Janet Z. Mackinlay, *Field Report, September 18, 1962. LSA and Tri-County Project Papers*, Trenton, NJ: New Jersey State Library.
19. "Editorial," *The Bergen Record*, April 18, 1963.
20. Dorothy Thompson West and David West, Telephone interview conducted bt Henry Michniewski, February 13, 1986.
21. Public and School Library Services Bureau, *Estimated Costs for Regional Library Operations*. Mimeographed, February 11, 1960.
22. Public and School Library Services Bureau, *Proposal for Establishing Cumberland County Library*, April 15, 1963.
23. Robert Staples, interview.
24. New Jersey State Library, *Library Grant Programs*, September, 1989: 13.
25. New Jersey State Library, "Newark-Based MultiMAC Benefits State's Non-English Speaking People," *New Jersey State Library Fleeting Impressions*, June 1993: 3.
26. New Jersey State Library, *Grant$ Bulletin*, August, 1995: 4–5.
27. New Jersey State Library, *Library Grant Programs*, May 1992: 11.
28. New Jersey State Library, *Grant$ Bulletin*, Aug. 1993: 10.
29. Ralph Gers, *The Need for Financial Assistance for the Construction of Public Libraries in New Jersey*, Library Development Bureau, New Jersey State Library, December, 1971: 2.
30. Gers: 8.
31. George S. Bobinski, *Carnegie Libraries*, (Chicago: American Library Association, 1969): 17.
32. New Jersey State Library, *Library Grant Programs*, June 1991: 16.
33. New Jersey State Library, *Grant$ Bulletin*, August, 1995: 2–3.
34. Oliver P Gillock, Jr. and Roger H. McDonough, "Micro-Automated Catalog of New Jersey," *Wilson Library Bulletin*, December 1970: 354–7.
35. Keith Michael Fiels, *Report to the LSCA Advisory Council*, June 3–5, 1985: 1–3.
36. New Jersey State Library, *Grant$ Bulletin*, November, 1994: 8.
37. New Jersey State Library. *Grant$ Bulletin*, June, 1993: 4.
38. New Jersey State Library, *Grant$ Bulletin*, August, 1995: 5–8
39. Turock: 127.
40. Peter Fuller, "The Politics of LSCA During the Reagan and Bush Administrations: An Analysis," *The Library Quarterly*, 64 (1994): 295.

7

Library Education and Professional Development

Patricia Reeling

Background

New Jersey's libraries date back to the colonial era and have long been part of the state's history and culture. However, even though the state's largest cities had developed major collections by the end of the nineteenth century, its formal library training and professional development programs lagged considerably behind and are largely a product of the twentieth century.

Elsewhere in the country, some states had already begun providing training/apprenticeship courses for their library staffs during the last two decades of the nineteenth century. These vocational courses were offered either by large public libraries or by technical institutes. Especially noteworthy in the annals of American library education was the establishment, in 1887 in neighboring New York City, of Melvil Dewey's School of Library Economy at Columbia University. Other area schools soon to follow included Pratt in Brooklyn (1890) and Drexel in Philadelphia (1893).[1]

Meanwhile, in New Jersey there was no real pressure to provide formal training programs for library personnel until the Public Library Commission's creation in 1900 with its mandate to establish free public libraries in the smaller communities in New Jersey.[2] One of the organizers of the Commission, Sarah Byrd Askew was a key figure both in the establishment of county library systems to provide rural library service and in the development of extension and

---

(The author is indebted to Mei-Mei Wu, Ph.D. '93, and Kathleen Reilly, MLS '96, whose Independent Study research proved valuable to this study.)

summer school programs to train public and school library personnel to staff these libraries.[3] These vocational programs would provide the bulk of local training for New Jersey's librarians until formal degree programs were established at state institutions of higher education.

Summer School Programs, 1906–1943

Under the auspices of the Public Library Commission and the New Jersey Library Association, the first five-week summer session for public librarians was held at Asbury Park in 1906, and by all accounts it was a great success. Tuition and supplies for the summer school were free, although students did have to pay for living expenses. They also had to be employed in a New Jersey library as a condition of enrollment. Distinguished lecturers in the early days included Clara Hunt, in charge of the Children's Department of the Brooklyn Public Library, James I. Wyer of Albany, John Cotton Dana of Newark, and Dr. John Erskine of Columbia University.[4] Lectures of the invited guest speakers frequently were published in the *New Jersey Library Bulletin.*

Typically, almost from its inception, the fifth week of the summer school program culminated in an institute, to which all of the state's librarians and trustees were invited, whether or not they had taken the preceding elementary course.[5] Themes for the popular institutes varied from year to year. By 1917, New Jersey's summer school elementary library science course was listed as having been approved by the American Library Association.[6]

After experimenting with various inland locations, the summer school was moved to the shore community of Ocean City in 1923, where it was able to offer an extensive repertoire of classes under the aegis of the Department of Public Instruction and the Public Library Commission.[7] Sarah B. Askew directed the program, assisted by Ora F. King, Principal of the Ocean City Library School. The public library program consisted of a four-year summer sequence of courses (a total of 430 hours of instruction, or 32 semester hours) not altogether dissimilar to those taken by today's practicing librarians. School library courses were similar in nature, but the program was only two years in length.[8]

Although there was still demand in the profession for students with specialized skills as late as 1931, the great Depression was beginning to make itself felt.[9] The following summer (1932) school was canceled altogether for economic reasons, and arrangements were made for students to attend either Drexel Institute or Columbia's School of Library Service; the latter institution granted ten $50 scholarships to New Jersey students. In 1933 the school made its final move to the State Teachers College in Trenton where it continued under the control of the Public Library Commission, which noted that eighty percent of the librarians of the little libraries in the state had been attendees. Certificates were now provided for the public library students who completed the four summers of instruction.[10]

In 1944 it was decided to discontinue the public library program. Its last students were admitted in 1943. World War II, following on the heels of the Depression, had added to the problems faced by the summer school. (The school library component would be continued by the Trenton State Teachers College.) Ultimately, as noted in the Commission's last report on the summer school program: "the demand for this type of course has diminished as the library schools in the colleges have grown stronger. The Commission could offer no degree for work covered in its school. Its courses served high school graduates, whereas standards have now risen so that a college degree is required for professional library positions."[11] By the time of the summer school's demise at the end of the 1945 summer session, altogether 1,600 librarians had been trained. With its closing, a distinct period of library training in New Jersey had come to an end.[12]

Extension Courses

In addition to the summer school programs sponsored by the Public Library Commission, extension courses in various library disciplines were also offered. As was the case with its summer school program, courses were taught by library practitioners and were open to graduate teachers, employees of public and school libraries, and those under appointment to such positions.[13] Classes were conducted in various libraries and schools located throughout the state. The Commission supplied the majority of books used for the classes, as the libraries usually did not have the necessary professional materials.[14]

By the early 1930s, credit was also being given toward library certificates, thereby guaranteeing the continued popularity of extension courses and the onset of rivalry with the summer school program. In the 1936–37 annual report of the Commission it was noted that a meeting of instructors of both the extension courses and the summer school classes was arranged by a Commissioner from the Department of Public Instruction and the Secretary of the Public Library Commission. In order to receive a state certificate that

could also be approved by ALA, students would need to supplement extension courses with summer school or resident work at an
approved institution.[15] Five years later, however, in its 1941–42 annual report, the Commission noted that Summer School enrollment
had continued to decline, a fact they attributed to Winter extension
courses offered throughout the state. In an argument somewhat
reminiscent of that currently being made against distance library
education programs, they noted:

> these extension courses are not adequate and so we have decided to
> discontinue them. The book collections for extension classes cannot
> begin to meet the needs of commuting students and we feel that it is
> not possible to keep the work up to the academic standard of the
> work done at the regular summer session. There is, too, a very great
> advantage in having librarians from all over the State meet and work
> together in a group so that there may be not only a learning of library
> theory but also an exchange of ideas and experiences which is invalu-
> able. It is this bond of having studied and learned together that has
> created the close cooperation that now exists between the libraries of
> the State.[16]

Certification and Its Impact on Library Education

With the growth of library training programs in the late 1920s, the
thoughts of library workers in New Jersey began to turn to the issue
of professional licensing. A plan for voluntary certification, initiated
by NJLA in 1936, specified three years of college work as preliminary to professional education and the completion of the four-year
liberal arts/professional curriculum as a requirement for personnel
in public libraries in cities having over 3,000 population.[17] By 1938,
the issue of professional certification had clearly surfaced as one of
serious concern, and the Public Library Commission noted: "The
problem which has absorbed most attention among librarians aside
from the regular work is the certification of librarians. It is felt that
this is one of the steps most needed in the state."[18]

By the early 1940s, librarians were hard at work designing a certification statute. In 1943 the Public Library Commission reported:

> One of the chief steps forward made during the year by the library
> profession as a body was in the preparation of a proposed law for the
> certification of librarians. This was submitted to and approved by the
> New Jersey Library Association at its annual meeting in May. It is
> hoped to introduce it as a bill during the next session of the Legisla-
> ture. The Librarian of the Commission serves as Secretary of the Cer-
> tification Board.[19]

Poised though the profession may have been for the institution of professional certification, it was not until 1947 that the Legislature actually passed the legislation creating such a system for public librarians. This first certification law was "permissive" only, and it was not until 1956 that the first "mandatory" certification law was enacted.[20] The 1947 legislation was important however, in that it established the principle of state certification for librarians, a concept that was undergirded by the passage of a companion bill which added a librarian to the State Board of Examiners, the certification board for teachers. State Education Commissioner John H. Bosshart immediately appointed the State Librarian, Roger McDonough, as the library representative to the Board, where he served until his replacement, Edwin Beckerman, was appointed to succeed him in 1967. It seems likely that no other single action of state government was as influential in assuring the presence of competent, trained personnel in New Jersey public libraries. This act did much to shield public libraries from the use of unbridled political influence in staffing professional public library positions in the state.

Since most professional public library certification throughout the country has been tied to professional library training in institutions of higher learning, the establishment of certification also acted to assure the value of four-year library degrees, and later, master's degrees, since it essentially required such degrees for certification, and this was the required route to professional employment in a public library.

Certificates were also required in the field of school librarianship, but implementation proved somewhat simpler when positions in school systems generally required some form of certification.

The effects of the law were immediate. Since the Summer School Program had ceased in 1943, the only in-state programs available were the ALA-accredited undergraduate program at the New Jersey College for Women and the summer school fifth year program at the State Teachers College in Trenton. Neither school was producing the number of graduates needed to fill the vacant positions in New Jersey libraries, and both offered undergraduate training only. New Jersey was ready to join the national bandwagon moving toward graduate library education.

Undergraduate Degree Programs

As early as 1883, at which time Dewey was already proposing the establishment of a School of Library Economy, there was much debate within ALA about the quality of available training for librarians, and by 1905 ALA had proposed its first formulated Standards of Library Training for Library Schools. A similar interest had developed in the Carnegie Corporation of New York which, after having built numerous public libraries around the country, realized the need for trained librarians to staff them.[21] Consequently, in 1919 the Trustees of the Carnegie Corporation authorized a study of library training to be carried out by Dr. Charles C. Williamson. His report[22] recommended complement (1) that professional library schools should be organized as departments of universities rather than under public, state, or municipal library auspices, and (2) that professional library training should be based upon a college education or its full equivalent. The report's final section dealt with "The Problem of the Small Library" and concluded: "General improvements in standards of service, through certification of librarians, strengthening of professional library schools, and the training of leaders, will accomplish more in the long run for the small public library than the multiplication of library courses and training schools of the usual type."[23]

It would not be until post–World War II, however, that the profession would be ready to endorse Williamson's recommendation to move library education out of baccalaureate programs, and press instead for the establishment of graduate programs offering the MLS degree. Meanwhile, some compromise was necessary. Faced with the diversity of existing training institutions, three "Types" of schools were ultimately recognized by ALA, based upon the extent of the professional courses offered and the number of years of college work required for admission. Type III schools called for a minimum of three years of college, and of the eleven which appeared on the national scene during the decade of the 1920s, one was the Library School of the New Jersey College for Women at Rutgers University.[24] The state's other baccalaureate program, intended primarily for school librarians, was housed at the Teachers College in Trenton.

Fifth-Year (BLS) Summer Program at Trenton State Teachers College, 1942–1957

When the Public Library Commission's Summer School Program moved to the State Teachers College in Trenton in 1933, the stage was set for the development of a second campus-based library training program in New Jersey. In 1942 Mary Gaver was appointed Director of the library at the State Teachers College, and shortly thereafter when the Commission decided to discontinue its summer school program, Gaver took over supervision of the school library educational component. By 1947 a fifth-year (summer only) BLS program for school librarians had been established at Trenton State Teachers College with Gaver as its part-time director, while she also continued her responsibility as Director of the College library. The BLS program produced 44 graduates, with the last degree awarded in the spring of 1957, by which time newly enacted state legislation mandated a master's degree for certification. After the highly-rated BLS summer program was discontinued in 1956, an undergraduate library minor for regular students in the College was established. (Gaver left Trenton State College in 1954 to accept an appointment at the newly established Rutgers Graduate School of Library Service.)[25]

The Library School of the New Jersey College for Women, 1927–1952

The New Jersey College for Women (NJCW) was founded in 1918 as a department of the State University of New Jersey. In 1924 the name Rutgers was adopted for the entire institution, although the public seemed to regard NJCW as separate from Rutgers College even though they had the same president and board of trustees. NJCW was the first and only publicly supported institution of higher education in New Jersey designed to accommodate women, and women—then as now—were the predominant enrollees in library science courses. In tracing the origins of the NJCW undergraduate library school, its former director, Ethel Fair, wrote:

> Four compelling factors brought the school into being: libraries were ingrained in New Jersey's culture; there was a resulting need for able librarians; the New Jersey College for Women sought to widen professional opportunities for young women; and the American Library Association had recently issued new academic guidelines for a library school's organization and curriculum.[26]

NJCW's Dean, Mabel Smith Douglass (for whom the college would later be renamed in 1955), believed librarianship to be a field in which women of the state could render outstanding service, and so in 1927 she arranged a consultation with two members of ALA's Board of Education for Librarianship: Harriet E. Howe and Adam Strohm (formerly librarian of the Trenton Free Library). Dean Douglass took their advice to appoint a full-time director to plan the new school and named Ada J. English, Librarian of the College, to this position. As a result of English's hard work, the School was able to open its doors almost immediately, and by 1929, following official visits by two more members of ALA's Board of Education, the new program was fully accredited.[27]

Students could follow a prescribed three-year course of liberal arts studies followed by library courses in their senior year, or for those who already had a degree, they could take the courses as a fifth-year and receive a second baccalaureate degree. Although the fourth-year curriculum was traditional, the faculty ultimately came to believe "that people as users of books should be the starting point for all courses." Classes sought to associate books with a variety of social concerns, including nutrition, housing, minority problems, wartime civil defense, etc.[28]

Practical library experience for students and faculty was considered essential. Students were expected to obtain unpaid library experience the summer before their admission to library school, and they also were required to complete a two-week field experience during the second semester of their senior year. Faculty and students regularly attended library meetings, and faculty also served as NJLA officers and committee members.[29]

NJCW's first library faculty consisted of: Alice G. Higgins, Polly Fenton (later replaced by Ruth Budd Galbraith), and Helen Chadwick. At the end of the first year of operation, Clara E. Howard was appointed Director and served for two years before resigning. She was replaced by Ethel Fair. Both Higgins and Fair deserve special mention.[30] Higgins was an outstanding teacher, having taught for the New York Public Library Training class and the New Jersey Summer School. Later, in her capacity as chair of the Certification Board of NJLA, Higgins guided the drafting of the state's certification standards.[31]

It is Director Ethel Fair, of course, whose name is so closely associated with NJCW's library school. Having been a faculty member at the University of Wisconsin's library school, she maintained strong national and international library education contacts. Fair is remembered by Mary Gaver as "one of the most generous-hearted persons I have ever met . . . undoubtedly the most professionally-minded person I ever worked with, absolutely committed to librarianship, the soul of integrity, and generous in her dealings with students and faculty."[32]

When Fair arrived at NJCW in 1930, the impact of the Depression had not yet been felt, but by the mid-thirties the Library School's situation was indeed precarious. Enrollment had declined dramatically. To save the School, college authorities reduced its budget by cutting Fair's salary by one-third, with the suggestion that she in turn reduce her responsibilities proportionally, a recommendation she steadfastly refused to heed. Indeed she took on more work since, throughout the Depression and war years, faculty replacements generally were not permitted, until finally only Higgins and Fair remained.[33]

Needless to say, resources for the new program were scarce. The School's professional collection numbered only 825 volumes in 1929, so faculty and students were forced to utilize the Rutgers Library as well as other local collections. Until 1947 students were required to pay a book selection fee.[34]

In the aftermath of World War II, with an improved economy and a burgeoning population of GIs seeking educational opportunities, a dispute developed over the admission of men into the program. The School began receiving requests from men for admission, but the organizational structure of Rutgers University did not allow for men to be admitted to the College for Women. Finally in September 1949 a university committee met to study the matter, and "there was general agreement that the curriculum in Library Service should be open to men as well as women."[35] By January 1950 the "tangle" of cross-registration was finally resolved and Rutgers College men were permitted to enroll in library service courses. But time had already run out for the undergraduate program.

The prevailing national trend was for a fifth-year graduate degree program, and twenty-six of the thirty-four ALA accredited schools had already adopted the new MLS degree by 1949. Early in 1950, alarmed by the results of an informal survey by the Bureau of Public and School Library Services which revealed a serious statewide shortage of librarians, State Librarian Roger McDonough urged State Education Commissioner John H. Bosshart to commission a full-scale study of library education needs. In July 1950 Bosshart appointed a "Committee to Study the Professional Education and Training of Library Personnel in New Jersey" and charged it "to examine the present facilities for training library personnel in New Jersey and to make such recommendations for future programs as the committee saw fit."[36] Bosshart's Committee (comprised of Rutgers University Librarian Donald F. Cameron, NJCW Dean Margaret T. Corwin, Newark Public Library Director John B. Kaiser, Assistant Commissioner of Education Robert N. Morrison, Trenton State Teachers College President Roscoe L. West, Summit Public Library Trustee Mrs. Gerald F. Winser, and Roger McDonough as Chairperson) called in an outside consultant, Dr. Robert D. Leigh, to gather data for them and assist with recommendations.

Coincidentally, at about the same time as Dr. Leigh was undertaking his study, ALA's Board of Education for Librarianship, under the chairmanship of Dr. Richard H. Logsdon, was making a preliminary report to the American Library Association indicating that future accreditation should be restricted to schools offering a five-year graduate program leading to a master's degree in library science. This development certainly influenced both Dr. Leigh's and the Committee's recommendations.[37]

In February 1951 Dr. Leigh submitted the results of his investigation to Dr. Bosshart's committee. The Committee then submitted its report together with Dr. Leigh's to the Commissioner of Education in March 1951. The report indicated some significant findings including: (1) that from sixty-five to seventy new library graduates each were needed each year in New Jersey; (2) that only five or six graduates each were being produced by NJCW and Trenton State; (3) that relatively few of the New Jersey residents who went out-of-state to gain library training returned to positions in the state; and (4) that 72 percent of the individuals occupying the 1,200 professional positions in New Jersey lacked the necessary professional education.[38]

Not surprisingly, the Committee's first recommendation called for "the establishment of a coeducational graduate school at Rutgers University, the State University, in New Brunswick."[39] Support for the proposed graduate school program also came from NJLA in the form of a resolution from its Executive Board.[40]

As a result no doubt of both the political pressure exerted from within the state and the national changes taking place in accreditation standards, as well as the retirements of both Fair (1950) and Higgins (1951), a plan was improved in principle by the Rutgers' Board of Trustees to end the undergraduate program and institute a graduate program in Library Services. In 1952 this was done and NJCW's Library School closed after twenty-five years of existence.

Active long after her retirement, Fair lectured abroad and also served as full-time Executive Secretary of ALA's Library Education Division. In 1970, she was awarded the Rutgers Medal in recognition of her outstanding service to education and to librarianship.[41]

Rutgers' Graduate Program in Library Service, 1954–

"Graduate Library Schools just don't happen, and that at Rutgers just didn't happen either," reminisced James E. (Ned) Bryan on the occasion of the School's 25th anniversary celebration, April 11, 1980. Bryan recalled a meeting in 1952 with Milton Gross, soon to become president of Rutgers, who said: "Ned, we want you to know that if Rutgers does get the Library School, it will not be just any library school; it will be . . . one of the best in the country."[42] And so it would come to be, ranking almost from the beginning among the leading ALA accredited library school programs. Officers of the New Jersey Library Association, under Bryan's leadership as president, aided by State Librarian Roger McDonough's political savvy, lobbied for gubernatorial and legislative support for the proposed graduate school. Ultimately $50,000 was appropriated for start-up costs,[43] and the following year NJLA again lobbied successfully for additional funding.

Although the Graduate School of Library Service (GSLS) was officially established in September 1953, it would not be until the following September that the School would open its doors to 104 students.[44] Lowell Martin (who was recommended for the deanship by NJLA in response to a request from Mason Gross)[45] served as GSLS' first dean from 1954 to 1959, and it was primarily he who laid out the blueprint for the School: to serve not only the State but also the Middle Atlantic region, and to attract students not only from other states but also from foreign countries. His guiding objectives for the School were threefold: (1) to establish a program of graduate instruction for librarians, at a high university level; (2) to organize training for librarians on-the-job in New Jersey and beyond, from sub-professional through administrative personnel; and (3) to engage in research designed to improve the diffusion and retrieval of knowledge through libraries.[46] All three objectives seemingly were accomplished during Martin's tenure as Dean.

Distinguishing features of the GSLS 36-credit curriculum included

(1) a foundation or "core" sequence of seven courses (21 credits), required of all students;

(2) provision of elective courses (12 credits) to meet specific library needs in New Jersey and the vicinity;

(3) avoidance of proliferation of courses, in order to make best use of the time of both faculty and students;

(4) stressing of close faculty-student relations, by means of small classes, limitations on faculty loads, and group and individual conferences;

(5) integration of classroom instruction and field experience, through a degree requirement of satisfactory field performance under supervision and a special "field" seminar (the final three credits). The student could satisfy the field performance either by service in an approved library for a period of 250 hours or by performance in a work-study program;

(6) enabling students to finance their professional education by means of a work-study plan with libraries; and

(7) supplementing of regular faculty resources with distinguished

librarians who visited at the School for periods of two or three days.[47]

Martin's well-planned program called for action on several fronts: improvement of the governmental structure for library service, increased local support for libraries, assumption by the state of its responsibility for sharing in the financial support of this part of its educational facilities, certification of professional librarians, and continued development of the library training center established at Rutgers.[48] The School received a large grant from the Council on Library Resources for 1957–58, and was able to to initiate its "Targets in Library Research" program. It also received a Carnegie Corporation grant which enabled it to establish a special seminar for advanced administrators of research libraries.[49] In Jana Varlejs' words:

> The School has had a major impact on state-wide planning since its inception. *Libraries for the People of New Jersey; or Knowledge for All*, familiarly known as the Martin-Gaver report, provided the framework for the funding and organization of cooperative library services . . . in New Jersey.[50]

In addition to Lowell Martin who was a recognized leader in public librarianship, the School's distinguished founding faculty would include three ALA presidents: Keyes Metcalf, a noted academic librarian; Ralph Shaw, expert in scientific management and research, who would later become GSLS' second dean; and Mary Virginia Gaver, whose expertise in children's and school librarianship has already been noted. Gaver also proved invaluable to the School because of her contacts in the State Department of Education and within the New Jersey library community. Four assistant professors, who were competent respectively in cataloging, reference service, book collections and adult library services, rounded out the founding faculty.[51]

At first, faculty and students met on the Rutgers College campus in a small house (now occupied by the Campus Patrol) on Huntington Street. Mary Gaver later recalled: "My most vivid memories of those early days is the exciting ambiance, collegiality, of the faculty and students, all crammed into that little building. . . . Margaret Monroe remembers this also, with the excitement of 'being in on the ground floor of an exciting new endeavor in library education'— all of us in it together with Ralph Shaw and Lowell Martin as the leaders."[52]

Later, although faculty continued to be housed at 5 Huntington

Street, classes would be held in the basement of the new Alexander Library building which opened its doors in 1956. The library science collection which had been carefully built over the years by Ethel Fair and her associates was transferred from Douglass College to the university campus and was later integrated into the university library.[53] (University policy prohibited the development of departmental libraries so there was no plan to develop a separate library school library, and it was also felt that students would profit by using the facilities of the entire university library.)

In October 1955 the Library School was visited by an ALA accreditation team. The faculty had prepared a substantial report, and the visitors were understandably impressed by the progress that the Dean and the faculty had made. In January 1956 the ALA Board of Education for Librarianship voted to accredit the Rutgers' MLS degree program.[54]

The School suffered a real loss in 1959 when Lowell Martin resigned to accept a position with the Grolier Company. Ralph Shaw succeeded him as Dean (1959–61). Shaw had earned his doctorate from the University of Chicago and had been Director of Libraries for the U.S. Department of Agriculture from 1940 to 1954. Twenty years later Ned Bryan would recall Shaw as "brilliant, a maverick. He had a mind of his own. He was innovative and perceptive. He was yeasty and abrasive. He added stature to the Library School and to the University, where he was held in great respect."[55] (While at Rutgers Shaw took a leave of absence to help found a library school at the University of Hawaii.)

Development of the new doctoral program, which graduated its first three Ph.D. students in 1961, generated much intellectual stimulation during Shaw's short tenure as dean. Curriculum innovation and experimentation could be evidenced in a successful exchange of faculty with Columbia in 1960–61. The addition of Richard Shoemaker and Paul Dunkin to the faculty resulted in both the MLS and Ph.D. programs having a strong bibliographical component. Another highlight of Shaw's tenure as dean was the publication of a ten-volume series on "The State of the Library Art," as well as a volume covering the Keyes Metcalf seminars in advanced library management, which brought many library leaders to the campus.[56]

One hundred and two students earned the MLS degree in 1960, compared with sixty-two in the preceding academic year, but still the state-wide shortage of librarians persisted.[57] The 1960s were years of extreme social unrest in the country, and Neal Harlow, who came from the University of British Columbia to assume the deanship, proved to be a capable administrator. He was fortunate to have the assistance of Professors Mildred Y. Johnson and Marian H. Scott (Assistant Dean and Placement Director respectively). Because massive sums of federal money was being allocated for educational spending and libraries, the shortage of librarians intensified. During Harlow's tenure as dean MLS enrollment steadily increased, and in 1967 there were 191 degrees awarded.[58] Thanks to the passage of the Higher Education Act with its Title IIB fellowships, the Ph.D. program also thrived. Likewise the faculty increased about three-fold during this time (Blasingame, Deininger, DeProspo, Reeling, Rehrauer, Simpson, Voos, and Weintraub, among others, were appointed). The ALA Committee on Accreditation noted with particular approval the high caliber of the GSLS faculty. (Ernest De-Prospo was the first non-librarian to be appointed to the GSLS faculty; Harlow and future deans would increasingly describe the MLS and Ph.D. programs as interdisciplinary in nature.)

Space to house the rapidly-growing School became a pressing issue, and Harlow was faced with the challenge of planning (and funding) a new building. A building request was presented to Mason Gross in 1962, and with his support $850,000 was earmarked for construction in a bond issue approved in November 1964. Additional funding resulted from a June 1965 grant under the Higher Education Facilities Act.[59] Finally, in December 1968, just in time to hold final fall semester classes, faculty was permitted to occupy the new three-storied building adjacent to Alexander Library.

Occupation of the new building with its ample laboratory space and technical staff changed the character of the curriculum. An unanticipated effect, often lamented at faculty meetings, was the weakening of communication. Faculty were no longer sequestered in a tiny house and lost their close camaraderie. The stage was now set for the friction that would later occur between the "library service" faculty housed on the bottom two floors and the administration and information science faculty on the top floor.

To celebrate the occasion of the new building, Dean Harlow organized a series of seminars in spring 1969, including "State-Wide Library Planning—The New Jersey Example," chaired by Mary Gaver. A number of other well-publicized conferences had been held during Harlow's tenure as dean, the most notable being a series of seven international seminars sponsored by the National Science Foundation and directed by Dr. Susan Artandi on the "Intellectual Organization of Knowledge," 1963–66. Proceedings were published by the Rutgers University Press.[60] The tradition of an annual Alumni/Faculty Symposium was also initiated in the early 1960s. (Since 1982 the proceedings have been published by McFarland & Co. under the editorship of Jana Varlejs.)

Having planned the new building, Neal Harlow announced his retirement. He left the School in excellent condition. Shortly after his departure, a study of accredited library schools showed Rutgers' Ph.D. and MLS programs ranked third and fourth respectively in the nation.[61] They were a source of great pride, both to the university and to the state.

On July 1, 1969 a new era was ushered in. Dr. Thomas H. Mott, formerly Director of the Center for Computer Studies at Rutgers, was appointed dean, a position to which Gaver and at least one other internal candidate had aspired. Shortly thereafter Gaver announced her retirement; others would follow. Mildred Johnson stepped down from her administrative post, and Richard Shoemaker died.

During the early 1970s the post-masters (continuing education) program received special attention. In 1972 Professor Dorothy Deininger was the first to serve as Director of Professional Development Studies (PDS). The PDS program was intended to provide "a forum for interaction between the field and the faculty, to the benefit of both, as well as an opportunity to experiment with new courses and teaching methods."[62] Over the years the number of courses and workshops offered in various locations throughout the state has continued to expand. A sixth-year certificate program was also developed under the leadership of PDS.

Tom Mott was the first non-librarian to become dean, and some on the faculty despaired that he would ever become an effective spokesperson for libraries and library education. During the latter part of his tenure the School, which changed its name to the Graduate School of Library and Information Studies in 1979, became mired in controversy, especially after a plan was unfolded to merge GSLIS with the undergraduate Department of Communication. GSLIS' relationship with its external constituencies had also soured and enrollment plummeted, especially after the MLS program was reaccredited only "conditionally" by ALA in 1980–81. Many feared the School might actually close its doors. In reviewing this period, an external panel found that there were "declines of unusual magnitude which we attribute primarily to a prolonged collective failure in leadership. . . ."[63]

Following an intensive debate regarding the reorganization of the School, with considerable input from NJLA, the School's Advisory Associates (notably Edwin Beckerman, John H. Livingstone, and Roger McDonough), distinguished alumni, and retired faculty, the Rutgers University Board of Governors approved, on June 11, 1982, a "Resolution on the Establishment of a School of Communication, Information and Library Studies" in order "to permit the University to meet more fully the technological needs of the State and Nation and the vocational needs of its students." The rationale for the new configuration was "a growing concern with the impact of electronic technologies on human communication and information processes and with the resulting complexity manifesting itself in information-related phenomena."[64] The last clause of the Board of Governor's resolution (much to the relief of this author who testified at the public session and requested support for the MLS program) read:

> BE IT FURTHER RESOLVED, that in establishing the School of Communication, Information and Library Studies, the University shall continue its commitment to maintain the excellence of the Master of Library Service program and to pursue full accreditation for the program by the American Library Association.[65]

Dean Mott announced his resignation as Dean shortly thereafter, and the following year, Richard Budd, Chairperson of the former Department of Communication, was appointed Dean of the new School (SCILS) which is comprised of three departments: Communication; Journalism and Mass Media; and Library and Information Studies. Much work needed to be accomplished to rebuild the MLS program. In 1984 Reeling was appointed Chairperson of the LIS Department (what was formerly the old library school) and, with the special help of Professors Daniel O'Connor and Benjamin Weintraub, took immediate steps to sooth external relations with the field. Renee Swartz, Trustee and Chair of the LIS Program Associates, was an invaluable source of support and a good friend to LIS. Dean Budd supported the hiring of two new faculty (Carol Kuhlthau and Kay Vandergrift) to develop teaching/research competency in the areas of children's and school media library service. Students were recruited to work in public libraries, and LIS faculty once again were visible within the state (as well as nationally and internationally).

In 1987 the LIS program was reassessed by both ALA and an external review panel, and received praise from both groups.

> We concur fully with the Department's own assertion that the MLS program has been substantially improved. This was also the opinion expressed by the alumni, students, and local employers with whom we had contact. The dedication, hard work, and leadership of the Department Chair, Professor Patricia Reeling, and the faculty who helped her, deserve praise and reward for an outstanding achievement.[66]

Professors Betty Turock and David Carr succeeded Reeling in the Chairmanship of the LIS Department. In a recent *U.S. News and*

World Report poll, Rutgers once again is listed as one of the top graduate library science programs in the country.[67]

Other Library Education Programs in New Jersey

In 1971, twenty years after the Committee to Study the Professional Education and Training of Library Personnel in New Jersey submitted its report, Roger McDonough prepared to undertake "a thorough review of present educational opportunities and inter-institutional practices . . . in the area of education for librarianship."[68] There followed a series of meetings culminating in the "First Library Education Conference—State Library" in October 1971, at which time a set of recommendations was issued aimed at developing a coordinated, state-wide plan. An outcome of this meeting was the formation of an Advisory Council of Library Education. The state-wide plan called for articulation among library education programs throughout the state at the two-year community college level, the four-year undergraduate level, and the graduate master's and Ph.D. levels. As background for later discussion, a handout was prepared showing the location of existing New Jersey programs. They included: (1) Graduate—Rutgers GSLS; (2) Graduate and Undergraduate—Glassboro State College; (3) Undergraduate—Caldwell College, Montclair State College, Newark State College, Trenton State College, College of St. Elizabeth, and William Paterson State College of New Jersey; (4) Two-year programs—Alphonsus College, Brookdale Community College, Camden County Vocational and Technical School, Cumberland County Community College and Mercer County Community College. (Appendix 2 contains updated information on currently available programs.)

Summary

Although the primary goal of the Public Library Commission, when it was created in 1900, was to establish free public libraries throughout New Jersey, it soon found itself assuming the "lion's share" of responsibility for training personnel to staff these libraries. Until the post–World War II era, summer school programs and extension courses offered under Commission sponsorship were the primary means of providing New Jersey librarians with practical training.

While neighboring states had already established formal library training programs in the late 19th century, New Jersey's first campus-based baccalaureate program did not open its doors until 1927. Housed at the New Jersey College for Women, the School managed to survive the lean years of the Depression and World War II only to find itself bucking the national trend toward a fifth-year graduate degree. At that time the state's only other undergraduate program was Trenton State's fifth year summer school program.

Following a formal study of library education needs in 1951 the Graduate School of Library Service was established at Rutgers University in 1953. Lowell Martin as the first Dean was instrumental in setting the "tone" for the new school, with Ralph Shaw and Mary Gaver also playing major roles as part of the original faculty.

One of the early characteristics of the School was its close connections with library practice and practitioners in New Jersey. Ties were particularly strong with NJLA and the State Library. In 1956 New Jersey enacted its first "mandatory" certification law, requiring thenceforth that library professionals hold a fifth-year master's degree.

Gradually GSLS faculty activities moved toward interdisciplinary research. In 1982 the University merged the Department of Communication with the Library School to form a new School of Communication, Information and Library Studies. The School houses the state's only ALA-accredited program. The Rutgers MLS degree continues to be a source of pride to its holders.

Notes

1. See Sarah K. Vann's *Training for Librarianship Before 1923* (Chicago, ALA, 1961), and Carl M. White, *The Origins of the American Library School* (New York, Scarecrow Press, 1961).

2. *Handbook of the Public Library Commission of New Jersey: Libraries and Library Laws of the State, November 1, 1901* (Trenton, N.J.: Mac-Crellish & Quigley, 1901).

3. In 1914 the law governing the Commission was amended to include responsibility for supervision of school libraries.

4. *New Jersey Library Bulletin*, 1:1, March 1912, 3:2, September 1913, and 3:1, July 1914.

5. *New Jersey Library Bulletin*, 1;1, June 1912.

6. *New Jersey Library Bulletin*, 6:1, April 1917.

7. *New Jersey Library Bulletin*, 11:5, November 1926.

8. *New Jersey Library Bulletin*, 1 new series: 3–4, April 1931.

9. *New Jersey Library Bulletin*, 1 new series: 5, April 1931.

10. Mary Virginia Gaver, *A Braided Cord: Memoirs of a School Librarian* (Metuchen, N.J. & London, Scarecrow Press, 1988), 70 and *New Jersey Library Bulletin*, 2 new series: 2, April 1932.

11. *Forty-fourth Annual Report of the Public Library Commission of the State of New Jersey, 1943–4*, 11.

12. Gaver, 71.

13. *New Jersey Library Bulletin,* 5 new series: 56, February 1937.

14. *New Jersey Library Bulletin,* 7 new series: 81, February 1939.

15. *New Jersey Library Bulletin,* 6 new series: 67–68, February 1938.

16. *New Jersey Library Bulletin,* 11 new series: 25, April 1943.

17. Ethel M. Fair, *The Library School of the New Jersey College for Women, 1927–1952: A 'Type III' School in Historical Perspective* (Unpublished manuscript), 48. (A shortened version of her manuscript is published in *The Journal of the Rutgers University Libraries,* 43:41–65, December 1981.

18. *Thirty-eighth Annual Report of the Public Library Commission of the State of New Jersey, 1937–8*, 1.

19. *Forty-third Annual Report of the Public Library Commission of the State of New Jersey, 1942–43*, 7.

20. NJSA 45:8A-1 (The statute currently mandates a professional certificate for all librarians working in libraries serving 10,000 or more persons.)

21. Again the reader is referred to Vann and White for lucid accounts of this early period.

22. Charles C. Williamson, *Training for Library Service: A Report Prepared for the Carnegie Corporation of New York* (New York, 1923).

23. *Ibid*: 146.

24. Fair, 5.

25. Mary Virginia Gaver, *Evaluation Report* (Graduate School of Library Service, Rutgers University, September 1, 1955), 1; and *The Professional Education and Training of Library Personnel in New Jersey: A Report to the Commissioner of Education* (March 16, 1951), 20.

26. Fair, 1.

27. *Ibid*: 3, 5–7.

28. *Ibid*: 38–39.

29. *Ibid*: 45, 55.

30. *Ibid*: 6.

31. *Ibid*: 27–28.

32. Gaver, 60–61; Fair, 30–32.

33. Fair, 68.

34. *Ibid*: 11,12.

35. *Ibid*: 20–21.

36. *The Professional Education and Training of Library Personnel in New Jersey: A Report to the Commissioner of Education* (March 16, 1951), 3.

37. Fair, 77.

38. *The Professional Education and Training of Library Personnel in New Jersey,* 14–15.

39. *Ibid*: 12.

40. Fair, 82–83.

41. Gaver, 61.

42. James E. Bryan, *Some Recollections and Comments Made at the Time*

of the 25th Anniversary of the Graduate Library School at Rutgers, April 11, 1980, 5.

43. A line in the Annual Appropriation Act (Chapter 102, Laws of 1963) allocated $50,000 to found the Library School. There was no actual bill authorizing its creation.

44. *Annual Report of the Graduate School of Library Service, Rutgers University, 1954–55*, 2.

45. Bryan, 6.

46. *Annual Report of the Graduate School of Library Service, Rutgers University, 1957–58*, 1.

47. *Annual Report of the Graduate School of Library Service, Rutgers University, 1954–55*, 1.

48. Lowell Martin, *Brief Review of Plans for the School*, (for meeting of the Trustees, January 1956), 2.

49. *Annual Report of the Graduate School of Library Service, Rutgers University, 1957–58*, 1.

50. Jana Varlejs, "Inside Our Schools: Rutgers," *Wilson Library Bulletin*, February, 1980, 381.

51. *Annual Report of the Graduate School of Library Service, Rutgers University, 1954–55*, 2.

52. Gaver, 79.

53. *Ibid*: 81.

54. *Report on Rutgers University Graduate School of Library Service*, (American Library Association Board of Education for Librarianship, February 1956, 14–15.

55. Bryan, 7.

56. *Annual Report of the Graduate School of Library Service, Rutgers University, 1960–61*, 1.

57. *Annual Report of the Graduate Library School, Rutgers University, 1959–60*, 1.

58. *Annual Report of the Graduate Library School, Rutgers University, 1966–67*, 1.

59. *Ibid*: 2.

60. Gaver, 77; *Annual Report of the Graduate School of Library Service, Rutgers University, 1965–66*, 3.

61. Ray L Carpenter and Patricia A. Carpenter, "The Doctorate in Librarianship and an Assessment of Graduate Library Education," *Journal of Education for Librarianship*, Summer 1970, 11:3–45.

62. Varlejs, 385.

63. *External Review Report*, (Department of Library and Information Studies, Rutgers University, 1987). 3.

64. James D. Anderson, Nicholas J. Belkin, Linda C. Lederman, and Tefko Saracevic, "Information Science at Rutgers: Establishing New Interdisciplinary Connections," *Journal of the American Society for Information Science*, 39:327, September, 1988.

65. Board of Governors, Rutgers University, "Resolution on the Establishment of a School of Communication, Information and Library Studies," June 11, 1982.

66. *External Review Report*, 1–2.

67. *U.S. News and World Report,*120:100, March 15, 1996.

68. *Library Education in New Jersey: Report and Recommendations*, (New Jersey State Library, August, 1972), 2.

8

School Library Media Centers

Arabelle K. Pennypacker and Anne Voss
(Revised by Marian Scott,
Mary Jane McNally and Carol Kuhlthau)

Early Days

School libraries in New Jersey have a comparatively short history, even though the first school in the state was opened in the mid–seventeenth century. On "October 6, 1662 Engelbert Steinhuysen was licensed to be a schoolmaster in the town of Bergen. . . . His was the first school in what is now the State of New Jersey."[1] Not surprisingly, there is no mention of a library or a collection of books, not even a word of *any* books.

On May 1, 1838 a law establishing common schools was passed stipulating that any library in a school district was to be of "equal benefit of all persons residing in the school district."[2] In 1839 the Trustees of the School Fund that was established under the new law suggested that provision be made for "supplying every district school with a small library together with a few globes, maps, and other similar aids in the acquisition of knowledge."[3] However, in 1840 the New Jersey Legislature had "passed no law relating to the establishment of school libraries."[4]

In his 1848 annual report T. F. King, the first State Superintendent of Schools, called for placing "within the reach of every individual . . . a large and judiciously selected assortment of books."[5] By the 1850s several legislative acts had provided that a "Webster's Un-abridged Dictionary," a gazetteer and a volume of New Jersey history be purchased and distributed to those schools that requested them. With the creation of State Superintendents of Schools in 1845, the establishment of the State Board of Education in 1866 and the appointment of county school superintendents in 1867, there were continued and diverse calls for school libraries. Despite this interest among the state's educators, it was not until the legislature established free public schools in 1871, and provided a uniform tax base that state aid for school libraries was established.

The law passed in 1871 authorized the State Treasurer to pay twenty dollars for library books to every public school upon order of the State Superintendent of Schools, providing there was money available and the district schools matched the funding. Assemblyman Nathaniel Niles of Madison, who was largely responsible for the passage of this legislation, was assisted by Maria Nixon, who prepared for buyers' reference "four lists of books suitable for libraries."[6] Despite this, "the condition of school libraries was disappointing as only a few districts even tried to introduce them. The explanation appeared . . . [to be due] to the unprecedented efforts to erect better school buildings which demanded all the financial resources of the progressive communities."[7]

Annual reports of State Superintendents of Schools mention continuing problems. In 1887 E. O. Chapman cited uneven development, with some districts having large collections and rooms in which to keep them, while other districts had not even applied for available state aid to establish school libraries.[8] In 1892 A. B. Poland highlighted another problem: "Too few [school district] trustees are able to make a wise selection of books."[9] Superintendent of Schools Charles Baxter, meeting with the newly formed New Jersey Library Association, sought the assistance of public libraries. The NJLA minutes of 1902 record a motion that the executive committee appoint "a committee of five to cooperate with the State Superintendent of Instruction on the revision of lists for school reading."[10]

Turn of the Century

The establishment of public high schools in 1895 and 1897 in first- and second-class cities brought a new dimension to the call for school libraries. By the early 1900s a few schools had begun to employ librarians.[11] Sarah Askew, Secretary/Librarian of the Public Library Commission, summarizing her evaluation of school libraries in 1912, recommended that their supervision be transferred from the Department of Public Instruction to the Public Library Commission, and that the Commission have greater power over school library operation than the Department of Instruction had held.[12]

By 1915 only eighteen school libraries had been established in the 115 high schools of New Jersey.[13] The relative influence of the pub-

lic library at the time is evidenced by the July 1916 requirement of
the New Jersey Public Library Commission that each school apply-
ing for library aid was:

> to submit in duplicate a list of intended purchases. This list must be
> approved by the librarian of the public library. . . . It is necessary for
> schools to own and keep in the school building certain books of refer-
> ence needed constantly by teachers and pupils. The greatest number
> of books needed by them are for temporary use and should be bor-
> rowed from the public library.[14]

This decree reflected a view of school libraries as branches of public
libraries.

What then gave impetus to school library development? Elizabeth
White, of the Passaic Public Library, invited librarians who were
working with schools to meet in the Passaic High School Library.
There, in March 1915, the New Jersey School Librarians' Association (NJSLA) was formed. The officers selected were Elizabeth
White, President; Ethel Fagin, Vice-president; and Dorothy White,
Secretary-Treasurer. The fifteen charter members represented a majority of the school librarians in the state. The NJSLA was only the
second school librarians' association in the United States, and it was
destined to be a potent force in school library development.[15] Also
in 1915 the Newark Board of Education approved the position of
school librarian. Previously librarians had been hired by the Board
of Trustees of the Newark Public Library, and the libraries in the
schools had functioned as branches of the public library.

In 1929 the New Jersey School Library Councils' Association
(NJSLCA) was formed, the first organization of its kind in the nation. It began in fifteen schools under the sponsorship of Mary Ann
Clark, Laura Faus, and Alice Bible. Its purpose was to create a "nu-
cleus for a real service group, to develop book lovers, and good
library users among young students."[16] By 1936, 75 percent of
schools reporting to the Public Library Commission indicated some
form of student assistance with library operations.[17]

From 1930 to 1950

The decades from 1930 through the 1950s brought growing strength
to New Jersey school libraries. As Margaret Lane reported in 1938,
many influences had

> worked together to raise the quality of the service given by the grow-
> ing school libraries. Opportunities have been offered for the training

of librarians; standards for the certification of librarians and the accreditation of libraries have been set up, the various library associations have increased professional awareness and the Public Library Commission has made advisory services available.[18]

Added to these influences were the changing trends in education and an increasingly supportive State Department of Education.

The New Jersey Department of Education over a period of years issued policy statements supporting the development of school libraries. In 1932, just twenty years after Sarah Askew recommended that only pedagogical books be kept in the schoolhouse, the State issued *A Manual for Secondary Schools* which stated: "It is impossible for a modern high school to function properly without a library planned and administered for the school. No public library however well run can take its place for the efficient school library is the center of the school and a laboratory for all."[19]

In 1945 when a state law reorganized the State Library as a division of the Department of Education, it established a Bureau of Public and School Library Service in the Library. Oscar McPherson, Librarian at Lawrenceville School and an active NJSLA member, hailed the new law. In anticipation of the projected demise of the "fit-all" textbook, McPherson suggested specific objectives to effect a "revolution in the attitudes of school librarians and school administrators, since New Jersey school libraries have at least been given the green light to effective educational accomplishment."[20]

In a speech delivered in 1947 State Librarian Roger McDonough proposed seven steps for the improvement of elementary and secondary school libraries. Funding the position of a school supervisor became the number one item in the State Library's 1948–49 budget.

The trend away from the textbook was closely allied to a growing interest in audio-visual resources. Edward Schofield, Director of the Newark Public Schools' Audio-Visual Aids Center, highlighted progressive education, the development of audio-visual resources and early technology, as well as the librarian's role as guide and counselor as factors in the "phenomenal rise in the provision of library service for schools."[21]

In 1948, Commissioner of Education John H. Bosshart also applauded the "emancipation . . . from the tyranny of the single textbook,"[22] and supported the appointment of professionally trained librarians school library service. Early training opportunities for school librarians included a summer school held in the Asbury Park Public Library, which was the genesis of the Trenton State Teachers College undergraduate library education program. By the 1940s the Trenton State program had been joined by programs at Newark

State Teachers College and the New Jersey College for Women in New Brunswick.

State Librarian Roger McDonough was also the prime mover in the establishment of the Rutgers University Graduate School of Library Service, with Lowell Martin as Dean and Mary Gaver as head of the School Library Department. Gaver was a distinguished teacher and the acknowledged mentor of New Jersey school librarians. The impact of her leadership on the development of school libraries and librarians cannot be overstated. Gaver's vision and the strength of her pronouncements persuaded many school library media specialists of the need to accept and use media resources in a variety of new formats. Eleanor McKinney, the founding librarian at Hanover Park Regional High School and Past President of NJSLA (letter to A. Pennypacker, November 30, 1985), described Mary Gaver's influence: "From the time she came into the State as head librarian at Trenton State to her retirement from Rutgers University she has been the most influential force in school media centers and in library education in the State." Dorothea Coachman, a Grolier Award recipient at Rutgers, and a past President of NJSLA (telephone conversation with A. Pennypacker, November 14, 1985), provided the following explanation, "Mary Gaver expected us to do better things than we believed ourselves capable of, and we did them in an attempt to live up to her expectations."

Professionalism raised the issues of certification and salaries. The NJSLA heeded the advice of Mildred Batchelder, School Library Specialist of the American Library Association (ALA), who, at a meeting in New Jersey, stressed the importance of working with other educational associations. In April 1949 the NJSLA adopted this approach: "Mr. Schofield was instructed to seek the help of the New Jersey Education Association (NJEA), through Dr. Hipp [NJEA Executive Director], in getting our recommendations incorporated in the certification regulations."[23] This was just one instance in which the NJSLA found an advocate in the NJEA.

The minutes of the NJSLA Executive Board meetings show that the Association was not reluctant to take a stand.[24] The Board authorized its certification committee to "word a well-considered blast" against proposed certification requirements, and established a committee to study the salary status of school librarians. Commissioner Bosshart applauded the effectiveness of the NJSLA's "well-considered" certification and salary efforts, and he gave the Association credit for its significant influence on the improvement of school libraries.

As statewide interest in school libraries grew, the State Library issued two documents in 1956, *Minimal Suggestions for Secondary*

School Facilities in New Jersey and *Elementary School Library Facilities in New Jersey*, designed to serve as planning tools for school libraries. The early trend in many communities seemed to be toward a supervisor for all the elementary schools in the town, with volunteers or parents staffing individual schools. Few towns could afford a professional librarian in every school, but parents were enthusiastic about the idea. And it had the strong support of the Congress of Parents and Teachers as well as the NJSLA, who were both inspired by Mary Gaver's publication, *Every Child Needs a School Library*.[25]

The 1960s and 1970s

Events through the 1960s and the 1970s brought growth, strength and change. Long-range planning and federal funding were powerful catalysts that fostered the growth and proliferation of school libraries in New Jersey. A Rutgers study showed that between 1962 and 1970 there was a 23 percent increase in the number of school libraries, as compared with a four percent growth in public libraries during the same period.[26]

An outside source of validation for secondary school libraries was the increased importance attached to the Middle States Association's evaluation of schools for accreditation. By the 1960s boards of education, superintendents and principals, who were anxious to meet accreditation standards, gave thoughtful attention to school library needs.

Long-range planning characterized the first half of the 1960s. The *Standards for School Library Programs*, published by the American Association of School Librarians (AASL),[27] recommended levels of achievement that were far above those of New Jersey school libraries. Whether looking at the ratio of librarians to pupils, number of books, or expenditure per pupil on libraries, New Jersey came up short.

Having identified the need to improve both teachers' use of the school library and their recognition of it as a teaching tool, the NJLSA proposed a demonstration project for teachers in training. In 1961 the Association received a School Library Development Project (SLDP) grant from the AASL to conduct such a project. Montclair State College agreed to send 75 students to the first demonstration lesson, which was conducted in the Hanover Park Regional High School in April 1962 by school media specialist Betty Torricelli and an experienced social studies teacher, who worked together in a team approach to use the resources of the library. This plan, the first of its kind in the country, was watched with great interest and duplicated at several locations.[28]

Both Eleanor McKinney and Margueritte Baechtold, Chairperson of the Library Science program at Newark State College, who helped develop and implement New Jersey's School Library Development Project, believed that the SLDP was "most effective in New Jersey and has had a lasting effect on the building of New Jersey school libraries."[29]

Title II

Long-range planning characterized the first half of the 1960s, federal funding dominated the latter half of the decade. The passage of the Elementary and Secondary Education Act (ESEA) of 1965, Title II, had far-reaching, and long-lasting effects on the development of school library media programs in New Jersey.

Any plan to distribute Title II funds had to include the following elements in the law:

1. This was a child benefit act. Every child, including those in non-public or private schools, was entitled to benefit.
2. Any school receiving funds must use the funds to supplement the program, not substitute for local funding. Local effort must be maintained.
3. There was to be equitable distribution of funding based on need.
4. The funds could be used only for printed materials, which, according to the Title II definition, included periodicals, films and filmstrips, as well as books. Shelving, furniture, and equipment were ineligible for purchase.
5. No more than 15 percent of the federal appropriation could be spent for administration.

State Librarian Roger McDonough assigned the Bureau of Public and School Library Service (later called the Bureau of Library Development) the task of preparing a plan within these basic guidelines. Anne Voss, of the Bureau's School and Academic Media Section, was named coordinator, and an Advisory Committee was formed. The Committee included county superintendents, principals, teachers, and public and school librarians. Non-public schools were represented by headmasters and librarians. Community members included representatives of the New Jersey Congress of Parents and Teachers, Federated School Boards and the New Jersey Education Association. High school students were included in later years.

The Committee first met in August 1965. Commissioner of Education Frederick Raubinger reminded the group that federal funding was a very small part of a district's budget; state aid was about 25 percent, and the rest was local funding. The Committee was cautioned that any plan had to conform to state law and that no plan would be acceptable that was contrary to Department of Education policy.

Discussion was vigorous. Although it was the first time for many to participate in a planning session with public and private school representatives, educational principles and respect for the learner were areas of common ground. The Committee adopted a set of fundamental policies for implementing ESEA Title II:

1. Textbooks as defined by the National Defense Education Act should be excluded from the New Jersey plan.
2. Every school was eligible, whether or not there was a librarian, or even a library.
3. The Advisory Committee should recommend to the New Jersey Department of Education indicators of need; schools had the responsibility for selecting materials appropriate to meet their need.
4. The formula for indicating need should be as simple as possible.
5. There should be an annual review and evaluation of the program by the Advisory Committee.
6. Schools must show maintenance of effort to receive funding.

In December 1965 the New Jersey plan was approved. The first applications were mailed to the 585 public school districts and the 675 private schools in January 1966. The first year's application used books per pupil as an indicator of need; the second year's used number of filmstrips per pupil.

Impact of Title II

The alternate use of books and audio-visual software as indicators of need encouraged many school libraries to build multimedia collections. The increase in expenditures for materials is apparent in the following figures of the State Department of Education.[29]

Audio-Visual Expenditures in Public Schools
| 1966–67 | $3,256,038 | Per Pupil | $2.31 |
| 1974–75 | $6,865,537 | Per Pupil | $4.69 |

Book Expenditures in Public Schools
1966–67 $5,794,167   Per Pupil $4.38
1974–75 $8,694,920   Per Pupil $5.94

The increase in the number of school librarians over a similar period indicated that districts saw the need for librarians to prepare purchases, to maintain an accurate inventory as required by law, and to organize collections for easy access by children and teachers.

1958–59   906, or 1 librarian for every 1,792 pupils
1974–75   1,755, or 1 librarian for every 860 pupils

A similar pattern of support is demonstrated by the figures for private schools.

In addition to the allocation of funds for the purchase of library materials, the federal law allowed unexpended funds to be used for special grants. In New Jersey these grants were used to supplement the allocation for urban schools, to begin a county audio-visual commission, and to establish Special Education Instructional Materials Centers. Established in 1968–69, these centers were among the first in the country where special education teachers could examine and evaluate library materials. The original centers, located at Glassboro State College and Newark State College, were the forerunners of the Learning Resource Centers at East Brunswick, East Orange, Morristown and Sewell.

In 1971–72 the first of an annual designation of demonstration media centers was established. The selection of the schools was based on a study sponsored by NJSMA, the New Jersey School Media Association (an updating of the name New Jersey School Library Association to reflect the growing importance of non-print media in school "libraries"), and conducted in 1970 by researcher Charles Curran.[30] Media centers were considered for inclusion according to the following criteria:

1. An effective unified media program
2. Strong administrative support
3. Extensive utilization of the collection by teachers and students
4. Relevance to the region
5. In-service training for teachers and librarians in the utilization of the media center
6. Qualified staff
7. Adequate space to support program and accommodate visitors

The final selection was made from schools identified through the Title II data bank and supported by recommendations of county and local superintendents. Those chosen were distributed geographically throughout the state, with urban, suburban and rural schools as well as elementary, middle and high schools represented. The *Blueprint for School Media Programs in New Jersey* was used as an evaluative tool when visits were made.[31] By 1977 every county had one or more schools designated for visitation.

The success of ESEA Title II was based on its ease of administration and the extent to which it reflected the best professional judgment of the New Jersey school community. Strong support by the State Library, particularly the consulting services provided by members of the Library Development Bureau, including Jean Harris and Selma Rohrbacher under the direction of Anne Voss, played a key role in this achievement.

Since 1958 the State Library had compiled statistics of public school libraries. Beginning with the 1965–66 Title II applications, it was able to add information for private schools. Local districts used the compilation of figures concerning librarians, size of collections, and expenditures for both evaluating and planning their programs. The 1973 *Annual report of the State Library* had the following comments:

> The evaluative data of Title II ESEA seems to have been generally accepted as one of the measurements of quality education. In addition to the New Jersey Department of Education's use of data for approvals, the statistical information was used in a court case to indicate that financial support of individual school districts is closely correlated with support of the school library. This was interpreted as showing that quality education was not available to all children. The courts have upheld that concept.

The case referred to was *Robinson v. Cahill* which resulted in the famous "Thorough and Efficient" law of 1975. That law began a major restructuring of New Jersey's method of funding public education.

Another factor contributing to the growth of New Jersey's school libraries during this period was the vitality of the school library profession itself. The professional association, by now called the New Jersey School Media Association (NJSMA), merged with the New Jersey Association for Educational Communication and Technology in 1977 to form the Educational Media Association of New Jersey (EMAnj). As its conferences, meetings, and publications grew in sophistication, EMAnj became a more potent advocate for the best of school librarianship in New Jersey. Both during the merger and after, EMAnj was able to benefit from its many outstanding leaders including Carolyn Markuson, Robert Ruezinsky, Ruth Toor, who later became president of American Association of School Librarians, and Albert Saley.

The 1980s and 1990s

How did the gains in school library service brought about by ESEA Title II fare during the 1980s and 1990s? Inevitably there was some slowing down. Title II, which was designated for school library development, gave way to Title IVB and later to Chapter 2, which had more funding options. With this development the school library media center had to compete against other school programs for the federal funding in a school district.

If rapid growth was the theme of the 1970s, cooperation was the watchword of the 1980s. The creation of the New Jersey Library Network in 1985 and the establishment of multitype Regional Library Cooperatives provided opportunities for cooperative efforts by academic, institutional, public, school and special libraries. School librarians have representation on each Region's Interim Planning Committee and Executive Board. Recruitment efforts resulted in many school libraries, both public and private, joining their cooperatives. Membership in the Regional Library Cooperative allowed a school library to benefit from belonging to a larger bibliographical network. Interlibrary loan mechanisms might vary from region to region, but the delivery service funded by network aid was a lifeline for school libraries that chose to participate.

In February 1989 more than 100 participants from all types of libraries met in Princeton for a three-day retreat to discuss the direction of library service in the state for the next ten years. The "Roadmap Conference," as this gathering was dubbed, formulated a vision statement and action plans for fourteen topics.[32]

Another variation on the theme of cooperation was the School/Public Library Cooperative Grants awarded annually by the State Library. Funding of these grants enabled school libraries to work with public libraries on various projects addressing local needs. Such projects ranged from a lecture series to the creation of an electronic database.

In 1985 the Educational Media Association sponsored the publication which was the final document of a complex project designed and organized by Carol Kuhlthau and Selma Rohrbacher.[33] Together they oversaw three regional committees that worked on the selection process for over a year to develop a list of exemplary media centers throughout the state. After being identified for possible inclusion, each nominated media center was visited and evaluated. The final list included thirty media centers, elementary, middle, and high school, distributed over the state. This guide was used by many media specialists who wished to see robust programs in action.

Under the leadership of State Librarian Barbara Weaver, the State Library undertook the process of defining the role of the school library media center in the educational process.[34] To that end teams of representatives from twenty-two school districts were invited to meet in Cape May in October 1987. Attendees were included in teams from each district which included a member of the board of education, a school library media specialist, a classroom teacher, and a school administrator. At the conference each team formulated a plan for strengthening school library media services in their district, and all of them contributed to a statewide vision of school library media services.

Following the conference forty-two school library media specialists met to develop new guidelines for New Jersey's school library media centers. The resulting document[35] replaced the *The New Jersey Blueprint for School Media Programs*, which had been revised in 1979. The "Guidelines" were more in keeping with the philosophy of *Information Power*, the landmark document issued in 1988 which was currently shaping school library media thought nationally.[36] *Information Power* stresses the centrality of the library media program to the learning process by clearly and unequivocally stating that "the mission of the library media program is to ensure that students and staff are effective users of ideas and information."[37] With this mission in mind, many library media programs addressed thinking skills and information skills as opposed to the more narrowly defined library skills.

The evolution of school library media programs incorporating various information technologies, learning strategies, and media formats made renovation of older school libraries and the construction of new library media centers an important concern. Some notable recent construction projects were carried out in Ewing Township High School, Hunterdon Central Regional High School, Sayreville War Memorial High School, and West Orange High School.

The economic and political situation in the mid–1990s has created challenging times for school libraries. Budget reductions at the State Library have resulted in a Library Development Bureau that is a shadow of its former strength. Where once there were six consultants working with school library media programs, now there is one. Budget problems also forced the consolidation in 1994 of the six Regional Library Cooperatives into four. The Department of Education's new long-range planning document[38] does not mention libraries and information skills as part of the core curriculum. In response, the Educational Media Association of New Jersey drafted a statement on the role of the library media specialist in preparing students for the Information Age, which was read at county hearings held by the Department of Education.

Without a doubt the technological advances and the need for information in this decade and the next will change the structure and function of libraries. The Internet Grants awarded to school libraries for the first time in 1995 are an acknowledgment of the future direction for the provision of information in school library media centers.

Summary

A concluding look at the past 150 years of school library growth in New Jersey would recognize the forces shaping that growth:

1. Interested and enlightened leadership from the State Library, especially the consulting services provided by the Library Development Bureau.
2. Funding such as SLDP, ESEA Title II, and Title IVB that was earmarked for school library development.
3. Establishment of the Rutgers Graduate School of Library Service, now known as the School of Communication, Information, and Library Studies, and professional education for school librarians.
4. The enthusiasm and vision of New Jersey school librarians themselves, who created the variously named professional associations, now known as the Educational Media Association of New Jersey, that took the initiative in bringing the school library media program into the mainstream of educational practice.

Despite the progress made so far, New Jersey has yet to meet the following 1977 goal of the New Jersey School Media Association:[39]

That every school building shall have a library media center staffed by a professionally certified media specialist, with supportive staff, and a collection of materials to meet the day to day needs of the school population.

With their characteristic professionalism and energy the library media specialists of New Jersey are ready to meet the challenge.

Notes

1. David Murray, *History of Education in New Jersey* (Washington, D.C.: U.S. Government Printing Office, 1899), 108, 109.

2. *Ibid*: 143.

3. Nelson R. Burr, *Education in New Jersey, 1633–1871*. (Princeton, N.J.: Princeton University Press, 1942), 186.

4. Margaret Lane, *Development of Library Service to Public Schools in New Jersey*. Master's thesis, Columbia University, 1948 (Reprinted serially in *School Library Quarterly*, 3, 1948), 4.

5. Ibid: 4.

6. Murray, 189.

7. Burr, 292.

8. Lane, 23.

9. New Jersey Department of Public Instruction. *Annual Report, 1892, Part 1*, 113.

10. New Jersey Library Association. October 15, 1902. Meeting of Executive Committee. *Untitled minutes of meetings, 1890 through October 28, 1903*.

11. Lane, 27.

12. New Jersey School Library Media Association, Archives Committee. *The New Jersey School Library Media Association, 1915–1971* (Sussex, N.J.: NJSLMA. 1971).

13. Lane, 18.

14. New Jersey Public Library Commission. *Bulletin 5, (July)*. (Trenton, 1916), 1, 2.

15. NJSLMA, 1971.

16. New Jersey School Library Councils' Association. *History of the New Jersey School Libraries Association, 1929–1945*. n.p., n.d. Typed copy noted in State Library catalog.

17. Lane, 24.

18. *Ibid*: 19.

19. State of New Jersey. Department of Education. *A Manual for Secondary Schools* (Trenton, N.J.: State of New Jersey. Department of Education. 1950), 99.

20. Oscar McPherson, "Now Let's Have Libraries in New Jersey Schools," *School Library Quarterly*, 1, May 1945, 6, 7.

21. Edward Schofield, "New Jersey Libraries . . . Fifty Years of Progress," *School Library Quarterly*, 5. Fall, 1949, 2.

22. John H. Bosshart, "The Role of the School Library in New Jersey Education," *School Library Quarterly*, 3, May 1948, 5.

23. New Jersey School Library Association. *Executive Board Minutes, 1948/49–1951/52*. Minutes of 1949, 20.

24. *Ibid*: Minutes of 1948.

25. Mary Gaver, *Every Child Needs a School Library* (Chicago, Ill.: American Library Association, 1962).

26. Philip Clark, Kay McGinty, and Ellen Clark. *New Jersey Libraries*

and the State Plan: Seven Working Papers on the Progress and Potential of Library Development in New Jersey (New Brunswick, N.J.: Rutgers, 1974).

27. American Association of School Librarians. *Standards for School Library Programs* (Chicago, Ill.: American Library Association, 1960).

28. NJSLMA. 1971.

29. Letter to A. Pennypacker from Eleanor McKinney, November 30, 1985.

29. New Jersey Department of Education, Division of the State Library ... Library Development Bureau. *School Media Statistics, 1974–77* (Trenton, N.J.: State Department of Education, 1977), i.

30. Charles C. Curran, *Identification of Effective Media Centers in New Jersey Schools.* (New Brunswick, N.J.: Ph.D. Dissertation, Rutgers University).

31. New Jersey State Department of Education, Division of the State Library ... Library Development Bureau. *Blueprint for School Media Programs in New Jersey* (Trenton, N.J.: Department of Education, 1970).

32. New Jersey State Library. *Charting the Future: A Roadmap for New Jersey Libraries.* (Trenton, N.J.: New Jersey State Department of Education, 1989).

33. Carol Kuhlthau, and E. Wallen. *Programs of Library Media Centers Recommended for Visiting and Observing* (Educational Media Association of New Jersey, 1985).

34. Jean Harris, "School Library Media Centers in New Jersey: An Educational Imperative." *Emanations 11,* Spring, 1987.

35. New Jersey State Library. *Guidelines for School Library Media Programs in New Jersey: A Planning Tool.* (Trenton, N.J.: New Jersey State Library, 1992).

36. American Association of School Librarians; Association for Educational Communications and Technology. *Information Power: Guidelines for School Library Media Programs* (Chicago, Ill.: American Library Association, 1988).

37. *Ibid:* 1.

38. New Jersey State Department of Education. *Strategic Plan for Systematic Improvement of Education in New Jersey* (Trenton, N.J.: Department of Education, 1995).

39. New Jersey School Media Association. Development of School Media Programs Committee. *Library Media and T&E* (Trenton, N.J.: New Jersey State Library, 1977), i.

9

Academic Libraries

Robert Van Benthuysen
(Revised and Expanded by Edwin Beckerman)

Of the nine American institutions of higher learning with a continuous past dating to pre-Revolutionary times, two, the College of New Jersey (Princeton University), founded in 1746, and Queens College (Rutgers University), founded in 1766, were in New Jersey, the only colony with two such institutions. In the past two centuries New Jersey has created an academic environment that now supports eight universities, fifteen four-year colleges, nineteen two-year colleges, two engineering/technical colleges, one medical and dental school, three proprietary technical schools and seven theological colleges. These fifty-five centers of higher education have put New Jersey in the forefront of public and private higher education.

Initially the two colonial colleges had libraries that were small, poorly organized and jealously guarded, but seldom used. Library budgets were small or non-existent. Most books were donated, although a few were purchased with money raised from special student fees and sometimes from lotteries. Students frequently brought the books they needed from home or purchased them from their predecessors. Since books were scarce, costly and in constant danger from the frequent fires that plagued the colonial colleges, the regulations governing their use were strict. While the library is the very center of modern campus intellectual life, this was not true at colonial Princeton and Rutgers. That role was assumed by the student literary societies, which established their own collections of books to meet the demands of inquiring student minds. It was only in the latter part of the nineteenth century, as more money became available to the schools and curricula broadened, that the two universities began to build extensive library collections and services.

Princeton University

The College of New Jersey was founded in 1746 by royal charter for the purpose of "encouraging and promoting a learned education of our Youth in New Jersey . . . wherein Youth may be instructed in the learned Languages, and in the Liberal Arts and Sciences. . . ."[1] It was the fourth college to be established in British North America, after Harvard, William and Mary, and Yale. The charter was issued to a self-perpetuating board of trustees who were acting in behalf of the evangelical or New Light wing of the Presbyterian Church, but the new college had no legal or constitutional connection with the denomination. Its doors were open to all students providing "that those of every Religious Denomination may have free and Equal Liberty and Advantage of Education in the Said College notwithstanding any different Sentiments in Religion."[2]

The first class of ten students met in the house of Reverend Jonathan Dickinson, the college's first president, in Elizabethtown. Dickinson died soon after taking office and was succeeded by the Reverend Aaron Burr, Sr., who moved the college to his parsonage in Newark, where it remained for the next eight years.

The first known mention of the library occurred on September 26, 1750, when the Board of Trustees "ordered that the President be allowed to Apply Certain Donations in his and Mrs. Woodruff's hands, to procure a book-case for the Use of the College."[3]

When the trustees decided to move the college to a place more convenient to eastern Pennsylvania, two towns, New Brunswick and "Princetown," were proposed. The trustees stipulated that the town chosen would have to donate 1,000 pounds New Jersey money, ten acres for a college campus, and two hundred acres of woodland to provide fuel. While New Brunswick was initially selected, Princeton eventually won out by convincing the trustees of its superior location. In 1752 they voted to locate the college at Princeton, and the move occurred in 1756. The college then had about seventy students.

In 1750 Territorial Governor Jonathan Belcher provided that his personal library be given to the college. He died in 1757, shortly after the completion of Nassau Hall, where the library was located after the move to Princeton. His bequest included 248 books (474 volumes), listed by size. Theology comprised a third, history a fourth, belle-lettres a fifth and law seven percent of the collection.[4]

On September 27, 1759, at the first meeting of the trustees after the newly appointed president, Samuel Davies, had arrived, they asked him to compile and publish a catalog of the college's library. The catalog which was printed four months later listed nearly 1,300 volumes and was one of the earliest library catalogs printed in America. It was used to solicit gifts for the library.[5]

In 1768 the Reverend Dr. John Witherspoon of Paisley, Scotland became president of the college and brought with him several hundred volumes, the gifts of friends. Later, when the college's straitened finances forced him to make frequent excursions to Britain for aid, he usually returned with books for the library.

Witherspoon not only brought back books; he also returned with the college's first librarian, Hugh Sim, whom he recommended as a person well qualified to serve as "librarian and inspector of rooms."[6] Sim was appointed at a yearly salary of five pounds. However, he was replaced in 1770 by William Huston, who served until 1786. Between 1786 and 1796 the college had four successive librarians, and no one held the office between 1796 and 1804.[7]

The library was essentially a circulating collection; only the college trustees were permitted to use books in the building. The circulation rules in 1770 provided that, "the librarian or his deputy were required to be in regular attendance twice in every week for the space of one hour for delivering the books to the students, who shall be allowed one book at a time."[8] In 1794 the hours of opening were reduced and the library was open only one day a week at noon.

The college suffered heavily during the Revolutionary War. Being on the main highway between New York and Philadelphia and in the path of both armies, the library was especially subject to the vandalism of war. Nassau Hall was despoiled by friend and foe alike, being used at times as a prison, stable, barracks and hospital. Library books were carried away wholesale by soldiers of Cornwallis; some were recovered as far away as South Carolina.[9]

In view of the war losses sustained by the college, the legislature in 1796 appropriated 1,800 pounds to the college for the "repairing of buildings and the increases of the library." The college itself inaugurated a student fee for the use of the library.

Despite its war losses, the library grew from the 1,282 volumes listed in the 1760 catalog to some 3,000 volumes by the end of the century. But war was not the only peril it faced. In 1802 a fire gutted Nassau Hall, destroying the library collection. Through the response of donors the collection was rebuilt, and by 1827 it had 7,000 volumes. Soon after the fire of 1802, the library was reestablished in Stanhope Hall, which was completed in 1803.

On the whole the first half of the nineteenth century brought the library little more than its new quarters. "The library was entirely inadequate throughout Carnahan's administration (James Carnahan, President, 1823–1854), and there seems to have been no attempt to make the few thousand volumes housed in Stanhope Hall the tools for undergraduate work. Students were admitted twice a week to take out a book if they could find anything of interest among (in the words of one student referring to the collection) "the dusty tomes—mostly polemical and controversial."[10] During this period the collection grew slowly. In 1839 there were 8,000 volumes; 9,131 in 1856, and 14,000 in 1868.[11]

Because of their limited access to the college library, students during the antebellum period turned more to the libraries of the student literary societies that flourished on the campus, especially the American Whig Society and the Cliosophic Society. "Fortunately, the boy who was discouraged by the shelf after shelf of theological works in the main library had only to climb the stairs to Clio Hall or Whig Hall to find more interesting reading. Here were hundreds of books which a boy could really enjoy. . . ."[12] In 1848 Charles C. Jewett, the Librarian of the Smithsonian Institution, undertook a national survey of library resources. He identified 142 student libraries in northern colleges with a total of 254,000 volumes, compared with 126 official college libraries with a total of 582,912 volumes; some colleges such as Princeton had more than one student library.[13]

The college library remained in Stanhope Hall until 1860, when it was returned to Nassau Hall, this time to larger quarters in the rear wing created as part of the building's restoration after another fire in 1855. In 1873, during the administration of President James McCosh, the library acquired a building of its own, the Chancellor Green Library. The building was donated by John Cleve Green, one of the college's principal benefactors, and named for his brother, Henry Woodhull Green of the class of 1820.

During the McCosh presidency the first professional librarian was engaged. Frederick Vinton of the Library of Congress brought with him long years of experience and wide acquaintance with books. With the completion of the new building and the transfer of the books from Nassau Hall, Vinton went to work to arrange, classify and catalog them. The modest collection of 14,000 books in 1868 grew rapidly to 25,000 in 1873, 60,000 in 1883 and 81,000 in 1884, a rate of increase unknown in earlier years.[14]

Vinton spent the years 1877 to 1884 preparing a subject catalog of the library's holdings,[15] one of the most scholarly and useful publications of its kind up to that time. Despite ill health, he was a man of great energy and devotion to his profession. He was one of the small group who founded the American Library Association in 1876.

In the meantime, changes were taking place in the library which were transforming it from a storage place for books into the very heart of the college, a center for undergraduate study and faculty research. It became necessary to add more reading tables, card files and shelves. The students, no longer content to depend entirely on textbooks for their reading, were demanding volumes of literature, history and philosophy. In 1888–89 the circulation was 16,939; by 1893–94 it had grown to 22,271.[16] The experiment of opening the library from eight o'clock in the morning until dark proved so successful that Ernest Cushing Richardson, who succeeded Vinton, predicted that if lights were installed students would come even in the evening.[17]

With library activity accelerating as the century moved toward its close, the Chancellor Green Library reached its limits and the new Pyne Library, the sesquicentennial gift of Mrs. Percy Rivington Pyne, was constructed in 1897. The old library, however continued to be used for library purposes. Together, the two buildings had a capacity of 1,250,000 volumes.[18] In the 1920s crowding again began to be a problem. In 1944 President Harold W. Dodd and Julian P. Boyd, the university librarian, invited representatives of fifteen institutions which were planning to construct new library buildings when materials became available after World War II, to meet in Princeton to share their experience and ideas. This group, meeting in various places during the next several years, became the Cooperative Committee on Library Building Plans and had an important influence on the revolution in academic library architecture that took place at that time.

In Princeton, the tangible result of this planning was the Harvey S. Firestone Library, constructed in 1948. Firestone was planned as the largest open-stack library in the world, a teaching library that would bring students, faculty and books together in ways that would encourage learning, intensive scholarship and casual browsing. With more than 2,000 seats dispersed throughout the stacks and in several reading rooms, the plan achieved a functional commingling of reader and collection space. Firestone became a model for other library buildings throughout the country. The Firestone Library has been expanded four times since its original construction, most recently in 1988, when a 50,000 square foot addition was completed.

Today, if you stand just inside the FitzRandolph Gates at Princeton University, you will behold a spectacle not to be seen on any other American campus. You will see all five of the buildings that have housed Princeton's library through two and a half centuries; Nassau Hall, Stanhope, Chancellor Green, Pyne, and Firestone, all save the last filling roles for which they were not originally designed, a testament to the changing scope of the academic library over the centuries.

From its original 474 books donated by Governor Belcher, Princeton's library has grown to a collection of five million volumes. They includes 2.2 million monographs, and 1.5 million bound journals, approximately ten million manuscript items, and smaller holdings of prints and coins, as well as phonograph records, microforms, maps and various other artifacts, including a collection of death masks.

While the Firestone Library is the dominant element in Princeton's library system, it houses only two-thirds of all items cataloged. There are also 19 smaller subject libraries, in close proximity to relevant departments, for the convenience of users and to encourage the greatest possible integration of teaching, learning and research.

There are a number of fields in which Princeton's collections are unusually rich. These include art and archeology, classics, medieval and Renaissance studies, English and American literature, American and European history, population research, East Asian studies, Near Eastern studies, mathematics, physics and plasma physics.

Rutgers University

Princeton's sister colonial institution was established by royal charter in 1766 as Queen's College (now Rutgers, The State University of New Jersey), the eighth institution of higher learning founded in the colonies before the Revolution. Although the college was established by members of the Dutch Reformed Church, it was neither owned by the church nor subject to its ecclesiastical control. The college was named in honor of Charlotte of Mecklenburg, the Royal Consort.

The first classes opened in 1771 in a tavern, the Sign of the Red Lion, in what is now downtown New Brunswick. Frederick Frelinghuysen, an 18-year-old graduate of Princeton, was named the first tutor. The first two decades were as turbulent for the college as they were for the nation. Queen's College was located in one of the principal theaters of the Revolutionary War; faculty and students often were forced to flee to neighboring villages, and many interrupted their studies for military service.

Early records are so meager that it is doubtful if the library's origins can be established.[19] The library collection was probably drawn from the private collections of the Dutch scholars who taught the first students. There is no reference to any book collection or room in the first college building. There is a record that during the college's wartime migrations books were kept in an "old chest" and a closet. Meager though those resources were, they were supplemented by the book collections of the Athenian Society and later, in 1811, of the Calleopean Literary Society, two student literary societies modeled on the Clio Society at Princeton.

The patron of the library at Queens College was Reverend Peter Leydt, class of 1782, whose life had been close to the college. His father, the Reverend John Leydt, had been influential in its founding, and his brother Matthew was the first graduate. In his will in 1791 Peter Leydt bequeathed all his Latin, Greek and Hebrew books to the trustees of Queen's College.[20]

The college had difficulty recovering from the havoc created by the Revolution. From 1785 to 1809, and from 1816 to 1825, it closed down completely. When it reopened in 1825, it had two new assets: a new name, Rutgers College, and a building, whose cornerstone had been laid in 1809. The new name honored Colonel Henry Rutgers of New York, a prominent leader of the Dutch Reformed Church and a wealthy philanthropist. Colonel Rutgers contributed a bell for Queen's Tower valued at $200 (now rung only on festive occasions) and a $5,000 trust fund.

With the completion of the building, the library, which was advertised in 1814 as "considerable,"[21] was given a new home. The books were under the care of a student in the Theological Seminary of the Dutch Reformed Church, who kept the library open only on Saturday mornings from 8:30 to 9:00, similar to the provisions made for student use at Princeton.

In 1825 two new literary societies, Peithessophian and Philoclean, were founded shortly after the re-establishment of the college as Rutgers. They zealously built their libraries, which before many years outstripped the college library in size. Featuring current works of literature, biography, history and travel, as well as important periodicals, they provided a basis for a very different kind of intellectual experience from that offered by the curriculum. Through them the students enhanced their knowledge of literature and contemporary affairs and acquired tastes and values not to be found in their formal studies. It was only near the close of the nineteenth century that books of the literary societies and the main college library were united.

From 1830 to 1860 the library operated under conditions that were far from ideal. A new set of rules was adopted in 1835 providing for the appointment of a faculty member as librarian. It was his assignment to arrange the books in proper order, maintain registers of loans and acquisitions, and serve borrowers during the limited time that the library was open. Members of the faculty held virtually unlimited borrowing privileges, while students were restricted as to the number of volumes they might borrow. Each student paid one dollar semi-annually "for the use and increase of the library." When Professor Alexander McClelland took charge in 1835, he found the books in complete disorder. Methodically he arranged all the volumes into ten classes, each in a separate portion of the shelves.[22]

From 1807, when the Theological Seminary of the Dutch Reformed Church was founded, until 1857 the college library and the Seminary library were arranged as one collection. In 1857 the Seminary split from the college when it acquired its own campus just north of the college and built its own building, Hertzog Hall. This building had its own library room. The books in the Queen's building were then divided; those belonging to the Seminary, or especially appropriate to it, were transferred to Hertzog Hall, to remain there until eighteen years later when a separate building was completed. It is now the Sage Library of the New Brunswick Theological Seminary.

The Rutgers College Library, thus reduced, remained in the Queen's building. In 1871 it was still open only a very limited time, from 3:00 to 4:30 p.m. on Fridays. In the 1870s money from the estate of Sophie Astley Kirkpatrick became available, and the college decided to build a chapel in her honor. Half of this building was set aside for the library. The building was dedicated in December 1873. In 1877 a student assistant was hired to keep the library open for two and a half hours each weekday and two hours on Saturdays.

By 1882 there were 10,000 books. Two years later a young man of the class of 1881, Irving Stone Upson, became the first full-time librarian.[23] While faculty members had hitherto spent some time occasionally on library duties, Upson brought the library to a new level of effectiveness. He and President Merrill Gates induced the Board of Trustees to increase the library's book allotment, and by 1890 the collection had grown to more than 26,000 volumes.[24] During his tenure as librarian Upson also filled the role of registrar.

Gradually, space in the Kirkpatrick Chapel became inadequate; books were behind one another on shelves and stacked on the floor. Their proper use was impeded, and service to students was inadequate. The need for a new library was brought to the attention of Mr. and Mrs. Ralph Voorhees, and in 1902 they offered $20,000 for the erection of a library building. Plans were drawn by Henry Rutgers Marshall, who designed a stone structure in keeping with the Queen's building. The costs proved to be greater than the gift originally announced, and the benefactors increased their donation to cover the increased costs, and increased it again when costs continued to mount. In November 1903 the Voorhees Library was dedi-

cated. Forty-six thousand volumes were moved into the new building, beginning a new era of library service at Rutgers.

In 1905 Irving Upson became the college's registrar and secretary
to the faculty. Acting Librarian George A. Osborn, who had become Upson's assistant just before his graduation from the college
in 1897, succeeded him as librarian in 1907.[25]

The library grew rapidly during the early years of Osborn's administration. The collection tripled between 1907 and 1922, expanding beyond the capacity of the building and requiring an addition
which was built in 1923.

Osborn served as librarian for thirty-seven years. During much
of his administration he was handicapped by an inadequate book
budget, small staff and an inadequate building. Toward the end of
his tenure the university turned its attention to scholarly activity
and recognized that it must enlarge the library to meet the needs of
growing graduate instruction. Expansion was delayed, however, by
the advent of World War II.

In 1952 and 1953, a new library building was proposed by Governor Alfred E. Driscoll and approved by the legislature. In November 1956 the new Rutgers University Library was dedicated, now
the Archibald Stephens Alexander Library, named to honor a long-
time member of the Board of Governors. The six-story building had
a capacity of 1,500,000 volumes and room for 1,000 readers. A major
expansion was recently undertaken, and in 1994 a large addition was
dedicated which enlarged the library by a third to over 200,000
square feet.

Mabel Smith Douglass Library

Across town from the Alexander Library is the Mabel Smith
Douglass Library of Douglass College. Douglass is the largest
women's college in the United States. Established as the New Jersey
College for Women in 1918, it was renamed in 1955 for Douglass,
who cooperated with the New Jersey Federation of Women's Clubs
in making the case for an institution of higher education for women
in New Jersey and who became the college's first dean. When the
trustees of Rutgers assented to the establishment of a women's college, they specified that it was not to be located on the Rutgers campus. The college was expected to secure its own buildings and funds
for maintenance and its own faculty. Rutgers library facilities, however, were to be available for its use.

The library of the New Jersey College for Women library began
in an old brownstone mansion known as College Hall, as did many
of the departments of the college. Here in 1918 a few books lent by

the Rutgers Library were placed on the desk of the registrar, who kept a record of loans on a slip of paper. From this desk the library expanded to a shelf, then to a locked closet. Library hours were whenever there was someone present to unlock the door. Later the closet was left unlocked, and the students kept the record of books borrowed on a card in the closet.

During its first few years the library seems to have had little appeal. Dean Douglass spoke of seeking a librarian of such personality that she could endow the library with an atmosphere that the girls would prefer of an evening to that of the movies. Although some of the students went to the Rutgers library, the library at the college was little used, as one of the early students remarked, except as a refuge from a noisy dormitory and by two commuting students who habitually awaited train-time there. As with Princeton and Rutgers, the early library was anything but a center of learning for the college community.

In May 1958 the legislature appropriated one million dollars for a library to be located on the Douglass campus. In April 1961 the new library was dedicated. Ada English, who was the librarian of the college for many years, had worked throughout her career at the college for this cause.

In 1975 the library was expanded by an addition. At the dedication ceremony William Dix, librarian of the Princeton University Library, noted that "this library is large enough to allow considerable 'exploitation,' yet small enough to permit easy browsing. It can remain conveniently small, backed as it is by the resources of the Alexander Library and the shared resources of the country to which we shall all have increasing access."[26]

The Rutgers library system is now a network of eighteen units, holding some 3 million volumes, with 23,993 periodical subscriptions and 2.5 million documents and adds more than 100,000 volumes to its collection each year, making it one of the nation's leading research libraries.

State College Libraries in New Jersey

New Jersey's state colleges begun as normal schools in the mid–nineteenth century to train teachers to staff the state's burgeoning school system. Gradually they have grown into a network of institutions that provide a broad range of curricular choices to New Jersey's students, and their libraries have grown to serve the changing needs of these academic communities.

Free public schools were established by an act of the legislature in April 1846. Dr. Theodore F. King, a physician from Perth

Amboy, was then appointed Superintendent of Public Instruction. In June 1849, at the Somerset County Courthouse in Somerville, the first teacher institute was held, led by two brothers, Charles and Joshua Saunders, both experienced teachers; about thirty teachers attended. Other institutes followed which provided training in the city in which the teachers were to serve.

A more regular pattern of teacher education began to develop and more permanent institutions called "normal schools" were established. One of the first in the country was the New Jersey State Normal School at Trenton, which opened in October 1855 in a temporary building with fifteen students registered. The Newark City Normal School operated from 1857 to 1913, when the state acquired its facilities for a state normal school. The same pattern was followed in other cities. The Normal School in Jersey City, founded in 1862, was transferred to the state in 1929; the Paterson City Normal School, established in 1855, was transferred in 1923. Elizabeth had a normal school from 1888 to 1917, but the state did not adopt it.

There were six normal schools in New Jersey in 1945 when responsibility for their support and administration was assumed by the State Board of Education[27] In the half-century that followed they grew from small teacher training institutions into colleges with broad missions and much greater resources. In 1945 only two of the schools were accredited; enrollments were so small that pressure was exerted to close two of them; the curricular offerings were narrow, and the faculty was underpaid. The state colleges are now vastly different. One of them, Montclair, has recently become Montclair State University.

Trenton State College

The first New Jersey state normal school, the ninth in the nation, was founded by the legislature in 1855 as the New Jersey State Normal School and Model School. It was designed initially to train elementary school teachers. In 1925 it began to train secondary school teachers as well, granting its first bachelor of science degree in 1926. In 1929 its name was changed to the State Teachers College and Normal School at Trenton; it became State Teachers College, Trenton, in 1937; and Trenton State College in 1958. These successive name changes reflect the changing role and mission of the institution. In 1947 the college awarded its first master's degrees in education.

The library of the New Jersey State Normal School and Model School in Trenton opened in the school's temporary quarters in 1855. By the close of the second year it had 3,762 volumes. After the purchase of a building for the school, plans were made to provide library and gymnasium space on the second floor.

In 1930 the college acquired its present 200-acre campus in Ewing Township and erected a library building in March 1932. Extensive remodeling was done in 1960–61, and an addition to the building was completed in 1969–70. When plans for the addition were proposed the temptation was great to make a new start and to move the library facilities to a different location. In the end the director of the library, Dr. Felix Hirsch, proposed a plan to use all available money to build a large annex. The plan was accepted and the result was a much larger building complex than could have been achieved otherwise with limited funds. The library, containing over 500,000 volumes, is named for Roscoe L. West, who served as president of the college from 1930 to 1957.

William Paterson College

William Paterson College was founded in 1855 as a city institution training teachers for the newly established public schools in Paterson. One of the pioneer city training schools, the college by the 1890s offered a two-year course. In 1923 it became a state normal school under the supervision of the State Board of Education. In 1937 it became the State Teachers College at Paterson, having offered a three-year program since 1929 and a four-year program since 1935. However, the college's physical facilities did not keep pace with its curriculum; as late as 1945 it was housed on the second floor of a fifty-year-old condemned public school.

In 1951 the college moved from School #24 in Paterson to a 217-acre campus in nearby Wayne. It was authorized to offer a master of science in education program in 1955. It changed its name to Paterson State College in 1958, began conferring bachelor of arts and master of arts degrees in 1960. And it changed its name to William Paterson College of New Jersey in 1965.

The 1922 catalog of Paterson City Normal School did not mention any room or facility set aside in School #24 for a library. A pamphlet published by the Student Government Association in 1934 mentions that the library was organized in the spring of 1924 by collecting 1,500 books from different classrooms. During the first year approximately $150 was spent for books and subscriptions to eight periodicals and one newspaper. By 1934 the library contained about 11,000 volumes, with a collection of 8,000 pictures available to the students for their practice teaching. A second room and space for stacks and a circulation desk were added in 1935.

After the college moved to Wayne in 1951 the library was housed on the second floor of the administration building, the former Hobart Manor, until a separate library building was constructed in 1956. The library director at the time was Juliette Trainor.

The library was moved in June, the students assisting by carrying all the books from the second floor of the administration building directly to the stacks of the new building, on which they were placed in proper order under the supervision of librarians and faculty members. At the time of the move the resources of the library consisted of 25,000 adult books and 3,500 children's books, 2,000 pamphlets, and other education material of various kinds. The library subscribed to 250 periodicals.

The new library seemed quite spacious in 1956, when the student body numbered 823, already above the maximum enrollment of 750 full-time students for which the building was planned.[28] It was located in the center of a broad expanse of lawn, on one side overlooking Paterson, Bergen County and the New York skyline.

The staff in 1966 consisted of eleven professional librarians and seven clerical workers, supplemented by a large number of student assistants. The total budget for 1965–66 was $45,000. The library, which had been adequate in 1956, was filled to overflowing with books and users by 1965. A bond issue in 1964 made possible a new building and audio-visual center. While planning for the new building the staff began converting its bibliographic records from the Dewey Decimal to the Library of Congress classification system. This decision anticipated a directive from the state, issued in 1975, that called for all state colleges to reclassify their collections. The new building was completed in 1967, and the old library was then converted to administrative offices. In 1992 the library expanded its building by the addition of 40,000 square feet. The library has been named the Sarah B. Askew Library in honor of the first director of the state's Public Library Commission.

In 1966, when the college admitted its first class of liberal arts students, the book collection consisted of 88,750 volumes. To serve the students it was necessary to expand and augment the collection rapidly. Ideas from the faculty were sought as the library responded to the changing educational landscape. By the end of the 1971–72 academic year the collection had grown to 180,000 volumes, including extensive back files of periodicals which had been acquired. Substantial growth has continued, and the library now consists of more than 307,000 volumes.

The William Paterson College Library has been in the lead in the adoption of automation and interlibrary cooperation. In 1972–73 it was one of two colleges to participate in the experimental CAPTAIN cooperative ordering and cataloging system located at Rutgers University; it participated for four years before the system was disbanded.

Kean College

The Newark Normal School, founded by the city's Board of Education in 1855, became a state two-year normal school in 1913, when it moved to new quarters at 187 Broadway in north Newark. It began to offer a three-year program in 1929, started a master of science in education program in 1947, and was authorized to grant bachelor of arts and master of arts degrees in 1960.

In 1937 the name of the college was changed to Newark State Teachers College; in 1958, when the institution moved from Newark to a 120-acre campus in Union, the name Newark State College was adopted; and finally, in 1973, the name Kean College of New Jersey was chosen. The college is located on the former estate of Hamilton Fish Kean, whose family had been active in New Jersey's social, political and cultural life since the Revolution.

The library building on the new campus, the Nancy Thompson Library, was dedicated in September 1959. Typical of the state colleges of this period, collection growth and increased enrollment soon made the library building obsolete, and a new building was constructed and dedicated in April 1969. A 16,000 square foot addition was built in 1996.

The library administered the college's Audio-Visual Center until 1972, when the Center was separated from it, although it continues to be housed in the same building. The Nancy Thompson Library now has a collection of over 250,000 volumes. Among its special collections are the papers of former Congresswoman Florence P. Dwyer.

Rowan College

New Jersey established two two-year normal schools in 1923, one in Glassboro and the other in Paterson, the latter being transferred from local to state administration. This action resulted from a 1912 study ordered by Commissioner of Education Calvin Kendall, who believed that New Jersey should not be dependent on other states to staff its schools. In 1917, a group of one hundred and seven Glassboro residents raised over $7,000 to buy twenty-five acres of the Hollybush land tract, which they offered to the state if a college were located in their town. This show of support and the natural beauty of the site convinced the state site selection committee.

The college became a four-year degree-granting institution in

1935. It adopted the name New Jersey State Teachers College at Glassboro in 1937. It changed its name to Glassboro State College in 1958, the year it was accredited by the Middle States Association; it assumed its present name in 1992, when it received a large endowment from Henry and Betty Rowan.

The college's library originally occupied two rooms on the second floor of College Hall, its administrative and classroom building, and consisted of 232 volumes. Its physical expansion was limited to two more offices until its own building was completed in 1956. By that time the collection was forty-thousand volumes. These were years of growth for Glassboro, and it was soon necessary to provide additional library space. In 1963 a new building was built, the Savitz Learning Resource Center, named after Jerohn J. Savitz, who was the president of the college from 1923 to 1937. The old library was then converted to administrative space. In 1968 a new floor was added to the library, increasing available space by 19,000 square feet.

In February 1995 a new 118,000 square foot building was opened, replacing the Savitz Learning Resource Center, and currently houses over 350,000 volumes. The library holds several outstanding special collections. In 1948 a collection of New Jersey history was willed to the college by Frank Stewart, a prominent Philadelphia businessman. This is one of the largest collections of Jerseyana in the state, including rare books, colonial documents and genealogical materials. The South Jersey Educational Improvement Materials Center, consisting of specialized audio-visual materials of interest to student-teachers and schools, is also located in the library.

Jersey City State College

One of the youngest of the New Jersey state colleges, Jersey City State College was founded in 1929 as the New Jersey State Normal School at Jersey City with two curricula, elementary and kindergarten education. It added health education and nursing in 1936 and a general curriculum in 1941–42. It changed its name to Jersey City State College in 1958. The college is the only one of the state colleges that remains in a large city, although a number of them began there. Its campus of fourteen acres is the smallest of all the state college campuses.

Beginning in 1959 the college began to offer a master of science degree in education for elementary school teachers; degrees of bachelor of arts and master of arts have been offered since 1960. The A. Harry Moore Laboratory School which was acquired in 1962, is one of the few demonstration schools for the mentally retarded and physically handicapped in the United States.

When the institution opened, the library consisted of two rooms in Hepburn Hall, which seated seventy-five and had a shelving capacity of 3,500 volumes. An expansion of the library into two floors was accomplished by 1954, increasing the shelving capacity to 50,000 volumes. In 1968, a new administration-classroom-library building was completed, providing relief from the crowding which occurred since the last expansion of facilities. The library now has some 245,000 volumes. It is named in honor of Forrest Atlee Irwin, a former president of the college.

Stockton and Ramapo Colleges

In 1958 the New Jersey Board of Higher Education recommended the creation of two new state colleges, one to be established in the northern part of New Jersey and the other in the southern part of the state. The aim was to create facilities in areas of high demand in order to permit students to live at home and commute to school.

A three-hundred acre wooded site was selected in the foothills of the Ramapo mountains in Bergen County, close to the New York state border. Ramapo State College opened in September 1971. Barrier-free buildings with exterior glass walls which reflect the wooded setting are a dominant feature of the campus.

The college's programs emphasize liberal arts, business, and other professional studies. Faculty members and students are organized in schools which focus on broad interdisciplinary themes: American and international studies, contemporary arts, social sciences and human services, theoretical and applied sciences, and administration and business.

The library of over 130,000 volumes is housed today in a centrally located four-story building. In designing the structure an overriding concern was to provide easy access to the library and its resources. Key elements of the library program, reference and circulation, are located on the main floor. Seating at tables is dispersed among the reference stacks, index tables, circulating collection, government documents collection and the periodical level to facilitate use of library materials.

Special facilities in the building include two seminar rooms, one of which has been converted into a Resource Center for Holocaust and Genocide Studies; a preview room, which also serves as the library's instruction classroom; a special services room for disabled students; a computer terminal room; a typing room; and a gallery for special exhibits.

Richard Stockton State College was founded in 1969 and named for Richard Stockton, a New Jersey signer of the Declaration of Independence. The college was located in Galloway Township on a 1,600-acre campus. The first students were enrolled in 1971.

Construction delays almost prevented the college from opening on time. Classes were held in the Mayflower Hotel in Atlantic City; the library was initially located in the dining room. Actually the college had more room for administrative space and recreational areas at the hotel than it would later have during the first phase of campus building.

In addition to the book collection, which now has some 237,000 volumes, Stockton maintains an extensive media center housing films, video-cassettes, filmstrips and audio tapes. A library of more than eight thousand slides forms a resource for faculty and student slide presentations. Situated on the fringes of the New Jersey Pinelands Reserve, the library maintains an extensive collection of material pertaining to the southern New Jersey area.

Other State Facilities

Montclair State University

The second state college in New Jersey opened in 1908 as a two-year normal school in Montclair. It has been noted for emphasizing the academic preparation of its students rather than concentrating on teaching methods.[29] Beginning in 1927 it trained secondary school teachers exclusively and had the reputation of being particularly strong in music, mathematics and foreign languages.

In 1929 the school changed its name to the New Jersey State Teachers College at Montclair. It granted its first master of arts degree in 1932 and was accredited by the Middle States Association of College and Secondary Schools in 1937. It was called Montclair State College from 1958 until its recent change to Montclair State University in 1995. Beginning in 1958 its academic emphasis has been more strongly on the arts and sciences.

The first library established in the school was far from adequate. The state provided the textbooks requested by the faculty, but the time lag between the requisition and appropriation for supplementary reading was such that many faculty members lent their own books to students for their assignments.[30] A survey in 1917 reported that the library occupied a room only 32 by 60 feet, and it expressed regret that, small as it was, the reference collection included duplicate copies. During the 1930s under the leadership of President

Harry A. Sprague, steps were taken to relieve the overcrowding by converting an auditorium into a reading room.

In 1963 a new library building was completed and named the Sprague Library. In 1973 a 15,000 square foot expansion was added. Twenty years later the building proved far too small for the school's needs, and in 1993 a 45,000 square foot addition was constructed. The Sprague Library now has some 380,000 volumes, including a number of special collections. One of these is the China Institute Library, a gift of the China Institute of New York, which contains many valuable books on Chinese philosophy, art and literature.

University of Medicine and Dentistry

The University of Medicine and Dentistry, New Jersey (UMDNJ) began in Jersey City in 1954 with the establishment of Seton Hall University's School of Medicine and Dentistry, which the state purchased in 1965. The present George F. Smith Library of the Health Sciences traces its origin to the Jersey City facility.

The UMDNJ Libraries, a statewide system, became operational in 1982–83. It now includes the Smith Library in Newark, the Robert Wood Johnson Health Sciences Library in New Brunswick, the Media Library at the Robert Wood Johnson Medical School in Piscataway, the Kennedy Memorial Hospital/University Medical Center in Stratford, and the Educational and Research Library in Camden. Cooperating libraries include the Cooper Hospital/University Medical Center in Camden and the Library of Science and Medicine, Rutgers University, in Piscataway.

New Jersey Institute of Technology

The New Jersey Institute of Technology (NJIT) started as the Newark Technical School. For most of its life it was referred to as NCE, the Newark College of Engineering. The technical complex today occupies a 34-acre campus in Newark's academic hub, which includes the Rutgers-Newark campus, the Seton Hall University Law School, and Essex Community College. NJIT's library resources are supplemented by the collections of these institutions and the Newark Public Library. The Institute's Robert W. Houten Library was relocated in 1992 to a new 50,000 square foot building. The library contains the rare book collection of Edward Weston, the inventor, with particular strength in the history of science and technology.

While the state government had given some funding to NJIT for several years, in 1996 the school became completely state supported, making it the newest addition to the state-supported system of higher education.

The New Jersey Academic Library Network

The state colleges, the University of Medicine and Dentistry, and the New Jersey Institute of Technology are tied together by the New Jersey Academic Library Network. The database for the cooperative venture consists of some 800,000 titles and 1,300,000 individual items, representing the holdings of all the member institutions, one of the largest groups of its kind in the country.

Independent College and University Libraries

Independent institutions of higher education in New Jersey began with the establishment of Princeton and Rutgers in the eighteenth century. The other independent degree-granting institutions currently operating in the state were founded during the nineteenth and twentieth centuries. From 1850 to 1900 nine were established, all but one, Rider College, under religious auspices. Three were founded by the Catholic Church, and five by Protestant denominations. In addition to the institutions described which provide a broad academic curriculum, New Jersey also is home to institutions with specialized curricula in religious studies, as well as several private proprietary schools providing training in business and technical subjects.

Seton Hall University

Seton Hall College was founded in Madison in 1856, the first Catholic diocesan college in the United States. In 1950 it became a university. Four years after its establishment, the college moved to its present location in South Orange. Its original site is now the home of the College of Saint Elizabeth.

The first half-century of the college's library were hampered by three disastrous fires, in 1866, 1886 and 1909. In 1909 students formed a hand-to-hand brigade and moved all the books to the administration building. In the early days of the library's existence there is no listing for a librarian in the college's catalogs. The catalogs do show that student librarians were selected by the three literary societies then active at the college: the Setonia, the Bayley, and the Reading Room Society.

As was common, students lived in a restricted environment. The college catalog for 1866–67 noted that "no books of any kind could be held by the students unless by permission of the President . . . students are not allowed to receive newspapers, except for their reading room, which is under the direction of the President." In 1884 the library was located in Alumni Hall on the same floor with two billiard parlors. A new library building was constructed in 1889. When the Reverend Thomas H. McLaughlin was appointed college president in 1922 he immediately showed interest in the library, and under his leadership it received its first approval from the Middle States Association in 1932. This despite the fact that when the Immaculate Conception Seminary, located at Seton Hall since 1862, was moved to Darlington in 1922 half of the Seton Hall library collection moved with it.

In 1941 the library was named the Marshall Library after the Reverend William Marshall, fifth president of the college. It expanded to occupy half of what had been an auditorium/gymnasium. In 1950 it expanded again to embrace all of the old gymnasium and the entire basement as well. The collection had grown from eight thousand volumes in 1941 to one hundred and ten thousand in 1949. While the size of the collection expanded rapidly, there were lingering questions of quality. A Middle States Association report in 1959 noted that the bulk of the collection could best be described as the result of either alumni solicitation or job lot buying.

Under the administration of the university librarian, Monsignor Murphy, the library improved in quality. In January 1955, a new library building with a capacity of more than 300,000 volumes was dedicated. In 1961 the building was named in honor of Bishop McLaughlin, the university's ninth president, who had earlier been so instrumental in improving the libary.

From 1974 to 1981 the library continued to grow and improve in quality, under the leadership of its director, Monsignor William Noe Field. Msgr. Field established strong special collections and archives in Catholic history, and was instrumental in the creation of the New Jersey Catholic Historical Records Commission at the University under the auspices of the Newark Archdiocese. When Robert Jones succeeded him as library director, Field became the University Archivist and Director of Special Collections.

Most recently, in 1994, a new 155,000 square foot library building was constructed, the Walsh Library. The combined libraries of the University now house over 400,000 volumes.

Drew University

One of the largest academic library collections in the state, now numbering 437,000 volumes, is owned by Drew University.

Founded in 1866 as Drew Theological Seminary of the United Methodist Church, the university consists of a college of liberal arts, a graduate school and a theological school.

Drew had a library before it had a faculty. Dr. John McClintock, the first president, sent a scholarly agent to Europe looking for the books that the president thought indispensable. McClintock saw the library as a "teacher's tool chest."[31] The strength of the early collection was in the fields of denominational, doctrinal and ecclesiastical literature. This established the basis for the present strong collections in subject areas such as church history, patristics and biblical archeology.

When the Rose Memorial Library opened in 1939 it was a spacious facility for a student body of less than five hundred. The building was a gift of Nellie K. and Lenox S. Rose. It was designed to hold four hundred thousand volumes, with ten times the space available in the institution's first library in 1888 and with twice the number of books the library held in 1938. In 1982 the library was renovated and expanded by the construction of a fifty-one thousand square foot addition, and the college's media center became a part of the library complex.

In 1981 the United Methodist Archives and History Center was added to the library, an acquisition that made Drew the research center for the denomination. The library is rich in the manuscripts of John Wesley and his associates and the letters and papers of the early bishops, theologians and preachers of the Methodist Church. It is particularly strong in the documents of early American Methodism, as well as the periodical and official records of the several Methodist churches. The library also contains an important collection of Black Methodism.

Centenary College

Centenary College Institute was founded in 1867 by the Newark Conference of the Methodist Episcopal Church to celebrate the one hundredth anniversary of the founding of Methodism in the United States. The earliest written accession records of the library date back to the early 1920s, when it was located in a small room on the first floor of the present Seay Administration Building. In 1954, a new library, the William H. and Mary D. Taylor Library, was constructed. Current plans include a new 4,000 square foot addition to begin construction in the summer of 1996. In line with current trends, the library is now called the Learning Resource Center. The library today consists of 58,000 volumes.

Rider University

The thunder of the Civil War was still echoing when a one-room private school specializing in business training was established in Trenton in 1865. Known as Trenton Business College, it later merged with the Stewart Business College. It became Rider College in 1921, when it broadened its curriculum and moved to a new location in the city. In 1959 the college moved to a 245-acre campus in nearby suburban Lawrenceville. The exclusive business and education curriculum was maintained until 1955; then it was gradually diversified. In 1994 the college became Rider University. Recently, Westminster Choir College in Princeton affiliated with Rider University, adding a highly regarded music program to the university's offerings.

During the early years of the college library, facilities were minimal. It was not until 1934 that Joseph W. Seay, the college's director of admissions, conceived the idea of appealing to colleges and universities, business, alumni and friends for contributions of books and money to improve the library.[32]

Response to the initial appeal was substantial; so great in fact that college officials were encouraged to believe that their goal of twenty thousand volumes might be achieved. The college administration had agreed that as soon as ten thousand volumes had been received, construction could begin on a building for the library. Remodeling and construction actually began in March 1934 on a building which was to be connected to the main college building by a ramp and was to have a capacity of twenty-five thousand volumes.

One of the events celebrating the institution's centennial year in 1965 was the dedication of a new library building, named for Franklin F. Moore, president of the college at the time and the driving force behind its relocation to Lawrenceville. The library's collection now consists of some 360,000 volumes; in addition there are some 56,000 volumes in the Talbott Library-Learning Center of Westminster Choir College.

Bloomfield College

Founded in 1868 in affiliation with the Presbyterian church, this small private college is located on a 12-acre urban campus in Bloomfield. The college has a current enrollment of over 2,100 students, many of them from minority backgrounds.

The George Talbott Hall Library, located in the center of the campus, has a current collection of over 60,000 volumes.

Fairleigh Dickinson University

Founded by Dr. Peter Sammartino, an educator, Fairleigh Dickenson Junior College opened for classes in Rutherford in September 1942, at a time when established colleges were considering closing because of the war. The first class consisted of fifty-nine female students and one male. Its library was purchased as a package from a defunct junior college and consisted of about four thousand volumes. The books were kept in one room of the building known as "the castle," the only building the college owned. A local woman volunteered her services as librarian two days a week. In appreciation the college sent a cleaning woman to her home once a week.

At the end of World War II the college grew rapidly, aided by an influx of veterans studying under the G.I. Bill of Rights. In 1948 four-year status was approved by the State Board of Education, and the name of the institution was changed to Fairleigh Dickinson College. In 1953 the assets and liabilities of Bergen Junior College in Teaneck were taken over and Fairleigh Dickinson's Teaneck campus was founded. In 1956 the State Board of Education approved university status for the college. A year later the university acquired the Florham-Madison campus, the estate of Florence Twombly, granddaughter of Commodore Cornelius Vanderbilt. It was a show place with considerable possibilities.

The library on the Madison campus opened in 1958. It is named the Friendship Library in honor of Fairleigh S. Dickinson, Jr., whose close friend, Samuel S. Silber, donated the building. The library stands on the site of the estate greenhouse. The large reading room at the front of the building was designed by the celebrated architect Stanford White. Still known as the Orangerie, it once held tropical plants and is all that remains of the original structure.

The library has special collections relating to printing and publishing. The Outdoor Advertising Association of America has designated the library as the official repository for historical material about its industry. The George H. Moss, Jr. Music and Theater Collection holds fifteen hundred pieces of sheet music, in addition to approximately two hundred and fifty catalogs. The Moss Collection provides a history of the music and theater industries from 1890 to 1950. In combination with the advertising collection it illustrates important aspects of American popular culture. The collections of the Fairleigh Dickinson libraries on both the Madison and the Teaneck-Hackensack campuses now total over 450,000 volumes.

Monmouth University

Monmouth Junior College was founded in Long Branch in 1933, one of six experimental institutions established during the Depression to improve access to education during a time of economic stress. By 1956 the college had outgrown its home in Long Branch and moved to its present Shadow Lawn location just down the road in West Long Branch. The present focus of the campus is Woodrow Wilson Hall. This ornate structure, built as a summer retreat by Theodore Parson, president of the Woolworth department store chain, was one of America's outstanding mansions. In March 1995 the college became Monmouth University.

The Guggenheim Memorial Library is located in a summer "cottage" (i.e., mansion) built by Murry and Leonie Guggenheim and donated to the college by the Guggenheim Foundation. After the building was converted to library purposes the collection grew rapidly, and in five years the shelves were filled to capacity. A donation of $625,000 from the Foundation and a grant from the federal government made possible the construction of a thirty-thousand square foot addition in 1968. In 1985 the original wing of the library was restored to its past grandeur through a bequest of one million dollars from Margaret O. Bruns to the Monmouth College Library Association. The Guggenheim Library now has some 245,000 volumes.

College of Saint Elizabeth

New Jersey's first Catholic college for women was established in Convent Station in 1899 by the Sisters of Charity. The inadequacy of the library, initially located in Santa Rita Hall, was of concern to the faculty and administration. The situation changed in 1969 when the college dedicated a new building named in honor of Sister Hildegard Marie Mahoney, who served for seventeen years as president of the college. The building was funded by private donations and by the 1963 federal Higher Education Facilities Act. It now has a collection of 187,000 volumes.

Georgian Court College

Georgian Court College is a four-year Catholic college for women situated on the north shore of Lake Carasaljo in Lakewood. It was founded in 1908 by the Sisters of Mercy of New Jersey as Mount Saint Mary College in North Plainfield. A growing student body forced it to relocate. In 1924, when Georgian Court, the Jay Gould estate in Lakewood, became available, the Sisters of Mercy purchased it for a new campus. Gould stipulated that the estate name be kept, and thus Mount Saint Mary became Georgian Court College. The 152–acre estate included four principal buildings, to which seven other buildings have been added over the years. The construction included the Farly Memorial Library, which was dedicated in 1951. In 1975 a new wing was added to the library, doubling its capacity. A new library building was constructed and opened in 1993. The collection has over 150,000 volumes.

Saint Peter's College

The charter for Saint Peter's College in Jersey City was granted by the New Jersey Legislature in 1872. However, the first class did not convene until September 1879 and the first commencement was not until 1889. The billboard in front of the college on Kennedy Boulevard says simply, "Saint Peter's College: New Jersey Jesuit College." The library collection which now totals 320,000 volumes is housed in the Theresa and Edward O'Toole Library, completed in 1967.

Caldwell College

Caldwell College for Women, a Catholic institution founded by the Sisters of Saint Dominic, opened in 1939. Its library, originally created to serve the sisters wherever they were studying, predated the establishment of the college by many years. The library also served high school students attending Mount Saint Dominic's Academy.

The collection, housed in the old Academy building, was primitive. Cataloging was non-existent or was confined to minimum author and title entries. The early librarians were untrained, and their duties consisted primarily of keeping track of the books that were borrowed.

With the construction of Rosary Hall in 1929, an era of improvements began. A room was designed for the library and plans were made to staff it with a certified librarian. The building was completed in 1931, and the librarian, not yet trained, faced the task of moving and organizing eight thousand books, largely unaccessioned, unclassified and uncataloged.

In June 1939 the Sister Librarian was told that the college would open in September. She was to go to Washington for professional training and remain there until her courses were complete. She did so and arrived back at the college in the spring of 1940 fully accredited.

The small size of the collection was a source of distress. Visitors admired the quality of what there was, but deplored the quantity. Funds for the purchase of books were scarce. As the student body grew, funds became more available and the size of the collection increased. With this came concern for space. "Inasmuch as there is but a limited amount of space for expansion in our library, it is our aim to proceed with systematic weeding until the quality of our book collection will partially make up for what it lacks in numbers."[33] This problem was solved by the construction of a new library in 1952. In 1992 a substantial addition of 32,000 square feet was constructed, including a multi-media center and a theater, and the building was renamed the Jennings Library in honor of the former college president, Vivien Jennings. The collection currently consists of 107,000 volumes.

Stevens Institute of Technology

During the 1960s many new academic libraries were constructed in New Jersey. One of these was the Samuel C. Williams Library at the Stevens Institute of Technology in Hoboken, which has over 100,000 volumes. The library also contains the Stevens Computer Center. The building's lobby is graced by a specially designed mobile contributed by its creator, Alexander Calder, class of 1919. The library's special collections include the Leonardo DaVinci collection, one of the finest collections of DaVinci prints, manuscripts in facsimile and books in the Western Hemisphere. Another special collection contains original manuscripts, drawings, artifacts and books by and about Frederick Winslow Taylor, class of 1893, pioneer in the theory of scientific management.

Felician College

Felician College is a small Catholic-affiliated institution established in 1942. It has an enrollment of about a thousand students, offers courses in education, the liberal arts and nursing, and is located in Lodi. The library currently consists of 113,000 volumes.

Community College Libraries

Higher education in early New Jersey was the province of a fortunate few. Until the mid–nineteenth century there were only Princeton and Rutgers. After 1855 came gradual expansion of educational opportunities, as the state normal schools and private colleges were created and eventually expanded into four-year programs and post-graduate programs to meet the demands of the economy for an increasingly well-trained work force and the demands of the population for more opportunity to participate in the economic expansion. Along with the growth of private institutions and the state college and university system to meet this increased demand has come the development of the two-year community college, to enlarge educational opportunity even further.

Community colleges in New Jersey serve the most heterogeneous student population in the academic world. Open admission to the institution, liberal admission policies throughout the curriculum, and vigorous recruitment among such disparate groups as the elderly, the disadvantaged, minorities, high school seniors (and juniors), and workers in need of retraining, create an "open door" to the world of higher education. The community college also serves as a point of entry for students who need to reduce educational costs by living at home and matriculating at a community college for two years before entering a four-year college. New Jersey's community colleges serve more than half the freshman and sophomores in the state. They offer a total of 145 separate programs that range from computer information systems to literature.

Grassroots support of public two-year colleges and the speed with which they opened in the 1960s were a direct result of conditions caused by the state's previous reluctance to support a widespread system of public higher education. There was an acute need for more college spaces in general and for technical-level occupational preparation in particular. Recognition of these needs led to the passage of the County College Act of 1962, committing state funds for the support of community colleges.

The forerunners of community colleges in New Jersey were the junior colleges, of which the first, Newark Junior College, was established by the Newark Board of Education. Classes met in South Side High School and used the high school's library collection and the ample resources of the Newark Public Library. The college ceased operation in 1922 because of financial difficulties. That same year Rider College became the first non-public college in the state to offer a two-year curriculum. In 1927 the College of South Jersey in Camden opened primarily as a two-year feeder to the South Jersey Law School. In 1929 Centenary College for Women opened, the first college to offer two-year programs exclusively.

The idea of publicly supported two-year colleges had been discussed since the 1930s, when a federal Emergency Administration (ERA) had funded six junior colleges in New Jersey. Establishing these colleges created jobs for unemployed college teachers. It also took young people off the job market and kept them busy. All but two of these colleges were phased out with the end of ERA funds. Monmouth Junior College and Union College are the two survivors.

In 1946, in an attempt to accommodate World War II veterans, the state passed legislation permitting municipalities to create two-year colleges. Bayonne and Jersey City established two-year units, and Rutgers established off-campus centers at Atlantic City, Englewood, Morristown, Trenton and West New York. All of these schools were discontinued when the rush of veterans subsided.

The library facilities at these early institutions were minimal. The situation at Monmouth Junior College was probably typical. The college began at the Long Branch High School in 1933 and was open each school day at 4:00 p.m. The high school generously permitted the junior college students to use the school library. The Monmouth County Library placed several hundred books at the college's disposal on long-term loan. Faculty members lent or donated books from their personal collections. One of the first full-time appointments to the Monmouth Junior College staff was a librarian, Isabel Cubberly.

Higher education in the early post-war years in New Jersey was characterized by the predominance of privately supported institutions, a mass exodus of students to out-of-state colleges, minimal state financial support, and the policy that students should be responsible for financing their own college education. Once legislation was passed in 1962, the establishment of a public, broad-based community college system of higher education was rapid. In the four years that followed, county boards of freeholders throughout New Jersey moved with unprecedented speed to carry out feasibility studies and establish community colleges. By 1966 two-year colleges had opened in Atlantic, Ocean, Cumberland and Middlesex counties. Fifteen additional county community colleges are now in operation in Bergen, Monmouth, Burlington, Camden, Essex, Gloucester, Hudson, Mercer, Morris, Passaic, Somerset, Salem, Sussex, Union and Warren counties.

The library at a New Jersey community college is typically called the learning resource center or the media center. These terms more clearly define the contents of the collections and the services. In addition to traditional print materials, these centers house a variety of non-print media and the equipment needed to use them.

In many cases, a media production department may be part of the learning resource center. The "LRC" staff works closely with the faculty in producing transparencies, slides, tapes and other material that supplement classroom instruction. The community college is frequently in the forefront of educational innovation, particularly in accepting multimedia teaching techniques.

When students use a learning resource center they are often served by media specialists. At Brookdale Community College, for example, the title "media specialist" is used to convey a philosophical as well as a practical emphasis: that the real world of teaching and learning is a multimedia world.

Summary

New Jersey academic libraries have progressed from beginnings in one-room facilities, open only a few hours a week, to their present complex organizations employing substantial staffs and housing thousands of volumes. The growth of these libraries has parallelled the growth of their parent institutions, and both have reflected the needs of a changing society. Throughout their history academic libraries in New Jersey have been part of that general movement in our culture toward greater access to education for ever greater numbers of people.

New Jersey's academic libraries, even those that pride themselves on their extensive collections, recognize that they can no longer acquire comprehensive book collections; that no library, however large, can afford to achieve self-sufficiency. Only through cooperation among all kinds of libraries, both within and outside of the state, will each institution be able to serve properly the needs of its students and faculty. Academic libraries generally are part of the New Jersey Network, cooperating with other libraries to share resources. This is true of Princeton and Rutgers in particular as providers of reference and research services for the state. Thus they support the information needs, not only of their own faculty and student bodies and those of other academic institutions but also of the general citizenry.

Notes

1. Thomas Jefferson Wertenbaker, *Princeton, 1746–1896.* (Princeton, N.J.: Princeton University Press, 1946), 396.
2. *Ibid:* 397.
3. College of New Jersey, *Board of Trustees Minutes,* I. 19.
4. Louis Shores, *Origins of the American College Library.* (Hamden, CT: Shoe String Press, 1966.) 262–268.
5. Alexander Leitch, *A Princeton Companion* (Princeton, N.J.: Princeton University Press, 1978), 285.
6. L. H. Butterfield, *John Witherspoon Comes to America.* (Princeton, N.J.: Princeton University Press, 1953), 83.
7. Shores. 270–271.
8. *Ibid*: 206–207.

9. John Rogers Williams, *The Handbook of Princeton* (New York: Grafton Press, 1905), 54.

10. Wertenbaker, 228.

11. *Ibid:* 55.

12. *Ibid:* 229.

13. Thomas D. Harding, "College Literary Societies: Their Contribution to the Development of Academic Libraries, 1813–1876" *Library Quarterly.* v. 29, 1959, 94.

14. *Ibid:* 311.

15. Frederic Vinton, *Subject-Catalogue of the Library of the College of New Jersey, at Princeton* (N.Y.: C.M. Green Printing Co. 1884).

16. *Ibid:* 350.

17. Princeton University, *Board of Trustees Minutes*, November 12, 1891.

18. *Ibid:* 352.

19. Shores, 44.

20. William H. S. Demarest, "History of the Library." *Journal of the Rutgers University Libraries*, v.1, 1937, 4.

21. Roy F. Nichols, "The Library We Dedicate." *Journal of the Rutgers University Libraries.* v. 20, 1956, 4.

22. Richard P. McCormick, *Rutgers, A Bicentennial History* (New Brunswick, N.J.: Rutgers University Press, 1966), 46.

23. McCormick, 103.

24. *Ibid:* 114.

25. *Ibid:* 139.

26. William S. Dix, "Dedication of the Mabel Smith Douglass Library, October 23, 1975." *Journal of the Rutgers University Libraries.* v. 39, 1967, 5.

27. Two new state colleges were authorized by the legislature in 1968, Ramapo College (in Mahwah) and Stockton State College (in Pomona). Their first students were admitted in 1971.

28. Kenneth D. White, *Paterson State College: A History, 1855–1966.* (Wayne, N.J.: Student Cooperative Association of Paterson State College, 1967), 113.

29. Earl C. Davis, *Origins and Development of the New Jersey State Teachers College, Montclair, 1908–1951.* (Ph.D. dissertation, New York University, 1954), 3.

30. Davis, 30.

31. John T. Cunningham, *University in the Forest: The Story of Drew University.* (Morristown, N.J.: Afton Pub. Co., 1972), 58.

32. Walter A. Brower, *Rider College: The First Hundred Years* (Trenton, N.J.: Publisher unknown, 1965), 141.

33. Sister M. Anne John O'Laughlin. *Profile of the Library of Caldwell College for Women* (Washington, D.C.: Catholic University of America, Degree of Master of Library Service thesis, 1965), 7.

10

Special Libraries

Susan Roumfort

What Is a Special Library

Special libraries have played an important part in the history of libraries in New Jersey, but only in the twentieth century has the term "special library" come into common use. It describes those libraries which are not public, academic or school libraries but are organized to serve a specific clientele, usually employees of the library's parent organization. In 1916 John Cotton Dana, director of the Newark Free Public Library and the first president of the Special Libraries Association, said the "the purpose of special libraries [is] to put knowledge to work." "Putting Knowledge to Work" became the motto of the Association.[1]

There are many definitions of a "special library," the most restrictive being that the library must serve for-profit businesses. Currently the most commonly accepted definitions are those used by the Special Libraries Association. The first appears in its *Bylaws*:

A special library is
  a) a library or information center maintained by an individual corporation, association, government agency or any other group, or
  b) a specialized or departmental collection within a library for the organization and dissemination of information, and primarily offering service to a specialized clientele through the use of varied media and methods.

A more informal definition appears in the Association's *A Visionary Plan for the Future: SLA's Strategic Plan 1990–2005*. It defines a special library as "an organization that provides focused, working information to a specialized clientele on an ongoing basis to further the mission and goals of the parent company/organization."[2] In this chapter, special units in academic and public libraries are not discussed since they are covered in other chapters. However, many of these units have played an important part in the development of specialized services and collections, and many of their librarians have had a significant role in special library services in New Jersey.[3]

The Development and Diversity of Special Libraries

Special libraries are created to meet the specific information needs of their organizations. These for-profit and not-for-profit organizations evolved as New Jersey's economy developed from an agricultural base, through an industrial and manufacturing phase, to one grounded more recently in service industries and high technology.

No one really knows how many special libraries there are in New Jersey.[4] New ones are being created constantly, while obsolete organizations die. It is especially hard to get a true count of special libraries since they often are not registered with organizations that produce library directories and statistics. Some published directories list only 400 or 500 special libraries in New Jersey. Yet the *1985 Official Directory of New Jersey Libraries and Media Centers* identified over 1,000.

The following overview describes how special libraries developed in response to economic changes in the state. It says little about the diversity of their purposes, individual collections or physical plants. In truth, there really is no typical or "model" special library. They come in all sizes and have many different missions or purposes. Generally they have relatively small but specific subject collections, and they adapt their services to support the research needs of their organizations. Some libraries maintain the archives of their organizations, others keep their organizations' technical research files. More recently, some have essentially done away with print collections and depend on online computer services to meet their clients' needs.

While many librarians in New Jersey can identify a few noteworthy special libraries, it is very difficult to obtain detailed histories of them. Most special libraries have no written history. Articles describing specific libraries appear in the publications of the Special Libraries Association and those of its chapters and divisions, but they are few and far between. Articles about special libraries have appeared in New Jersey periodicals and newspapers, but these are hard to locate since there are few indexes to these sources. The following history has been compiled from a variety of sources (library directories and publications of the Special Libraries Association and its New Jersey chapters) and from the author's more than thirty years as a special librarian.

There are three general types of parent organizations for special libraries: 1) for-profit, 2) not-for-profit, and 3) governmental. The for-profit group consists of industrial, commercial and professional services organizations. The not-for-profit group includes foundations, associations and non-profit research organizations. The government group consists of libraries developed to serve all levels of governments: federal, state, county, local and intergovernmental agencies.

Early Roots

We know of only a few special libraries in New Jersey before 1850. The best known were the State Legislature's library (now the State Library), established in 1796, and the New Jersey Historical Society's library, established in 1845. Other organization libraries may have existed, but little trace of them has been found.

In the latter half of the nineteenth century, libraries serving the professions and the specialized needs of their parent organizations began to appear. A major reason for this growth was the need for unique or technical information often not found in the academic and public libraries of the day. Both academic and public libraries had to establish collections to meet the general needs of their users, and could not afford to spend their limited resources on the specific needs of for-profit businesses or the professions.

The largest number of newly established special libraries identified in this period were attached to historical societies. They included the Vineland Historical and Antiquarian Society (1864), Hackettstown Historical Society Museum Library (1874), Salem County Historical Society (1885) and Camden County Historical Society (1899). New professional and business libraries included those of McCarter & English (Newark, law firm, 1870), James T. White & Company (Clifton, publisher, 1873), Camden County Bar Association (Camden, 1880), Paterson News (newspaper morgue, 1890), and the Helene Fuld School of Nursing (Camden, medical library, 1894). The historical record describing these libraries is very limited. Most of the founding dates for the libraries in this chapter were found in library directories published by national and state library associations and commercial publishers. Citations for directories used for this chapter can be found in the notes for this chapter.[5]

From 1900 to 1920 there began a steady growth of industrial and commercial businesses in New Jersey, and with it the need for information to support business decisions. Since then, the progress of special libraries in New Jersey has mirrored the progress of its economic environment from industrial to business to a high technology and service economy. Libraries were established to serve the growing number of industrial firms, public utilities and insurance companies. These libraries provided the information not only to further business needs, but also to help businesses respond to the increasing number of government regulations.

Surprisingly, the early creation of special libraries in New Jersey was nurtured by two public librarians, John Cotton Dana and Sarah B. Askew, who realized that public libraries could not meet all the information needs of the expanding business world. Dana, the director of the Newark Public Library, and Askew, director of the New Jersey Public Library Commission, provided business with as much information as they could, but they also prodded the larger business and industrial firms to establish their own technical libraries. In 1904 Dana provided a model for business information services by creating the Business Branch of the Newark Public Library. He and Sarah B. Ball, the head of the Business Branch, built a collection of business directories, catalogs and newspaper files. Both also were actively involved in the establishment of the Special Libraries Association, a professional organization devoted to promoting special libraries and the training of librarians to serve the information needs of business and industry. Dana served as the first president of this association from 1909 to 1911.

Early in the century several major corporations based in New Jersey organized libraries. Among them were Prudential Insurance of America (Newark, 1903), Public Service Company (later Public Service Electric & Gas, Newark, 1911), U.S. Rubber Company (Wayne, 1914), Calco Chemical Company (later a division of American Cyanamid, Bound Brook, 1916), Engelhard Industries (Newark, chemicals, 1916), Bell Telephone Company (Murray Hill, 1917, one of five known Bell Telephone libraries in the United States) and Esso (later Exxon, Linden, 1919). In 1917, two military libraries were established: the U.S. Army Morale Support Post Library, Fort Dix (a general library which later provided job training manuals to those on the base), and the U.S. Naval Engineering Center (Lakehurst, aeronautics).

A variety of other types of libraries were also created before 1920, including five more historical society libraries, two museums (at Montclair in 1916 and Newark in 1909); a newspaper library (Asbury Park Press in 1907); a medical library (St. Paul's Medical Center, New Brunswick, 1907) and a theological library (Seventh Day Baptist Historical Society, Plainfield, 1916). In 1917, the New Jersey Zinc Company at Palmerton established an employees library that included a good collection of Hungarian and Slavic books. This library was one of several corporate libraries set up to provide educational and general study materials to employees in towns which did not have public libraries. About 1910 the State Library established a legislative reference unit. In 1914 legislation was passed to sanction this service, but for years it suffered from funding problems.

The 1920s

By 1920 a new pattern of special library growth had emerged. The majority of new special libraries were in the manufacturing industries, and most were located in New Jersey's northeastern, heavily populated cities. At the same time, many academic and large public libraries began to create business and local history collections, and many librarians in these units joined the Special Libraries Association. Sarah B. Askew, whose job was to further advance public libraries, found that the State Library staff could not handle all the requests received from business firms, so she called upon businesses to establish technical libraries to meet their increasingly specific needs. In her 1921 annual report she reported that her Commission had received nineteen requests for advice on how to set up a special library, and that four business firms had hired librarians in spite of the current business depression.[6]

A spurt in the growth of industrial and corporate libraries occurred in the 1920s. Those established in 1920 were at such firms as the Allied Chemical Corporation (Morristown, chemicals), the Congoleum Corporation (Trenton, flooring), and the National Lead Industries (later NL Industries, chemistry, paints and metals). From 1921 to 1929 new corporate libraries in many major industries appeared, including the Western Union Corporation (Upper Saddle River, 1921), the Mutual Benefit Life Insurance Company (Newark, 1922), the Hercules Powder Company (metallurgy, 1925), the E. R. Squibb & Sons (1925), and the RCA Corporation (Camden, 1927).

Medical libraries were established by the Academy of Medicine (Newark, 1921), the Holy Name Hospital (Teaneck, 1925), and the Mercer Hospital—School of Nursing (Trenton, 1926). In 1921 the National Council on Crime and Delinquency set up its library in Hackensack. Several more historical societies also established libraries during this period. Government agencies that established libraries included the Newark Board of Education and the U.S. Army's Research and Development unit at Picatinny Arsenal (Dover, 1929).

Two important leaders of the special libraries movement emerged in the late 1920s and early 1930s. They were Alma C. Mitchill of the Public Service Company and Marion C. Manly of the Business Branch of the Newark Public Library. Both were strong supporters of the Special Libraries Association and worked actively to promote its growth and that of special libraries in New Jersey. They were the driving force in establishing the Association's New Jersey Chapter in 1935, and through it they fostered interlibrary cooperation and professional growth of special libraries nationwide.

The Depression Years

Even during the "Great Depression" of the 1930s, special libraries were being established and were working to help their organizations weather those difficult years. Some represented the firms of the emerging electronics industry. Among them were Western Electric (Kearny, 1930), RCA Tube Division (Harrison, 1931), RCA Industrial (Clark, 1931) and Bell Telephone Company Laboratory (Whippany, 1940). The pharmaceuticals industry also began to grow. Among the firms establishing their own libraries were Merck & Company (two libraries in Rahway, 1933 and 1938), Waller and Tierman (Newark, 1936), Ciba Geigy Corporation (Summit, 1937), Knoll Pharmaceutical Company (Whippany, 1938), and the Schering-Plough Company (Bloomfield, 1940).

Other industrial libraries opened as well, including the U.S. Testing Company, Inc. (Hoboken, Engineering, 1930), Mobil-Research and Development (Plainsboro, 1931), the Diamond Shamrock Corporation (Morristown, chemistry, especially paper and textiles, 1934), the Bendix Corporation (Teterboro, aeronautics, 1940), E .I. DuPont De Nemours Company (Parlin, chemistry, 1940), and American Cyanamid-Agricultural Division (Princeton, 1940).

Thus, by the time the United States went to war in 1941, New Jersey had developed both the industrial and information resources to provide the materials and technology to support the country's World War II effort.

The War Years

The war years produced great growth in many technologies. Research became a major component of New Jersey business as its industries were pushed to produce the weapons and materials needed to win the war. Over two dozen new special libraries were established between 1941 and 1945. Heavy industry and engineering libraries were created at Transamerica DeLaval Turbine Labs (Trenton, 1943), the General Cable Corporation (Bayonne, 1943), the Foster Wheeler Development Corporation—R & I Center (Livingston, 1944), and the Ajax Engineering Corporation (Trenton, 1945). The postwar electronics and communications industries were served by new wartime libraries opened at Bell Telephone Labs (Murray Hill, 1941), RCA Corporation—David Sarnoff Research Center (Princeton, 1942), and IT&T's Laboratories (Nutley, 1945).

In 1941 the U.S. Army established its Communications Systems Center Library at Fort Monmouth, and Curtiss-Wright opened an aeronautics library in Caldwell. New chemical research libraries included M & R Chemicals, Inc. (1942), GAF—Technical Center (Wayne, 1942) and J. T. Baker Research Laboratory (Phillipsburg, 1945).

New pharmaceutical libraries included Carter Products' Hartman Laboratory (Raritan, 1944) and Warner-Lambert (Morris Plains, 1945). Health science libraries for psychiatric care were set up at Trenton Psychiatric Hospital (Trenton, 1944) and at the New Jersey Neuro-Pychiatric Institute (Princeton, 1945). Representing the growing diversity of New Jersey's businesses, libraries were established for the Campbell Institute for Research and Technology (Camden, food, 1941), the Textile Research Institute (Princeton, 1945) and Hammond, Inc. (Maplewood, cartography, 1945).

The Early Post-War Period

By the end of the war New Jersey had become a major center for research and development. The postwar years through 1949 brought a gradual but continuing decline of heavy industry in New Jersey. However, new special libraries were created for the new and expanding sectors of the state's economy. Five new pharmaceutical libraries were established: Bristol Myers, Johnson and Johnson (two), Warner Lambert and Carter Wallace. The chemical industry began developing new applications and products, and libraries were created to service researchers at such firms as the American Cyanamid Agriculture Research Center, and Thiokol Corporation Chemical Division. In the related fields of plastics and textiles, libraries were created by Celanese Corporation of America and J. P. Stevens and Company. Johns Manville set up a library for its Research Center dealing with asbestos. In the service sector, the Labor Management Relations Institute at Rutgers University opened a library in 1947 to service its researchers and business clients. The same year the Educational Testing Service created the Carl Campbell Brigham Library to further its work.

The 1950s

During the 1950s, over seventy new libraries were established. At least ten health science libraries were created during the decade, as well as a research library at the Institute of Microbiology at Rutgers University. Pharmaceutical company libraries continued to increase, with new libraries at White Laboratories, Inc., Pfizer Therapeutics Institute, Ethicon, Inc., and Merck & Company (for patents). There were five new chemical libraries and one for petroleum, but there were also eight new libraries to serve the fast growing electronics industry. RCA led with three (missile guidance and radar), and libraries were opened at Lockheed (radar), EMR Photoelectric (a division of Schlumberger Ltd.), Allen B. DuMont Laboratories (missiles), Singer Company's Kearfott Division, Perlin-Elmer Technical Systems Division, and Western Electric. In 1959 the Institute for Defense Analysis library was established in Princeton, as the defense industry and military libraries continued to flourish.

During the late 1950s the concept of the "organization man" and the emergence of middle managers brought about the development of libraries to serve professionals whose concerns centered on management of corporate resources, program development and financial service. American Cyanamid, Celanese Corporation and Allied Corporation were among those that established corporate management libraries.

The 1960s

The 1960s were marked by the continued expansion of the communications and electronics sectors and the emergence of many social service industries. The introduction of business computers began to change the way corporate librarians acquired and controlled their library materials. Special librarians began creating computer-generated indexes and catalogs, and produced computer-generated bibliographies for their clients.

By the middle of the decade, many research and service industries were moving to the area around Princeton University. Later known as the "Route One Corridor," former farmlands gave way to campus-style research centers and corporate headquarters. There was a similar expansion of government agencies just south in Trenton. These new organizations created a massive demand for information, and this resulted in the creation of many new small special libraries. Many were one-person libraries with few resources. Their librarians often had to depend upon the resources in the libraries of Princeton University and local colleges in order to obtain needed information. To provide mutual support, about fifty of these librarians formed PAL (Princeton Area Librarians), a forerunner of the Princeton–Trenton Chapter of the Special Libraries Association.

The rapid growth of the communications firms and their in-house library networks may have provided the model for public library networking in New Jersey. AT&T, Bell Telephone, Western Electric and RCA had large networks of special libraries. Many of their concepts of resource sharing and interlibrary loan were mirrored in New Jersey's public library network created in the 1970s.

Of the seventy or so new special libraries created in the 1960s, many were branches of corporations, but suddenly governmental libraries began to bloom, reflecting the growth of governmental and social services in the state. State agency libraries were established for the Attorney General, the Health Department, the Transportation Department, the Labor Department and the Delaware River Basin Commission. The federal government also set up libraries in New Jersey for the Environmental Protection Agency and the Marine Fisheries Agency. Several lesser known libraries were established by the Society for the Investigation of the Unplanned (UFO's), the Education Foundation for Human Sexuality, and the Motion Pictures Services (AV).

The 1970s

During the 1970s industrial manufacturing in New Jersey suffered a severe decline from which it has never recovered. At the same time this was balanced by explosive growth in the communications services industries. Many new ventures involved small professional offices and businesses which relied heavily on current information. Many established special libraries had to reorient their service programs to reflect the new directions their organizations were taking. To do this quickly and efficiently, special librarians embraced new microform and computer technologies which gave them an edge in the race to obtain high-quality current information for their clients.

During this decade AT&T continued to build one the nation's largest corporate library systems, adding at least five libraries in

New Jersey. A number of associations, educational organizations and health science centers organized libraries of their own. At least a dozen health science centers were established, and by the end of the decade they had grown so numerous that they formed a support group of their own. A sampling of other new libraries includes those of the National Adult Education Clearinghouse, the New Jersey Optometric Association, the Unexpected Wildlife Refuge (beavers), the Center for the American Woman and Politics (Eagleton Institute), ERIC Clearinghouse on Tests, Measurements and Evaluation at ETS, and the Global Education Association.

The 1980s and Beyond

By the beginning of the 1980s, New Jersey had developed a strong service-based economy, with heavy emphasis on communications and research. The state government made a strong commitment to support this trend through programs and grants to stimulate and assist scientific research and related educational organizations.

However, the decade of the 1980s became an economic roller coaster, with periods of economic contraction surrounding periods of unprecedented expansion. The effect of these rapid changes forced corporations to look more closely at their financial "bottom line." "Cost effective" and "cost benefit" became the watchwords of the time. Consolidation of services and the effective use of all resources became a necessity as money grew tighter. The federally mandated breakup of the "Ma Bell" system and the deregulation of many industries also forced many of these organizations and their libraries to do more with less.

Toward the end of the 1980s, only the legal and health sciences libraries were showing much growth. The remaining special libraries had to find creative new ways to serve their clients. By the end of the decade corporate library networks in New Jersey had been greatly reduced in size and some libraries were closed as corporations were "downsized." Eventually the slowdown in the economy affected the public sector and caused similar cutbacks in services and resources in many governmental libraries.

To survive, special libraries had to become more cost-effective within their organizations, and their librarians were expected to be good managers as well as expert researchers and information gatherers. "Value added service" (good value received by the client for the cost incurred) and "cost recovery" (fees charged to the client's unit for services rendered) became popular ways to show management that the library was a true "profit center." To meet service demands, special librarians found new ways to obtain information. Online computer services were becoming an economical way of quickly retrieving the information clients needed. The library "rented" information by paying only for the information or articles it wanted from a database instead of buying large numbers of books and serial publications.

Special librarians also found new ways to network with other libraries. Many special libraries contain proprietary information and must quietly acquire information supporting new research projects. Their organizations are therefore reluctant to open their libraries to the public, and they often refuse to allow their collections to be listed in generally distributed union lists. These policies prevented many special libraries from joining formal library networks. The State Library addressed this problem when a new statewide, multi-type library network was created. Its structure permitted libraries to join and use network services even if the library could not provide full reciprocity for services received. As a result, many of the state's special libraries were able to join this network and thus enlarge their access to information and other library services. In return, most special libraries have been able to provide not only considerable network support from their non-restricted collections, but also have provided in-kind management services and support for many of the network's projects and educational programs.

In the 1990s the number and size of special libraries continued to shrink. The introduction of PCs and computer work stations connected to commercial online data bases gave many computer-literate researchers direct access to needed information. Special librarians were no longer the gatekeepers of information. Once again they had to adjust to a changing reality. Some libraries closed; others became the archives of past records and research; still others used online data services to carve a new place for themselves. Some became teachers and guides for their organization's researchers, showing them how to get the most information from an online service at the best price. Others became part of a research team as the point person for gathering information. Still others struck out on their own and opened information research businesses to serve small firms.

Characteristics of Special Libraries

A major characteristic of special libraries is their emphasis on providing up-to-date information quickly. Personalized service to clients is paramount. Special librarians often not only collect needed information and materials in response to a request, but also organize, abstract and/or evaluate the information. Many libraries offer SDI (Selective Distribution of Information) services to their clients. The librarian establishes a profile of a client's needs and then automatically sends the new information to the client. By the mid-1990s much of this work was being done online by computer, with client profiles stored in the library's office work stations.

Special librarians have always been heavy users of new technologies. Beginning with the telephone and typewriter, they have been quick to adopt any new technology that promised faster or more efficient access to needed information. Benefiting from the growing use of computers in business and industry, special librarians became early and enthusiastic users of computer-generated data. Many library computer applications were developed by special librarians working with their firm's data management staff.

By the late 1980s the heavy emphasis on electronically produced information and a concomitant decline in the use of books as a primary information source convinced many special librarians that the term "library" no longer accurately described their work place or their job. For them the terms "information center" and "information manager" or "information specialist" were better descriptions. These terms are now included in the definition of a special library in the Special Libraries Association's *Bylaws*.[7]

One hallmark of special librarians is their willingness to help one another. The desire to cooperate with and learn from one another was a major factor in the formation of the New Jersey and Princeton/Trenton Chapters of the Special Libraries Association. Even though many special libraries could not join most interlibrary projects, one of the first cooperative activities among New Jersey special librarians was the creation in the late 1940s of a union list of serials in their libraries. The list was sponsored by the New Jersey Chapter of SLA. At first the list was a card file kept at the Newark Public Library. It became so useful that it was finally published in 1958, although its distribution was restricted to participating special libraries. A second edition was published in 1961. By 1962 it was too large to be maintained as a volunteer project, and the union list was transferred to a commercial publishing firm.

Who are these special librarians, and where do they come from? Some are full-time managers, but most are reference librarians and technical searchers. Many are people with advanced subject degrees who were attracted to library service. Many have master's degrees in library science, often combined with graduate or undergraduate degrees relevant to their organizations' interests. Still others are highly skilled paraprofessionals who have acquired library research and organizational skills.

Where are special libraries placed within their organizations? Since they are created to serve a specific clientele, a library is usually a part of the work group it serves. The libraries come in all sizes from a one-person library to one with a large staff of professionals and paraprofessionals. Some are the only library unit within their organization; others are a branch of the organization's library network. Some are general business libraries serving management; others are attached to specific departments, such as research, legal or public relations. Some are separate cost centers funded directly by their organization; others are funded by the unit they serve. Increasingly, libraries serving the whole organization must earn their money through charge-back fees received for services rendered to units within the parent organization. In the late 1980s a new trend in special libraries was the emergence of independent firms marketing special library services to businesses and other organizations for a fee. These information brokers rarely have library collections but rather, depend heavily on commercial databases and other libraries. They pay information sources for the raw data they use, reorganize the information, and present the new product to their clients with a bill to cover the costs.

No matter what type of special library we consider, special librarians are increasingly called upon to prove the cost effectiveness of the services they offer. Good management skills have become a necessity for special librarians.

The Influence of Professional Organizations on Special Libraries

While some special librarians prefer just to get on with their jobs, many have found the time to promote the growth of special libraries and the professionalism of their staffs. There are now hundreds of librarians working to spread the service concepts that have made special libraries a force within the library world. Thus it is difficult to select just a few librarians as leaders of the special libraries in New Jersey. The best known and the most critical in the special libraries movement were the leaders and early members of the Special Libraries Association. In New Jersey, SLA members organized local librarians and put their imprint on the purpose and the developing goals of the Association. Over the years, seven New Jersey librarians have served as presidents of SLA. They are John Cotton Dana, Newark Free Public Library (1909/10 and 1910/11), Alma C. Mitchill, Public Service Company (1938/39 and 1939/40), Betty Joy Cole, Calco Chemical Company (1946/47), Katherine L. Kinder,

Johns Manville Research Company (1956/57), Dr. Frank E. Mc-
Kenna, Air Reduction, Inc. Research Center (1966/67 and later Executive Director of the Association), Efrem W. Gonzalez, Bristol
Myers Products (1966/67) and Frank H. Spaulding, Bell Laboratories (1986/87).[8]

The Association was organized in 1909 to meet the need for professional interaction among librarians providing information and research materials to researchers and managers in business and industrial companies. It became a focal point for these librarians and a
mechanism for bringing them together to discuss mutual concerns.
The Association also provided training opportunities for librarians
to improve their skill and services. John Cotton Dana was instrumental in forming the Special Libraries Association under the um-
brella of the American Library Association. The fledging organization held its first conference in November 1909, with fifty-seven
members attending. Mr. Dana was elected its first president.[9] There
were three other charter members of the Association from New Jersey: Sarah B. Ball, Business Branch librarian, Newark Public Library; Frances L. Rathbone Coe, East Orange Public Library; and
Beatrice Winser, Newark Public Library.[10]

As the Association grew, SLA members in New Jersey began
meeting informally several times a year. At first there was no state
chapter, so New Jersey members traveled to New York City or Philadelphia for meetings. By the early 1930s, librarians in the northeastern part of the state were meeting informally in Newark and
nearby cities to talk about mutual concerns and to tour each other's
libraries. They also discussed forming a state chapter. In 1935 Marian Manley (Business Branch, Newark Public Library) and Alma C.
Mitchill (Public Service Company) invited sixty people to a meeting
in Newark to be held in April. Twenty-six of these librarians signed
a petition requesting chapter status, which was approved by SLA.
Mitchill was elected the first president of the New Jersey Chapter
and served two terms from 1935 to 1937.[11]

Among the original twenty-six members were librarians from the
Atlas Corporation (Jersey City), Newark Board of Education,
Montclair Free Public Library, New Jersey Telephone Company,
Newark Free Public Library-Business Branch, Public Service Com-
pany, Rademackers (Newark bookbinder), Standard Oil Develop-
ment Company (Elizabeth), Bakelite Corporation, Calco Chemical
Company (later a division of American Cyanamid), Stevens Insti-
tute of Technology, Western Electric Company, Mutual Benefit Life
Insurance Company, New Jersey State Emergency Relief Associa-
tion, Newark College of Engineering, and United States Rubber
Company.[12] Special libraries in New Jersey received additional rec-

ognition when a seat on the New Jersey Library Planning Commission was assigned to a special librarian.[13]

Among Alma Mitchill's accomplishments as president of the New Jersey Chapter were a ten-session training program for special librarians and the creation of a joint committee of SLA and the New Jersey Library Association. The committee's tasks were to study interlibrary relationships, to assemble information about special collections in the state, and to establish a close working relationship between the two organizations. The first training course, with twenty-nine registrants, was under the direction of Margaret Smith and was held at the Newark College of Engineering in February 1936. This was the start of a continuing education commitment that remains strong today. The Chapter worked with the New Jersey Library Association on several professional training projects and joint meetings. Chapter meetings were held almost every month and often included tours of members' libraries. In 1935 the Chapter began to publish a formal bulletin. These are still the basic activities of both New Jersey chapters.

Marion Manley of the Business Branch of the Newark Free Public Library was the second president of the Chapter, serving from 1937 to 1939. She continued and expanded Mitchill's programs. She was also a prolific writer and editor of many publications of the Chapter and of the Association.

In 1939 Betty Joy Cole of Calco Chemical Company became the third president. She was a chemist and a technical research librarian with close ties to the chemical researchers she worked with. During her presidency the Chapter held its first joint meeting with a technical society, the New Jersey Chapter of the American Chemical Society. Joint meetings with technical societies and associations became an important part of Chapter activities and were considered a good recruiting tool for special librarianship.

Cole was a strong representative of science and technical librarianship. Until then most special librarians in New Jersey had come from business or the social sciences. She saw the need for an organization which would support the concerns of technical research librarians. In 1937 the Chapter supported the formation of a Science-Technology-Biology Group. Later a College and University Group was organized. The Special Libraries Association itself soon also modified its structure to provide for two types of groups: at the local level, chapters which serve specific geographic areas, and at the Association level, subject divisions to support the various disciplines of the Association's members. Each member is affiliated with both a Chapter and at least one Division. Over the years, the number of

Chapters and Divisions have grown as the needs of the membership changed.

After World War II the New Jersey Chapter grew as many new libraries were established. The Chapter joined with the Philadelphia Chapter as host of the Association's 1959 annual conference in Atlantic City, the sixth time the conference was held there. At that conference five New Jersey members were inducted into the Association's new Hall of Fame. They were John Cotton Dana, Marian M. Manley Wisner, Sara Ball, Alma C. Mitchill and Linda Morley (Industrial Relations Counselors). The Hall of Fame honors members for an "extended and sustained period of distinguished service to the Association."[14] Other New Jersey members so honored are Betty Joy Cole, Katharine L. Kinder, Dr. Frank E. McKenna (Air Reduction Inc., Research Center, Preident NJ/SLA 1959/60, President SLA 1966/67, Executive Director of SLA 1970–1987), Robert Krupp (American Cyanamid, NJ/SLA president 1964/65), Ellis Mount (NJ/SLA president 1963/64) and SLA Executive Director 1967–1970), and Efrem Gonzalez.[15]

In the 1960s many librarians were working in the growing number of business and research centers clustered near Princeton University, and a new group, the Princeton Area Librarians (PAL), was organized. While many of these librarians were members of the New Jersey or Philadelphia chapters of SLA, they liked meeting locally with people they knew and worked with. Princeton University librarians were instrumental in the PAL's formation and supported its resource-sharing activities. Eventually the PAL group realized it needed a more formal structure to operate efficiently, and in 1967 it became the Princeton-Trenton Chapter of the SLA with members representing about fifty libraries. William Fisher of Western Electric was elected president.[16]

From the beginning, the Princeton-Trenton members represented mainly organizations working in basic research, government, education and social services. The Chapter's small geographic area encouraged large attendance at its meetings. Initially the New Jersey Chapter was concerned that this new chapter would diminish the effectiveness of its activities, but within a few years both chapters were growing vigorously. The 1993/94 edition of the SLA's *Who's Who in Special Libraries* lists 472 members of the New Jersey Chapter and 215 members of the Princeton-Trenton Chapter.

Both chapters have benefited from the support given their activities by for-profit and not-for-profit organizations in the state. Many organizations not only provide space for meetings and subsidies for chapter activities, but also encourage their librarians to work on

SLA committees and as officers of chapters. Without such support these activities would be substantially reduced.

Continuing education opportunities for their members has been a priority for both chapters. They have presented informational meetings devoted to new library concepts and technologies, sponsored SLA's continuing education courses, and co-sponsored seminars and workshops with other library groups in the state. In the late 1980s New Jersey librarians began enrolling in SLA's new middle-management continuing education program, which was designed to provide special librarians with the management skills now required in both the public and the private workplace. By 1990 the Association was considering making continuing education a requirement for continued membership, recognizing that its members need to keep their skills up-to-date in order to provide high quality services.

While the Special Library Association and its chapters in New Jersey have been responsible for significant growth in the number of special libraries in the state, they are not the only organizations that help to develop special libraries in New Jersey. Several other groups foster libraries in their special disciplines. One such group is the American Association of Law Libraries. In 1989 its New Jersey Chapter had about 100 members representing over eighty libraries.[17] The New Jersey Health Sciences Group had 100 libraries listed as members of the New Jersey multitype library network. Many special librarians belong to the American Society for Information Science, which supports specialists primarily interested in computers and computer-generated information. There are other small associations which support art, music and theology librarians.

The Future of Special Libraries

Special librarians recognize that current and accurate information is essential in a highly competitive world and that they will be working in an environment of "downsizing," tough fiscal constraints and ever broadening direct online access to information. They will continue to do more with less—fewer people and fewer resources. They may change their titles to "information specialists" working in "information centers" in order better to identify their objectives. Special librarians are used to coping in a world of constant change. The world of special libraries will no doubt offer them further opportunities to hone their skills in crisis management.

Notes

1. "The Annual Conference." *Special Libraries* (September 1916) 7:127.
2. *Who's Who in Special Libraries, 1993/94* (Washington, Special Libraries Association, 1993) "Chapter Number of Members": 11).
3. *Ibid*: 11.
4. *The Official Directory of New Jersey Libraries and Media Centers* (New York, LDA Publishers 1985):95–153.
5. Because they contained founding dates for libraries, the following directories were most useful: *Directory of Special Libraries and Information Centers* 7th ed. (Detroit, Gale Research Co., 1982), Vol. 2, and *Special Libraries Association-New Jersey Chapter Membership Directory 1960/61*, 1960.
6. New Jersey. Public Library Commission. *Annual Report 1920 and 1921* (Trenton, typewritten):3.
7. *Who's Who in Special Libraries, 1993/94*, 18.
8. *Ibid*: 30.
9. Alma Carvoe Mitchill, ed. *Special Libraries Association-Its First Fifty Years 1909–1959* (New York, Special Libraries Association, 1960), 5.
10. "Special Libraries and the Special Libraries Association, Appendix 1 Charter Members of SLA: 1909" *Encyclopedia of Library and Information Science* (New York, Marcel Dekker, 1987) 28:436–437.
11. Mitchill, 39.
12. "Chapter Notes [for New Jersey]" *Special Libraries* (March 1936) 26:77.
13. "Chapter Notes [for New Jersey]" *Special Libraries* (October 1935) 25:234.
14. Mitchill, 40–41.
15. "Know Your Chapter" *Special Libraries Association New Jersey Chapter Bulletin* (January 1986):11.
16. Special Libraries Association. Princeton/Trenton Chapter, *Princeton-Trenton Miscellany, Reminiscences of the First Twenty Years, From PAL to PT/SLA* (May 1987): 3. (This was a booklet prepared on the occasion of the twentieth anniversary of the Princeton/Trenton Chapter of SLA.
17. Robert Bland, of the New Jersey State Library and then editor of the AALL New Jersey Chapter's *Newsletter*, conversation with the author, 1989.

11

The New Jersey Library Association

Mary Joyce Doyle

Early History

The New Jersey Library Association was founded on December 29, 1890 by 39 charter members meeting in the state headquarters of the Women's Christian Temperance Union Building in Trenton, which also housed the Union Library Company, forerunner of the Trenton Public Library.[1] Melvil Dewey had sent a telegram of regret. He was prevented from attending by an ice skating accident[2] (although he did attend a meeting of the Association a few months later, bringing with him a delegation of nineteen people from Albany).[3]

B. B. Hutchinson was made temporary chairman and Martha F. Nelson secretary. "Mr. Hutchinson in his address of welcome spoke of the 'Public libraries of our time being among the most valuable and effective agencies, hand in hand with the church, the home and the school, in the promotion of the spiritual, mental and even physical welfare of all classes of people. . . .' He regretted that here in the Capital city of the State we are unable to point out a free library."[4] A committee of three (the Misses Hill of Newark, Marshall of Woodbury and Stratton of Trenton) was appointed to propose a name for the association and to present a constitution and bylaws. The committee reported that the association should be called the New Jersey Library Association with the constitution and bylaws drawn from those of two similar organizations in New York and Massachusetts. They were read and immediately adopted.

After various remarks, it was resolved that this December 29 meeting would be recorded as the first meeting of the New Jersey Library Association. The following officers were elected: President—Rev. William Prall of West Orange, a clergyman and State Assemblyman from Passaic County who had introduced the State Library Law in 1884; Vice-Presidents—Frank P. Hill of Newark and Ernest Richardson of Princeton; Secretary—Martha F. Nelson of Trenton; and Treasurer—George F. Winchester of Paterson. President Prall gave an address on library work and education. Annual dues were set at 50¢ per member.[5] The Association held its second meeting in April 1891. Membership was opened to any person, organization or library interested in the objectives of the Association.

Beatrice Winser, one of NJLA's charter members, recalled in 1940 that the original purpose of the Association was "to instill in the minds of assistants a love of work in which they were engaged."

One early focus of attention of the NJLA were the laws that governed the organization and operation of New Jersey libraries. At the Association's first meeting in 1890 this concern was expressed and a committee was appointed to review and codify the state's library laws. In its concern for improving libraries and encouraging the creation of library service in areas which did not have it, the association was joined by such organizations as the State Federation of Woman's Clubs, one of the most active groups in the state involved in starting new public libraries.

In cooperation with the Federation, the Association obtained passage of the Traveling Library Law for rural districts in 1899. In 1894, the NJLA began to urge the establishment of a state library commission to promote the development of public libraries,[6] pointing to the success achieved by similar measures in Massachusetts and New Hampshire. By 1896 a bill to form such a commission had been introduced. Miss Horton, Vice-President of the Federation of Women's Clubs, relayed a message to the association from Governor Griggs, saying "he would give the subject his careful consideration"[7] The Governor did indeed do so but he finally vetoed a bill passed by the legislature; it eliminated a provision for a modest amount of financial aid to public libraries, which he regarded as necessary to the bill's effectiveness. The library association vowed to continue the fight for the original bill.[8] After continuing agitation by the Association and the Federation, the measure was finally enacted in 1900. With the Public Library Commission's guidance and encouragement, 145 public libraries were established between 1904 and 1915.

The Association established close relations with organizations in neighboring states. Joint meetings with the Pennsylvania Library Club were held regularly for many years. In 1899 a joint conference was held with the Pennsylvania Library Club and the New York Library Club. In 1900 the Association went farther afield and held a conference in Washington, D.C., together with the Washington Library Club and the Pennsylvania Library Club. The all-expense cost of travel, room and board was advertised at $12 from New York but only $9 from Philadelphia. In 1913 a meeting was held with librarians from New York (presumably New York City) and Long Island.[9] As late as 1927 the Association was still holding joint conferences with Pennsylvania.

The Association operations in its early years were conducted on a modest scale. In 1920 the treasurer's report noted a balance on hand of $49.60.[10] By 1921 it swelled to $85.65.[11] As the decade passed the balance approached $200, hardly a magnificent sum by today's standards.

Perhaps it says something of the place of New Jersey in the cultural history of the times that the meetings of the association during the early post-war years through the mid–1920s (with the exception of the annual conferences normally held in Atlantic City) were regularly held in New York City, first at the Tally-Ho Club on East 34th Street and later at the Town Hall Club.

Topics addressed at the annual conferences tended to be practical. The 1916 conference was typical. Topics chosen for discussion were how to use fiction as reference materials, the small library helping the teacher with her geography lesson, and why to continue the fines system. The cost of funding the annual conferences was raised and the association advised on how to curtail expenses. "Mr. Katzenbach said that he did not think it ought to be necessary to pay out money for speeches at the yearly meeting, as high-grade speakers should feel it an honor to address a meeting of this kind."[12] At a later conference "it was planned to invite Miss M. L. Provost, of the Newark Public Library, to present good, concise book-reviews on the best of the present-day fiction to date. . . ."[13]

From the beginning the Association was concerned with the education and training of the library assistants needed to staff the expanding libraries. In 1905 it aided in establishing a "summer school for librarians." During the early days of Sara B. Askew's tenure at the Public Library Commission, NJLA closely cooperated with her efforts to establish summer institutes and training sessions for library personnel. In 1922 a "graded summer school for library service" was established with the Association's assistance. In 1927 the Public Library Commission, with continued support from NJLA, helped to establish a library school at the New Jersey College for Women (now Douglass College) in New Brunswick, as a regular part of the curriculum. The Graduate School of Library Service at Rutgers University was established in 1953 with enthusiastic support from NJLA and was accredited by the American Library Association in 1956.

Before 1920 NJLA also worked to create a structure that would promote improved library service in the less populated areas of the state. The Association was instrumental in effecting the passage of the County Library Law in 1920, the greatest single step taken to promote library service to rural areas of New Jersey.

Organizational Structure[14]

Today's NJLA constitution states five objectives as they have developed since 1890:

1. To advance the standards of librarianship in New Jersey;
2. To promote library science and to grant scholarships in connection therewith;
3. To promote the progress and welfare of all libraries in the state: public, school, academic and special;
4. To encourage the use of libraries for educational, scientific and literary purposes;
5. To engage in such other educational, charitable, scientific and literary enterprises as the membership shall elect from time to time.[15]

The Charter, Constitution and Bylaws and the Code for Committees define the structure of the Association. The Executive Board of Officers was initially elected by the membership and installed at the annual conference. The roster of officers serving one year terms were the President, Vice President/President-Elect; 2nd Vice President; Immediate Past President; Secretary; and Treasurer. As time went on it was decided to add ten Members at Large with three-year terms, elected by the membership, in order to provide continuity on the Board. A parliamentarian, appointed by the President, was also added.

The Association was incorporated in 1951. From 1968 to 1979 an Administrative Secretary, Pauline Schear, handled all administrative and office functions. In 1980 the Association hired an Executive Director. Three librarians have served in this position: Abigail Studdiford, Danielo Figueredo, and currently, Patricia Tumulty.

Membership in NJLA is now open to all who work in libraries—public, school, academic and special—as well as library trustees, Friends of Libraries, and commercial vendors. Members may become involved in one or more of the ten sections: Administration,

Adult/Young Adult, Audiovisual, Automated Library Services, Children's Services, College and University, History and Bibliography, Preservation, Reference, Technical Services and Urban Libraries. Most of the Association's work in continuing education and publication work is accomplished through section activities.

Any member of NJLA may volunteer for assignments to serve on one or more of the 30 committees. The President makes these committee appointments for one year following the annual election. The Executive Board approves only the appointment of the chairperson for each committee. In addition to the regular standing committees, ad hoc groups and task forces are appointed as needed to deal with immediate concerns.

The diverse interests represented in NJLA come together each year at the annual spring and fall conferences. The fall meeting, originally a one-day conference, served as a business report to the membership, as well as an occasion for a substantive informational program. It is now a three-day conference held in conjunction with the Educational Media Association and the New Jersey Library Trustees Association.

The longer conference in the spring, usually held in Atlantic City, provides an opportunity for sections and committees to present their particular concerns through speakers, workshops and special programs, in addition to their business meetings. It provides an opportunity to exchange ideas, to hear notable speakers on topics of national interest to libraries, and to gain a wider look at the state of libraries in New Jersey. Employment opportunities are made known at the conferences and new members are recruited.

Publishers and suppliers participate actively. A continuing good relationship between exhibitors and NJLA personnel has assured the conventions of financial stability and has provided commercial exhibits that reflect a wide range of interest to the library community.

Association Committees and Round Tables

Without describing the myriad projects carried on by the Association's committees, a list of them will indicate their scope: Archives; Committee on Organization (formerly the Code for Committees); Conference; Constitution and Bylaws; Education; Elections; NJLA/EMANJ Joint Committee; Employee Relations; Finance; Government Relations; Honors; Awards and Resolutions; Institutes; Intellectual Freedom; League of Municipalities; Library Development; Membership; New Jersey Libraries; NJLA/NJLTA

Joint Committee; Past Presidents Memorial Fund; Nominations; Past Presidents; Personnel Administration; Planning; Public Relations; Publications; Scholarship; Scholarship Trust Funds; Section Coordination; Special Populations; Ways and Means.

In addition to these committees, there are three active Round Tables: Small Libraries Round Table, Bookmobile Services Round Table, Junior Members Round Table. There is also an Aids Task Force.

A Planning Committee was established in 1967 for the purpose of reviewing the overall program, objectives and activities of the association. Chaired by the incoming President, this committee establishes goals for action and the means of accomplishing them. In 1995/96 the Planning Committee, chaired by Lynn Randall, NJLA 1st Vice President/President-elect, was directed by the Executive Board of NJLA to begin work on a strategic long-range plan for the association. A consultant, Kermit Eide, was hired to work with the committee. A series of focus groups, telephone interviews and a visioning session have been held in 1995 and 1996. A final report was presented to the membership at the 1996 Spring Conference.

The Library Development Committee[16]

Since the early 1930s a Library Planning Committee has existed within the framework of the NJLA. Now called the Library Development Committee, it became a standing committee in 1955. Representing all types of libraries and interested lay groups, the committee is charged with the responsibility "to study the status and condition of libraries in New Jersey and to recommend appropriate steps to the Association for improving and developing library service." Working in cooperation with the State Library, this committee has spearheaded the Association's efforts to effect major changes in the library structure of the state. The Director and other State Library personnel are members of the committee. Its reports and surveys have been financed cooperatively by the State Library, the Rutgers Graduate School of Library Service, and NJLA.

In addition, the Library Development Committee and the Executive Board have used a variety of special reports, initiated and funded through the State Library and/or the Rutgers Graduate School of Library Service, as a base for further efforts to promote the progress and welfare of libraries. Noteworthy among such studies are *A Regional System Reorganization Plan for New Jersey County Libraries*, by Nelson Associates (1967), and the study conducted by the Gallup Organization, Inc., *The Use and Attitudes Towards Libraries in New Jersey*, (1976), both of which were commissioned by the State Library. A third significant study was published in 1967 by the Bureau of Library and Information Science Research, Rutgers Graduate School of Library Service: the *New Jersey Measurement Study* by Phillip Clark, Ellen Clark, Mary Jo Lynch, and Ernest DeProspo.

Chaired by Mary Gaver, the Library Development Committee completed a study in 1952 which presented data about the services provided by public and county libraries. This report was published in 1953 as Part I of the report, *Library Service for the People of New Jersey*. It formed a solid base for a wave of serious agitation from the library community, long hampered by the generally inadequate public library services in New Jersey. Within a year a Commission to Study Libraries in the Counties and Municipalities of New Jersey had been formed, and by 1956 it issued its report with recommendations for action. In 1959 the first state aid law providing funds to New Jersey libraries was passed. The leadership of NJLA, acting largely through the Library Development Committee, was crucial to the success of the effort.

By 1962–63 the Library Development Committee began to move ahead once more to produce, in cooperation with the State Library, the first overall plan for library service in the state. Margaret E. Monroe chaired the LDC in 1963, when it presented a comprehensive report by Lowell A. Martin and Mary V. Gaver, *Libraries for the People of New Jersey; or Knowledge for All*, to the Executive Board for approval. The final report was published in 1964. Its recommendations resulted in the creation of a three-level library network: local libraries; 25 strategically located Area Libraries; and specialized services provided by the State Library, the Newark Public Library, Princeton University Library and Rutgers University Libraries. An important change introduced by the state aid law of 1967 allows state aid to be withheld from those municipalities and counties which do not conform to the state regulations. These regulations have become part of the administrative code of the state and have the effect of law.

Since the enactment of the state aid law, the Library Development Committee has been engaged in a continuing review of library performance. The review process has included the publication of several significant reports. For example *Interim Goals for a New Jersey Library Development Program*, which was published in the summer of 1977.

Government Relations[17]

In 1975 the Executive Board appointed Roger McDonough, recently retired State Librarian, as its Government Relations Consultant, reflecting the importance the Association had always placed on legislative action as a cornerstone of improvement in library services. When McDonough retired from the position its responsibilities were merged with those of the Executive Director.

The Government Relations Committee keeps NJLA members informed about the need for legislative action. Telephone chains have performed effectively on a number of occasions in requesting library and citizen support in the form of letters to legislators, the Commissioner of Education, and the Governor. Reports coming back from the Legislature leave no room for doubt that the work of NJLA has resulted in increased public awareness and support for New Jersey libraries.

Other tasks undertaken by the Government Relations Committee include reviews of all bills and issues before the U.S. Congress and the State Legislature that affect libraries, with recommendations for action. The committee also keeps the membership informed about library-related legislative changes in other states.

With active support and participation on the part of NJLA, legislation was also passed to permit the establishment of library federations, in particular the State Library Aid Act that enabled the State Library to apply for federal funding for libraries. Another important piece of legislation, the Library Construction Act, assisted many libraries in the renovation of old buildings and construction of new ones. Recently, with NJLA support, the passage of the New Jersey Network Law created six regional library cooperatives, provided additional funding for libraries, and mandated certain levels of service for the citizens of New Jersey. In response to this new level of service, NJLA formed the New Jersey Library Network Committee.

Another successful legislative effort by NJLA was the passage of a law which exempts library trustees from liability damage.

Public Relations and Publications[18]

From its earliest years NJLA has recognized the importance of an active public relations program. Through its Public Relations Committee, the Association has expanded its activities to include workshops in publicity techniques, an annual public relations contest, production of publicity kits for use by public libraries, and production of radio spots promoting library service which are distributed to all radio stations in New Jersey and the Philadelphia area.

In 1976 the Association hired an advertising agency for a short period to mount a statewide campaign of television, radio, and newspaper coverage aimed at effecting an increase in state library aid.

In 1977 the National Library Week Committee of NJLA won the annual Grolier Award, which is sponsored by the ALA for the best public relations program promoting public library use. Activities supported by the award included workshops for libraries on their relationships with their municipalities, distribution of special publicity materials, and distribution of plans for user testimonials on "what my library does for me." In 1976 the NJLA National Library Week project involved selection of a "Library Family of the Year." Presentation of the family to the Governor highlighted the ceremony proclaiming National Library Week, which for a number of years took place at the State Library or the State Capitol.

NJLA's publications communicate ideas and ways and means to carry out its objectives. *New Jersey Libraries,* its professional organ, is currently published eight times yearly and has appeared continuously in a variety of formats since 1911. Its present small-magazine format is illustrated by graphics and black-and-white photos. The staff consists of members of NJLA who have been chosen to serve on the New Jersey Libraries Committee. Policy matters are determined by an Editorial Advisory Board. The magazine's features include: a continuing calendar of future library meetings and events, "Out-of-State Job Hotline," "New Jersey Bibliographer," the "State of the State" column from the State Library, registration and program information for workshops, editorials, professional articles, and letters to the editor. The Publications Committee approves any proposed publications prepared by sections or committees, and it solicits, edits and publishes original material of interest to the membership.

In addition to its professional publications, the NJLA has published three books about the history of New Jersey and its libraries: *Public Libraries in New Jersey, 1750–1850,* by Howard L. Hughes (1965); *New Jersey and the Negro: A Bibliography, 1715–1966,* compiled by the NJLA's Bibliography Committee (1967); *New Jersey Libraries: A Bibliography of Their Printed Catalogs, 1758–1921,* compiled by Donald A. Sinclair (1992).

Honors and Awards Committee

The Honors and Awards Committee has for many years recognized the contribution of librarians and trustees to the improvement of library services. Two annual awards are presented at the annual conference. One is given to a trustee for promoting use of the library and developing recognition of its place in the community, county, state or nation. A second award is given to any person on a library staff who has made a notable contribution to the furthering of library services. Nominations are submitted to the committee by the membership.

Intellectual Freedom

Libraries may call upon the Intellectual Freedom Committee for information and assistance. This committee is empowered to act in emergency situations without prior approval of the Executive Board. It became a Standing Committee in 1962. Its activities over the years have included programs at the annual conference and special educational workshops, as well as the presentation of testimony before state legislative committees in opposition to obscenity and pornography legislation. The committee is regularly available for calls regarding intellectual freedom and has currently been working on the issue of children's literature and censorship.

Recruitment

Recruitment of members has for many years been the responsibility of the Membership Section. A New Member Section was formed in 1974 but is no longer active. The Membership Section distributes NJLA literature and contacts those not renewing their membership.

In 1973 NJLA established a "Job Hot Line" telephone service for listing job opportunities and positions wanted. The service is located in the offices of the Library Development Bureau of the State Library and maintained by a State Library clerical staff member and an NJLA liaison member.

As part of its commitment to the recruitment of professional librarians, NJLA established a scholarship fund in 1923 and has awarded two or more scholarships annually at the spring conference. The Scholarship Trust Fund Committee oversees the management of scholarship funds contributed and the investment of these funds.

Personnel Administration Committee

From its inception the Association has worked consistently to advance the employment standards of librarianship. A good example of these efforts is in the area of salaries. A beginning New Jersey librarian in 1890 could look forward to a good salary of $35 a month. An annual salary of $1,200 to $2,000 was considered "fairly munificent." The Personnel Administration Committee publishes an annual salary guide and a report, *Employment Standards for New Jersey Public Libraries.* The committee also assisted in a statutory revision of requirements for public library certification. Since 1978 professional library certification in New Jersey requires a master's degree in library science from an accredited graduate program of library services approved in New Jersey.

Grievance Committee

For many years NJLA had a Grievance Committee that would examine any grievance submitted by its members. After meeting as needed with all parties involved, the committee would recommend appropriate action to the Executive Board, whether disclosure, censure or legal action. Several years ago the Board eliminated the committee, since it was determined that most of its members had access to other, more formal grievance procedures through Civil Service, a staff union or a staff association, and through the grievance procedure of the American Library Association.

Human Relations Committee

In 1949 the NJLA established a special committee to work with the Division Against Discrimination of the State Department of Education and later the Attorney General's office. It was changed to a standing committee in 1962 and over the years has been called the Human Relations Committee, the Committee for Services to the Disadvantaged, the Outreach Services Committee, and currently the Special Populations Committee. The committee has undertaken a variety of activities to promote library service to prison inmates, to the physically and mentally disadvantaged, to the elderly, and to the various ethnic communities in New Jersey.

NJLA, ALA and Other Associations

In 1927 the Association became a chapter of the American Library Association. It is represented by an ALA Councilor, elected by the membership for a four-year term, who reports regularly to the Executive Board and to the membership. The first gesture of cooperation with ALA was the newly-elected Board's decision in 1891 to contribute $100 to the ALA's Endowment Fund. In addition, individual contributions were raised in the amount of $110. NJLA has made annual donations from $100 to $500 for the support of the ALA Washington Office.

228 • MARY JOYCE DOYLE

Eight New Jersey librarians have served as ALA Presidents: John Cotton Dana, 1895–96; Ralph Shaw, 1956–57; James E. Bryan, 1962–63; Mary V. Gaver, 1966–67; Roger McDonough, 1968–69; William Dix, 1969–70; Eric Moon, 1977–78, and Betty Turock, 1995–96. Other ALA Presidents have had strong connections with New Jersey—Arthur Curley (1994–95), for example, is a former director of the Montclair Public Library.

Several times the NJLA hosted the American Library Association's annual conferences; in 1916 when 1,400 librarians gathered in Asbury Park; in 1919; in Atlantic City in 1926, when ALA celebrated its 50th Anniversary; in 1948; and in 1969 when two New Jersey librarians were being honored. Roger McDonough was completing his year as ALA President, and Dr. William Dix of Princeton University was assuming the presidency. The attendance at this conference marked a new high of 10,000.

The 1960s and early 1970s were periods of radical change in all professions, and President Dix stated, "This is a time no one wants to be president of anything." He survived—and so did NJLA and ALA.

NJLA has always been actively involved with other professional organizations. It cooperates with the New Jersey Chapters of the Special Libraries Association, the Educational Media Association, the New Jersey Library Trustee Association, and the New Jersey League of Municipalities. For many years NJLA was a member of the Mid-Atlantic Regional Library Federation, which included New Jersey, Maryland, Pennsylvania, West Virginia and Delaware. (New York was a member in the early years.) NJLA also works cooperatively with the Continuing Library Education Network Exchange and the National Committee for Library and Information Sciences. It is a member of the Freedom to Read Foundation, and it participated in the White House Conferences on Libraries in 1979 and 1985.

The New Jersey Library Trustee Association

The association with which NJLA has been most closely allied over the years is the New Jersey Library Trustee Association. NJLTA was formed in March 1936, at a meeting of interested trustees during an NJLA Conference in Atlantic City. Before the conference a letter had been sent by NJLA President James Thayer Gerould to the presidents of all public library boards in the state. In the letter he said that a number of trustees had suggested the formation of a trustee organization, that this topic would be addressed at the conference, and that the idea had the endorsement of Miss Sarah Askew, Director of the State Public Library Commission. Trustees from 32 libraries were represented at this initial meeting. William E. Marcus of Upper Montclair was elected temporary chairman and later the association's first president. Dues were set at $1 for individual membership, and a constitution and bylaws were adopted. The group decided to hold a spring and fall conference annually in conjunction with NJLA. They adopted the name, *The Trustee Section of the New Jersey Library Association.*

At its first meeting in October 1936 the new organization addressed several issues: ways of increasing support for libraries; problems of teenage behavior in the libraries; theft of library materials. It sent letters to libraries asking their trustees to join, and held dinner meetings to encourage cooperation. In December it was made a regular section of NJLA.

At the March 1937 meeting of the trustee association Marcus proposed establishing a council to coordinate the work of NJLA, the Public Library Commission and the Trustee Section. He also proposed that county chairmen be appointed to act as a liaison to the trustees in each county.

In May 1943 NJLA adopted a revised constitution which made provision for cooperating members. In October the trustee organization changed its name to the *Library Trustee Association of New Jersey* and became a cooperating member of NJLA.

In 1946 NJLTA President Samuel L. Hamilton, Professor of Education at New York University, sent a letter to Ethel M. Farr, President of NJLA, in which he suggested several issues that both associations should address: classification and pay plans; securing larger appropriations from local town councils; implication of the State Library Law for trustees; and employee pension plans.

Over the years NJLTA has actively pursued and supported legislation on behalf of libraries. For example:

- representatives of NJLTA met with Governor Robert Meyner to urge support for the Library State Aid bill
- in 1958 the Association mailed postcards to all library boards asking support for the State Aid bill
- telegrams were sent statewide in support of the proposed law permitting the federation of libraries and a bill removing the ceiling of $15,000 that a municipality could appropriate to an association library
- NJLTA's legislative committee supported legislation permitting the option of library boards having either seven (7) or nine (9) members

- NJLTA urged statewide support for Senator Feldman's *Privacy of Records* bill
  In 1957 Senator Thomas Hilliard of Morris County addressed the Association during a trustee program and stressed the importance of speaking with one voice to the legislators. The New Jersey Library Trustee Association has cooperated closely with NJLA over the decades since its establishment
- In the 1950's they worked for the establishment of a library school in New Jersey
- NJLTA assisted in determining the proper method of obtaining pensions, specifically by having librarians join the New Jersey State Pension Fund
- Each year the trustees have co-sponsored the NJLA's booth at the League of Municipalities annual conference.
- In 1959 NJLTA distributed Pocket Guides for New Jersey Library Trustees
- In 1978–79 the Association published a *Handbook for Trustees.*
- In the 1980's NJLTA co-sponsored the popular T.O.P. (Trustee Orientation Program) with the State Library
- In 1984 NJLTA sent letters to all New Jersey mayors reminding them of the importance of appointing qualified citizens to local library boards

From a membership of 38 in 1936, NJLTA has grown to 1,205 members. One of its major goals is to have every library trustee in the state a member.

In 1979 NJLTA was honored to have its President James Hess elected President of the American Library Trustee Association.

Other NJLA Initiatives

In 1976 NJLA adopted a resolution that its documents must avoid terminology which perpetuates sex stereotyping, and that as current publications and official documents are revised they would be changed to omit such terminology.

NJLA worked closely with the Department of Education in changing the title of the position of the State Librarian to an Assistant Commissioner of Education, which became law in 1978. The new position would no longer come under Civil Service regulations but would be filled through appointment by the Commissioner of Education.

In 1990 NJLA celebrated its 100th anniversary with a series of activities that included a traveling exhibit that toured the state, a series of lectures that focused on books and library-related issues, and a Centennial Ball with the actress Celeste Holm as the keynote speaker.

Some of the many activities and accomplishments of NJLA since its centennial in 1990 include: the continued support of the NJLA booth at the League of Municipalities Convention; the Eagleton Survey of New Jersey voters on their use of libraries; the establishment of Patron Behavior guidelines by the Personnel Administration Committee; the sponsorship of two Building Fairs; a statewide New Jersey Libraries Change Lives contest; an annual Books for Tots program; a Ways and Means sales table at NJLA conferences and workshops; support of the newly formed State Friends of Libraries; and organization of a postcard campaign that resulted in the legislative restoration of funds for regional services.

New Directions

In the fall of 1995 NJLA began a strategic planning process to develop a long-range plan for the Association. Members believed that as NJLA approached the year 2000 it needed to redefine its mission if it was to continue to serve the needs of the library community. For many years the bureaucracy of the organization had been growing larger and it was becoming too cumbersome to serve its members effectively.

Approximately 100 NJLA members participated in the year-long strategic planning process. The resulting plan was adopted in May 1996. Among the goals adopted were the following:

Advocacy: NJLA, joining with others, will be an effective voice on issues affecting libraries.
Vision and Leadership: NJLA will help members develop a collective vision for libraries.
Partnerships: NJLA will pursue alliances to pursue its aims.
Public Opinion: NJLA will attempt to influence public opinion in favor of libraries.
Member Service: NJLA will concentrate efforts to enhance member benefits.

In order to accomplish the aims of this revised plan alterations were made in the organization's structure. The plan compressed the Associations 32 standing committees into just four major committees:

Public Policy Committee: To develop the legislative agenda and public policy positions for NJLA; to study and recommend action on bills and issues affecting libraries and librarians; to alert membership on pending issues; to plan legislative activities; and to train members to be effective advocates.

Member Services Committee: To study membership "market" and recruit new members; to study institutional and member benefits and recommend needed action; to follow-up with members who don't renew memberships and look at nonmembers to determine the reasons affecting their decisions.

Public Relations Committee: To educate and inform the public about library issues.

Professional Development Committee: To identify and enhance professional development opportunities, to coordinate continuing education opportunities within the Association, to develop leadership training, to develop continuing education standards for the profession and to plan NJLA conferences.

NJLA is looking to the future needs and concerns of its members, conscious that as time passes it needs change. It approaches the year 2000 making the kinds of organizational adjustments that can provide the flexible framework needed to deal with emerging issues.

Notes

1. *Encyclopedia of Library and Information Science,* v. 23 (New York: Dekker, 1980), 43.

2. *This Is Your Life; New Jersey Library Association, Century of Service, 1890–1990,* 1. This information sheet was prepared by the New Jersey Library Association on the occasion of its one hundredth anniversary and is located in the archives of the association at the headquarters of the association in Trenton.

3. *Minutes of the New Jersey Library Association,* April 3, 1891.

4. *Minutes of the New Jersey Library Association,* December 29, 1890. The minutes of the New Jersey Library Association are located in the arcives of the association at the association headquarters in Trenton.

5. *Encyclopedia of Library and Information Science,* 43.

6. *Minutes of the New Jersey Library Association,* October 31, 1894.

7. New Jersey Library Association, *Executive Board Minutes January 30, 1896.*

8. New Jersey Library Association, *Executive Board Minutes May 20, 1896.*

9. New Jersey Library Association, *Executive Board Minutes August 2, 1913.*

10. New Jersey Library Association, *Executive Board Minutes September 15, 1920.*

11. New Jersey Library Association, *Executive Board Minutes January 6, 1921.*

12. New Jersey Library Association, *Executive Board Minutes January 5, 1916.*

13. New Jersey Library Association, *Executive Board Minutes January 6, 1921.*

14. *Encyclopedia of Library and Information Science,* v. 29 52–54.

15. *Ibid:* 43.

16. *Ibid:* 47, 48.

17. *Ibid:* 49.

18. *Ibid:* 50, 51.

12

The Road Ahead

Edwin Beckerman

Predicting the future of anything is always likely to be a risky business. The only thing certain about the future is its very uncertainty. The future of libraries may prove no exception to the rule. Still, there are some general directions in which one might well look. In viewing the influences that are likely to shape the future of libraries in New Jersey, a number of discrete areas appear relevant; some of these are broad societal concerns which will shape the entire American culture, others are more local influences peculiar to New Jersey, and still others, specific to the nature of libraries as service institutions. Let us begin our look at the future of libraries in New Jersey with a review of the broad societal influences that are changing the United States and seem likely to exert a heavy influence in the future.

Societal Influences

Attitudes Toward Public Funding. This is written at a time when the Republicans have retained control of Congress and a Democrat has retained the Presidency; and after both have agreed on a conservative agenda of balancing the budget by the year 2002. Governor Whitman in New Jersey has fulfilled her pledge to reduce the income tax by a third and is preparing to run for a second term in 1997. While the "Republican revolution" proclaimed by Newt Gingrich never quite lived up to all of its hype, the conservative fiscal agenda it incorporated, has. This retained fiscal program seems likely to be with us for a while, if not permanently, and will affect the funding of libraries, especially in the public sector.

Views of the Electorate toward Government. Closely linked with negative reactions toward public spending is a loss in faith that government is capable of acting effectively to solve societal problems. Whether this perception is accurate matters less than the fact that it is widespread. Government is increasingly distrusted and so are public officials who scramble furiously to cut public spending to convince the electorate that they are on the side of the angels. We are in a period where notions of conspiracy abound, and dark forces are imagined waiting to subvert our liberties. In the minds of many, the media, once our most trusted source of reliable information now can no longer be trusted. It matters not that most people do not accept these ideas as literal truth: such speculations cast a pall over the public dialogue and the shaping of public policy.

The Posture of Libraries in the New Age. Where does this leave libraries with respect to public support? Libraries in the United States come in all shapes and sizes and as institutions are both public and private. For public institutions the financial future seems uncertain. With pressure increasing on local school and municipal budgets, the road ahead seems destined to be bumpy, as governmental agencies scramble for limited municipal dollars. Local officials and boards of education increasingly recognize that the primary method of retaining voter loyalty from election to election is to hold spending and taxes to an absolute minimum.

This general condition seems likely to persist, even though libraries of all kinds are widely used and held in high esteem by the electorate.[1] In library jurisdictions such as New Jersey, where funding is approved primarily by local political bodies, libraries, however popular they may be, are not likely to be considered essential by either elected or appointed officials. In such a climate publicly supported libraries are apt to suffer substantial funding limitations, if not actual losses. This may well include public libraries, school media centers, and libraries in public institutions of higher education, which already face limited state funding and tuition increases. Many of these limitations apply as well to private institutions of higher learning, as they struggle to remain financially stable.

On the other hand, despite the general skepticism toward public institutions, attitudes toward public libraries (and, by extension, all kinds of libraries) remain positive. When the public is able to consider them as a separate issue, more often than not it will support its libraries.

The case of special libraries is to some extent different, although they may face the same limitations affecting other kinds of libraries. Some special libraries are either wholly or partially dependent on public funding, and these are likely to share the general fate of public institutions. Corporate libraries also are likely to be affected by

economic trends, although the prospects of an individual corporation may differ from general trends, and this may prove to be the
dominant influence on the corporation's library. Thus it is fair to
say that corporate libraries have been adversely affected generally
by the recent trend toward corporate retrenchment occurring in the
business world, though each corporation has its own method of assessing the value of such components as the corporate library. A
corporation may determine in evaluating its own situation that its
library service needs expansion, general trends notwithstanding.

Technological Change

The second major influence on the future of New Jersey's libraries
will be the nature and speed of technological changes. This will have
profound effects on the nature of the services offered by libraries in
the years to come. To understand these changes and their effects
requires a close examination of the kinds of services currently offered by libraries, something which is not always done either by
library professionals or by the general public. Recently, I talked
about the future of libraries with an acquaintance who had begun
to make extensive use of his home computer in searching the Internet. At one point he exclaimed: "You know, soon we will not
need the library! We'll connect directly with the Internet ourselves
for all the information we need." Though such speculation is increasingly heard, sober reflection suggests it is inaccurate. Even if
computer researchers do by-pass the library—which to some extent
is already happening—the library will continue in some form, if
not as a prime information resource. Surveys of public library use
repeatedly confirm that most users still use the library as a source
of reading for entertainment and general enlightenment. It seems
unlikely that this activity will disappear even with automation. Libraries may change in their collections and their services but they
are likely to endure.

What is at issue is the capacity of the library to survive as an
information system. The future of libraries in this connection is
more uncertain. The survival of libraries in the form we now know
them appears to be related to a number of issues, to which I will
now turn.

The Ultimate Question of Information Mediation. It has been estimated that about 23 percent of American homes now have a personal computer.[2] This number will grow, as will the use of these
computers to access electronic databases directly, the Internet in-

cluded. Is there a continuing information role for libraries in this future?

The answer appears to lie in the degree of mediation needed to negotiate the electronic information universe and the amount of mediation that libraries are prepared to supply. An important aspect of this issue relates to the extent to which society is willing to provide entrée to the electronic universe of information for the information poor and economically deprived, who otherwise may lack a means of entry. While almost one in four American households has a home computer, this number drops drastically for adults earning less than $25,000 annually, down to less than ten percent of households with annual incomes under $15,000.[3]

Many of the information needs of patrons are still addressed to libraries, who meet them from traditional in-house information sources, or through the referral to cooperative networks that have emerged in recent years, or from electronic sources which with increasing frequency now include the Internet. This will change as more patrons acquire the capacity to connect directly to the Internet and other electronic resources without recourse to a library. However, as has been traditionally true of any kind of reference searching, the more knowledgeable the searcher, the more likely the success of the search. This is certainly true today of electronic searching for information. Given the present state of the electronic "highway," an experienced guide is useful, and often essential. Even in a better regulated electronic universe, experienced mediators are likely to be needed, even by the average searcher with some facility in the use of personal computers. It is in this area of reference and information mediation by trained library searchers that the major opportunity for libraries is likely to exist.

The mediation by librarians in electronic information searching will certainly be crucial to those who otherwise will likely not enter the electronic information universe. This group includes the economically deprived, who lack the resources to pay for hardware and software and the cost of connecting to the Internet and other electronic sources. It also includes the millions of adults who resist technology and are unskilled in its use and therefore unlikely to become more conversant with modern information technology without the assistance of a familiar institution.

If libraries are to play a significant role in supporting the efforts of patrons to negotiate the electronic information universe, they clearly will need the resources to do so. This means not only the resources to acquire the hardware and software to support information searching, but a sophisticated level of staffing. The question is whether society is prepared to support such a role, while at the same time maintaining support for the traditional roles that libraries fulfill.

Will Librarians Be Able to Retain Their Positions as Information Experts? For librarians to play an active role in assisting patrons in their information searching, it follows that they must become the community experts in electronic searching. This suggests an enhanced level of training, as well as both an interest in information technology and constant practice in the use of electronic systems. All of these suggest an enhanced level of resources needed to accomplish these purposes. This undoubtedly relates ultimately to the importance the public assigns to such a role by libraries.

Will the Information Highway Become So Simple to Negotiate That No Mediation Help Will Be Needed? Without doubt attempts will be made to make the electronic highway easier to use, resulting in less need for mediation on the part of librarians in the future. However, the information universe is not static. As more user-friendly tools are generated to make information searching simpler, the information universe will change and make searching more complex and uncertain. How these processes proceed and interact will help to determine what kind of mediation is needed from librarians.

Will For-Profit Businesses Alter the Need for Library Information Mediation? We have already seen many cases of for-profit enterprise entering the marketplace to supply the needs of clients with special information needs that could not be adequately met by public sector libraries. Is this process likely to expand in the future, eliminating the function of reference mediation by libraries and turning it over to for-profit organizations? Certainly this may occur, either by design or if libraries do not perform adequately. Much will depend on the view that society takes of the responsibility of public institutions in a democratic society to provide the public with the kinds of information they need to make informed decisions.

The Funding of Publicly Supported Libraries. Ultimately, the question of the library's role in the nation's information future may come down to the public's recognition that such a role has importance for them. This assumes the ability of the library community to bring the question clearly before the public and, assuming a favorable answer, to translate the public will into action. In this connection it is useful to repeat the observation made earlier, that libraries are more popular among the public, who use them, than they often are among politicians, many of whom do not.

The New Jersey Factor

Thus far we have talked about general factors, which will influence the future of libraries in the United States, wherever they may be located. There are additional factors which are peculiar to New Jersey.

Levels of Local Support. New Jersey over the years has done reasonably well in providing support for its libraries in both the public and private sectors, at least during periods of economic prosperity. What is the future likely to bring?

In the public sector long-term trends in New Jersey tend to follow the national pattern, toward limiting the role of government programs and expenditures, both local and state. Much of this in recent years has been rhetorical, but this may well have been a precursor to action. Experience seems to indicate that governmental funding will likely be extremely limited for the foreseeable future. Part of this pattern seems to involve the passing down to lower levels of government responsibilities for funding which higher levels now find inconvenient to fund if they are to meet their targets for budget cuts. Thus the federal government helps to balance its budget by passing down responsibilities to state government, which in turn passes down responsibilities to local government. Local government has no recourse but to cut services or raise taxes. Federal and state governments compound the problem by assuring the public that there would be no need for any additional taxes if only local government were as frugal as they. In fact, a sizable process of governmental retrenchment is now occurring (equivalent to the process of corporate "downsizing" which is also occurring currently). Some of the effects of this are apt to be good, as inefficiencies are wrung out of the system. However, there is a tendency also to discard many effective programs along with the useless.

The future of library funding in such a climate is uncertain. Libraries are generally popular in New Jersey, as they are in the nation, and this tends to help them in times of economic crisis. On the other hand, libraries are not viewed as essential by politicians generally, and this tends to hurt them in times of declining governmental revenue. (The decline in revenues may be relative rather than absolute, but the effect is the same.) At present libraries in the public sector appear to be holding their own as a group, but examples abound of institutions experiencing extreme hardship, a statewide phenomenon reflecting a broader national picture. It is hard to see a reversal of this trend, given present methods of financing libraries as agencies of local government or educational institutions. Given the pressures on local financing, politicians are unlikely to change their funding priorities regarding libraries, unless they see some compelling reason to do so.

Perhaps the most disturbing element in the New Jersey public funding picture has been its continuing reliance on the property tax.

This is particularly a problem in communities with large numbers of senior citizens, where the limited income of retired citizens tends to reduce tax revenue. As long as tax collections are based on the value of property rather than the ability to pay, local funding will be at hazard in communities where income is limited by large numbers of retired citizens. With reductions in the state income tax under the Whitman administration, the tendency to increase reliance on property taxes to fund governmental programs appears to be gaining strength. In the long run this is unlikely to prove helpful to libraries.

The one force capable of changing the funding priorities of local government concerning libraries is the force of public opinion. The main bulwark of a thriving library is its public. The only way of changing budget priorities to improve the lot of libraries is to enlist the public in the cause of maintaining and improving a service in which they take pride, and from which they derive benefit. This will require a recognition on the part of libraries that the success of their institutions is directly tied to their ability to activate their public on the library's behalf, energizing them to communicate their support to government officials. One other possibility may lie in creating opportunities for public libraries to organize as special library districts, similar to school systems, as is possible in some other states, relying on public referenda rather than local governmental action to set library budgets. Failing either of these alternatives, public libraries seem destined for some difficult times.

The future of school libraries/media centers seems equally unsettled. Given state constitutional mandates, the amount of money flowing from the state into local school districts has increased over the years. Improvements in secondary media centers have been significant; but after some initial improvement in the 1960s and 1970s, we seem no closer in the last decade to assuring the presence of such centers in primary schools, with qualified full-time personnel, than we were several decades ago. At best we appear to be developing a pattern of part-time professional staffing in primary schools, with staff often splitting their time between two schools. In some quarters there seems to have developed a belief that with the advent of the classroom computer, media centers may no longer be required at all. This reflects a lack of understanding on the part of some educators of the function of the media center, and of the limitation of computers as information tools if they are not adequately supported by trained media staff. What makes the future of the media center so tenuous is that as units of a school district they may not lobby independently in their own behalf and are often not a potent force in lobbying within the school system. This leaves advocacy, in large part, in the hands of statewide groups, the Educational Media Association and the New Jersey Education Association. NJEA is certainly one of the most potent advocacy groups in the state, and where it takes up the issue of media centers its support can be powerful. At the same time, it is a large organization with many other interests, and this may limit the help it can extend. The Educational Media Association, while it is centered on the issues of school media service, lacks the power of the larger NJEA and must struggle to make its voice heard, not only among the general public but within school systems themselves.

The Structure of Service. One of the major questions about library service in New Jersey's future relates to the way in which service will be structured. Since New Jersey is a "home rule" state, its library services have always emphasized the local political or school district as the appropriate base from which to extend service. From time to time, people concerned with the problems of public service have suggested consolidating smaller districts into larger units of service, but such efforts have been sporadic and largely ineffectual. While the impetus for change may gradually alter the scene to some extent, it is fair to assume that the local community will continue to provide the basis for service in the foreseeable future.

It is in the state's move to create networks of cooperating libraries that the future of coordinated effort appears to lie. We are currently served by the New Jersey Network, which includes four coordinated regions serving all areas of New Jersey, as well as the State Library as administrator of a number of statewide contracts it negotiates with independent libraries to accomplish needed statewide tasks. In the past some librarians were unimpressed by the system, particularly by the performance of the four regions, whose administrative structure they viewed as duplicative, and whose decision-making process, they believed, often led to faulty judgments. The State Library at times appeared to share this view, which led it to reduce the number of library regions from six to four. The "regions," for their part, believed that the State Library was lacking in clear direction and did not adequately appreciate that regional decisions are made by regional boards representing the will of libraries in the region, many of which are not public libraries, this being a multi-type library network. At the present time this issue still appears to be unresolved.

One thing seems certain. In a state which is likely to continue its basic pattern of local government, cooperative ventures like the present New Jersey Network provide the only method of coordinating the efforts of libraries throughout the state and making the best use of total resources, at a time when these resources may be in short supply. The interests of library patrons throughout New Jersey demand that differences be resolved, and that patterns of cooperation be continued and strengthened.

The Future of Private Libraries in New Jersey. The position of privately supported libraries in the state closely resembles that of school media centers. Private libraries are normally agencies of a larger entity, a corporation or an institution— just as school media centers are part of a school system. Decisions regarding the library are normally made by the management and they derive from the perception of the interests of the corporation or institution. In almost all cases the library forms a tiny part of the organization, and this means that decision making regarding the library is often pushed down the chain of management. However, with the powerful information tools becoming increasingly available to libraries, and with trends toward corporate and institutional retrenchment (particularly in the middle management), libraries may find some improvement in their position. Still, the place of libraries within larger corporations or institutions is most likely to reflect specific corporate and institutional imperatives concerning the nature of the enterprise and the perception of the usefulness of the library in reaching its goals, as well as the general economic climate of the time.

Notes

1. Richard B. Hall, "The Vote Is In: Undeniably Operational." *Library Journal*, v. 20, no. 11, June 15, 1995, 40–45. In this review of voter actions in 1994 relating to proposed public library expenditures, 50 of 54 referenda for operating funds were approved by voters throughout the United States, while 38 of 53 referenda for capital construction were passed during the same period.
2. U.S. Department of Commerce. Bureau of the Census. *Monthly News from the U.S. Bureau of the Census*, v. 30, no. 6, June 1995, 1.
3. *Ibid:* 1.

Appendix 1

Tenured Faculty and Administrators Rutgers "Library School," 1953–

Name Changes of the "library school"

Graduate School of Library Service, 1953–1978
Graduate School of Library and Information Studies, 1978–1982
School of Communication, Information and Library Studies, 1982–
    Composed of:
        Department of Communication, 1983–
        Department of Journalism and Mass Media, 1983–
        Department of Library and Information Studies, 1983–

Deans

Lowell Martin, 1953–1958
Ralph Shaw, 1959–1961
Neal Harlow, 1961–1969
Thomas H. Mott, 1969–1982
William A. Stuart (Acting Dean), 1982–1983
Richard Budd, 1983–

Chairpersons, Department of Library and Information Studies

James D. Anderson, 1983–1984
Patricia Reeling, 1984–1989
Betty Turock, 1989–1995
David Carr, 1995–

Directors of Professional Development

Dorothy Deininger, 1971–1976
Ilse Moon, 1977–1979
Jana Varlejs, 1979–1995
Karen Novick, 1995–

Tenured Library and Information Studies Faculty

James D. Anderson, Professor
Susan Artandi, Professor (retired)
Nicholas Belkin, Professor
Ralph Blasingame, Jr., Professor (retired)
David Carr, Associate Professor
Dorothy Deininger, Associate Professor (retired)
Ernest R. DeProspo, Jr., Professor (deceased)
Paul S. Dunkin, Professor (deceased)
Hendrik Edelman, Professor
Mary V. Gaver, Professor (deceased)
Neal Harlow, Dean/Professor (retired)
Mildred Y. Johnson, Associate Professor (retired)
Paul Kantor, Professor
Herbert R. Kells, Professor (retired. In March 1996 to February
    1997 he again returned to the Woodbridge Public Library as
    interim director until a permanent director was chosen in
    February 1997.)
Donald R. King, Associate Professor
Carol C. Kuhlthau, Associate Professor
Lowell Martin, Dean/Professor (resigned to take another position)
Sarah J. Miller, Associate Professor (retired)
Margaret Monroe, Associate Professor (resigned to take another
    position)
Thomas H. Mott, Jr., Dean/Professor (deceased)
Daniel O. O'Connor, Associate Professor
Patricia Reeling, Associate Professor
George P. Rehrauer, Professor (deceased)
Pamela S. Richards, Professor
Tefko Saracevic, Professor
Marian Scott, Associate Professor (retired)
Thomas Shaughnessy, Associate Professor (resigned to take another
    position)
Ralph Shaw, Dean/Professor (deceased)
Richard Shoemaker, Professor (deceased)

Elaine Simpson, Associate Professor (deceased)
Betty Turock, Professor
Kay Vandergrift, Associate Professor
Phyllis VanOrden, Associate Professor (resigned to take another position)
Jana Varlejs, Associate Professor
Henry Voos (deceased)
Benjamin Weintraub, Associate Professor (retired)

Appendix 2

Current Library Science Programs[1]

Rutgers University

MLS	Library Services Information Science Educational Media Services Library Administration
Certificate	Library Services
M. Phil.	Communication Information Library Studies
Ph.D.	Communication Information Library Studies

Rowan College of New Jersey

M.A.	School and Public Librarianship

Jersey City State College

Option	Library Media Specialist as option in M.A. in Urban Education

Trenton State College

B.S.	Elementary School Teacher/Media Specialist

Brookdale Community College

A.A.S.	Library/Information Science Technician

Appendix 3

Library Science Degrees Awarded by All New Jersey Colleges

Year	Bachelor's	Master's	Doctoral	Total
1971–72	26: KC8,TS8 WMP10	194	3	223
1972–73	84: KC48,TS20,WMP16	229	5	318
1973–74	47: KC18,TS15,WMP14	192	1	240
1974–75	59: KC41,TS18	199	5	263
1975–76	48: KC27,TS 21	196	1	245
1976–77	43–	183	7	233
1977–78	45–	159	4	208
1978–79	31: KC17,TS14	173	3	207
1979–80	28: KC18,TS10	166: G24,RU142	8	202
1980–81	17: KC7,TS10	160: G19,RU141	3	180
1981–82	16: KC8,TS8	117: G8,RU109	6	139
1982–83	6: KC2,TS4	112 RU	4	122
1983–84	8: KC2,TS6	126: G12,RU114	5	139
1984–85	9: KC8,TS1	101: G9,RU92	2	112
1985–86	4KC	95: G13,RU82	3	102
1986–87	12KC	124: G12,RU112	5	141
1987–88	3KC	128: G4,RU124	3	134
1988–89	1KC	145: G9,RU136	—	146
1989–90	1KC	149: G15,RU134	—	150
1990–91	—	137: G9,RU128	—	137
1991–92	—	154: G15,RU139	—	154
1992–93	—	187: G9,RU178	7	194
1993–94	—	191: G8,RU183	3	194
Totals	**488**	**3,617**	**78**	**4,183**[2]

Legend:
KC   Kean College
TS   Trenton State College
WMP   William Paterson College
G   Glassboro State College/Rowan
RU   Rutgers Unviersity

Notes

1. Source: State of New Jersey Department of Higher Education, *1995 Inventory of Degree Programs and Options Offered by New Jersey Institutions of Higher Education.*
2. Source: State of New Jersey Commission on Higher Education, *Degrees and Other Formal Awards Conferred by New Jersey Colleges and Universities.*

Appendix 4

State Librarians of New Jersey

William Livingson Prall	1822–1823
Charles Parker	1823–1828
William Boswell	1829–1833
Peter Forman	1833–1836; 1843–1845
Charles C. Yard	1837–1842
William DeHart	1845–1852
Sylvester VanSickle	1852–1853
Charles J. Ihrie	1853–1866
Charles J. Mulford	1866–1869
Jeremiah Dally	1869–1871
James S. McDanolds	1872–1883
Morris Robeson Hamilton	1884–1899
Henry C. Buchanan	1899–1914
John P. Dullard	1914–1919; 1924–1929
Francis E. Croasdale	1919–1924
Charles R. Bacon	1929–1934
Haddon Ivins	1934–1941
James E. Downes	1942–1943
Sidney Goldmann	1944–1946
Roger H. McDonough	1947–1975
David C. Palmer, Acting	1975–1978
Barbara F. Weaver	1978–1991
Donna Dziedzic	1991–1992
Louise Minervino	1992–1995
John H. Livingston	1995–

Index

About the Contributors

Edwin Beckerman (editor) served as the director of the Wood-bridge Public Library for twenty-seven years until his retirement in 1991. He has also been active as a library consultant. He is the co-author with Alice Gertzog of *Administration of the Public Library* (Scarecrow Press, 1994) and the author of *Politics and the American Public Library* (Scarecrow, 1996).

John T. Cunningham is the author of *This is New Jersey*, now in its 6th edition, and more than thirty other books. Through his books, articles, lectures and films he has done more than anyone else to make New Jersey history a vital, living thing to countless thousands of New Jerseyans.

Bruce E. Ford has been Assistant Director for Access Services at the Newark Public Library since 1987 and a member of the Newark staff since 1971. He began his career as a cataloger and worked subsequently as a reference librarian, as head of the Catalog Department and later as the head of Technical Services.

Robert K. Fortenbaugh has been a member of the New Jersey State Library staff since 1975 serving as a government reference librarian providing reference, research and interlibrary loan library service to state government employees; and as Head of Lending Services. Since 1987, as Assistant Coordinator, Library Programs, he has administered the $7.7 million state per capita aid program to local libraries.

Mary Jane McNally is a library media specialist at Ridge High School in Basking Ridge and a doctoral candidate at Rutgers University. She is a past president of the Educational Media Association of New Jersey.

Henry Michniewski headed the Library Development Bureau of the New Jersey State Library for a number of years until his retirement in 1984. He received his graduate degree in library service at Rutgers University, and worked at both the Brooklyn Public Library and the public library in Flint, Michigan before joining the New Jersey State Library Staff to administer programs under the Library Services and Construction Act.

Carol C. Kuhlthau is Associate Professor at the School of Communication, Information and Library Studies at Rutgers University where she coordinates the School Library Media Certification Program. She is known for her research and writings on the information search process and is a frequent lecturer on school library media centers in the information age school and information literacy. Her most recent books are *A Process Approach to Library and Information Services* and a second edition of *Teaching the Library Research Process.*

Roger H. McDonough served for almost thirty years as the Director of the New Jersey State Library. Upon his retirement he served for a number of years as the Legislative Advocate for the New Jersey Library Association. He also served as President of the American Library Association during one of the most contentious periods in its history.

Arabelle Pennypacker was the supervisor of library media services in the Lenape Regional High School District in Medford, N.J. for fifteen years during the 1960s, 1970s and early 1980s. A graduate of Douglass College and Drexel University, she was regional editor, Middle States bibliography, *Reading for Young People* (A.L.A., 1980).

Patricia Reeling is Associate Professor at the Rutgers University School of Communication, Information and Library Studies, and a past Chair of the Department of Library Studies. She was one of the early founders of the Government Documents Association of New Jersey.

Wenda Rottweiler is a graduate of Swarthmore College and Rutgers University School of Communication, Information and Library Studies. Prior to her present position as a reference librarian at the Woodbridge Public Library, she served as Supervisor of Extension Services at the South Brunswick Public Library.

Susan Roumfort retired from the New Jersey State Library where she managed its Law, Reference and Interlibrary Services. A member of the Special Libraries Association since 1961, she was active in its New Jersey Chapter and a founding member and a past president of its Princeton/Trenton Chapter.

Marian Scott has been a school librarian in the Westfield School District, as well as a faculty member at the School of Library Service at Rutgers University. Well known to many New Jersey librarians she has been active in the Educational Media Association.

Robert Van Benthuysen joined the staff of the Monmouth College Library from 1957 until his retirement in 1990. He served as director of the library from 1969 until 1985. During his time at Monmouth College he was one of the most active academic librarians in the New Jersey Library Association.

Anne Voss has had a varied career as a school librarian, educator and state government official. A graduate of the Columbia University School of Library Service she served as a school librarian in East Rutherford and Edison; Chair of the undergraduate minor for teacher librarians at Trenton State College; and Coordinator of School and College Services at the New Jersey State Library.